SCIENCE ENCYCLOPEDIA

SCIENCE
ENCYCLOPEDIA

B ARNES
& N OBLE
B O O K S
NEW YORK

Copyright © Miles Kelly Publishing 2004

This edition 2004 Barnes & Noble, Inc. by arrangement with Miles Kelly Publishing

Library of Congress Cataloging-in-Publication Data
on file at the Library of Congress

ISBN 0-7607-5260-5

Printed in Slovakia

1 3 5 7 9 10 8 6 4 2

Barnes & Noble, Inc., 122 Fifth Ave, New York, NY 10011

Editorial Director Anne Marshall

Editor Jenni Rainford

Editorial Assistant Teri Mort

Design Concept Debbie Meekcoms

Design Stonecastle Graphics

Copy Editor Rosalind Beckman

Consultants Sue Becklake,
Robert Birke, John Farndon,
Steve Parker, Chris Pellant,
Helen Pellant, Dr Kristina Routh,
Richard Tames

Proofreaders Margaret Berrill,
Hayley Kerr

Indexer Hilary Bird

Color Separations DPI Colour, Saffron Walden, Essex, England

www.mileskelly.net
info@mileskelly.net

Third-party website addresses are provided by Miles Kelly Publishing
in good faith and for information only, and are suitable and accurate at the time of going to press.
Miles Kelly Publishing Ltd disclaims any responsibility for the material contained therein.

Contents

Plants

Wild Animals

How Animals Live

Human Body

How Things Work

Inventions

Great Scientists

How to use this book

CHILDREN'S SCIENCE ENCYCLOPEDIA is packed with information, color photos, diagrams, illustrations, and features to help you learn more about all aspects of science. Do you know what the Earth is made of or which animal develops from eggs inside the male? Did you know that skin is the heaviest organ in the human body or that time is the fourth dimension? Enter the fascinating world of science and learn about why things happen, where things come from, and how things work. Find out how to use this book and start your journey of scientific discovery.

Main text
Each subject begins with an introduction to the different subject areas.

It's a fact
Key statistics and extra facts on each subject provide additional information.

Main image
Each topic is clearly illustrated. Some images are labeled, providing further information.

Check it out!
Find out more by surfing the Internet.

26

Energy and work

ENERGY IS the ability to make something happen. It is not just the light that comes from the Sun, or the heat that comes from a fire. Scientists say that energy is the capacity to do work. It is involved in everything that happens everywhere in the universe, however tiny or gigantic, from grass growing to stars exploding. All substances have energy locked up inside their atoms and molecules. Energy comes in many different forms and it can change from one form to another.

BRIGHT SPARKS

• Energy can never be created or destroyed; it can only be changed from one form to another. So, all the energy in the universe has always existed no matter what form it is in now.

• Scientists define work as a force multiplied by the distance a load moves when the force acts on it. In the metric system, the unit of energy is called the joule. One joule is the work done when a force of one newton moves an object a distance of one meter, or a meter-newton. The foot-pound is the imperial energy unit used in the U.S.A.

IT'S A FACT

• All the energy in the universe may eventually turn to heat. This is called the "Heat Death of the Universe" theory.

• Walking needs about five times as much energy as sitting still; running needs about seven times more energy.

▾ For a split second, as sprinters come off the starting blocks, they accelerate faster than an average sports car.

Movement energy

A moving object has a type of energy called kinetic energy. The more massive the object is and the faster it moves, the more kinetic energy it has. When runners start at the beginning of a race, they convert chemical energy in their muscles to kinetic energy. The faster they can change chemical energy into kinetic energy, the faster they run. At the end of the race, they stop producing kinetic energy. Air resistance and friction between their running shoes and the ground slow them down.

▶▶ Read further › chemical energy
pg16 (d2)

▶ At the end of the race, runners quickly lose their kinetic energy and stop.

Check it out!
• http://www.eia.doe.gov/kids/
• http://www.energyquest.ca.gov

▶▶ SUN see pg42 (k2) ▶▶

1   2   3   4   5   6   7   8   9   10   11   12   13   14   15   16   17

Cross-references
Attached to captions and pictures are cross-references that use the unique coordinates grid system. These lead you to related subjects within the book.

a b c d e f g h i j k l m n o p q r s t u v w

Converting energy
The heat generated by power stations is transferred to water. This changes into steam, which is released out of large, concrete chimneys. The kinetic energy of the steam makes a turbine spin. The rotational (spinning) energy of the turbine drives a generator, which changes the rotational energy into electrical energy for us to use.

Read further > chemical energy
pg16 [d2]

▸ When ocean waves crash onto a shore, the energy they carry can move sand and stones, and even make some cliffs collapse.

er stations are giant converters: they rt chemical, or nuclear, y in a fuel into heat.

Potential energy
Things can have energy because of where they are. This kind of energy is called potential energy. It is stored energy. A crane has to work against gravity to lift an object high off the ground. The object stores the energy needed to lift it. If the crane drops it, its potential energy changes to motion as it hurtles toward the ground.

◂ When something is lifted, it stores the energy used to lift it as potential energy.

Read further > gravity
pg24 [m12]

Making waves
All waves, including water waves and electromagnetic waves, carry energy. When waves hit something they give up some or all of their energy. If a pebble is thrown into water, the vibration travels outward as a wave. When light waves strike the back of our eyes their energy affects the retina (the light-sensitive part) so we see things. When infrared waves hit something their energy changes into heat. When radio waves hit the antenna of a radio, their energy changes into electric currents that the radio converts to sound.

Read further > gravity / waves
pg24 [m12]; pg31 [o22]

Photos and artworks
Illustrations and photographs accompany each caption. Diagrams are labeled to give more detailed scientific facts and information.

▸▸ EYES pg168 [o13] ▸▸

20 21 22 23 24 25 26 27 28 29 30 31 32 33 34 35 36 37 38 39

Cross-references
Look out for the references to related sections of the book that run along the bottom of each page.

The grid
The pages have a background grid. Pictures and captions sit on the grid and have unique coordinates. By using the grid references, you can move from page to page and find out more about related topics.

Solids, liquids, and gases

NEARLY EVERY substance in the universe is either a solid, a liquid, or a gas. These are called states of matter. For example, rock is solid, water is liquid, and oxygen is a gas. A substance can change from one state to another by gaining or losing energy. Heating water gives it more energy. The extra energy makes the water particles move faster. If they have enough energy, they can escape from the water and form a gas—steam.

Some of the substances in lava (liquid rock) are heated so much that they change to gas

Warm air rises and cools

Gas (atoms or molecules) can move fast. They spread out to fill the space they are in

Water (liquid) cools and freezes as it becomes ice (solid)

Gas

Liquid (atoms or molecules) can move about enough to flow past each other

Liquid

Solid (atoms or molecules) stay in the same positions

● Rock, air, and water

Solids, liquids, and gases are everywhere in the world. The land is made of solid materials, such as rock and earth. Oceans and rivers contain water, which is liquid. The air consists of many different gases (see pg35 [h25]). They may seem unchangeable, but their states can all be altered by a change in temperature or pressure.

▶▶ Read further › air / water / gases
pg34 [m11]; pg35 [b22; b34]

Solid

So solid

Nearly every substance is made of tiny particles called molecules, too small to see with the eye. Solids have strength and a definite shape. The molecules are firmly bonded in a regular framework. All molecules move non-stop, but in a solid they simply vibrate on the spot. The hotter the solid becomes, the more they vibrate. If it gets hot enough the molecules vibrate so much that the framework breaks down and the solid melts, like when ice turns to water.

▲ *Each substance changes its state at different temperatures. For example, ice melts at a higher temperature than ice with lemon added.*

Read further › molecules
pg12 (j15); pg28 (n2)

Boiling and melting

The temperature at which a substance melts from a solid to a liquid is called its melting point. The highest temperature a liquid can reach before turning to a gas is called its boiling point—although some of the liquid may evaporate (turn to gas) before it reaches this point. Each substance, like water or chocolate, has its own melting and boiling point. Water melts at 32°F and boils at 212°F. When a gas cools down enough, it condenses into a liquid, such as when steam turns to water. When a liquid cools down enough, it becomes solid, or freezes, such as when water turns to ice.

Read further › heat
pg28 (d2)

Going liquid

Unlike solids, liquids such as water, have no shape of their own and therefore take on the shape of any container they are poured into. The molecules in liquids are partly bound together in clusters. Liquids flow because these bonds are loose enough for the molecules to move around. The clusters roll over each other like dry sand, allowing the liquid to flow freely and quickly.

▲ *Water, like all liquids, takes the shape of whatever it is poured into.*

▶ *The particles in solid chocolate gain energy as they are heated—breaking away from each other as the solid melts.*

Read further › moving molecules
pg12 (j15)

◀ *The molecules in water flow freely over each other allowing liquids to pour quickly, such as the water in this waterfall.*

What a gas

Like liquids, gases have no shape or strength of their own. Unlike liquids, they have no fixed volume (mass or amount of space they fill) either, so they spread out to fill any space they are put in. In the same way, they can be squeezed into a much smaller space.

◀ *Airships float because the gas (helium) inside is lighter than the air outside.*

Read further › gases / air
pg15 (d29); pg33 (b22)

▶▶ FLOATING see pg189 (b31) ▶▶

1   22   23   24   25   26   27   28   29   30   31   32   33   34   35   36   37   38   39

a b c d e f g h i j l m n o p q r s t u v w

The tiniest bits of all

MATTER IS every substance in the universe—everything that is not just empty space. Yet matter itself, even the most solid rock, has a lot of empty space. All matter is made of tiny particles, atoms, with empty space between them. Atoms, and the spaces between them, are far too small to see except by using amazingly powerful microscopes. You could fit two billion atoms on the following period mark. Even atoms are not solid, though. They are more like clouds of energy, dotted with tinier particles, called sub-atomic particles.

IT'S A FACT

• By smashing atoms together at very high speeds, scientists have found over 200 sub-atomic particles, but few last more than a fraction of a second.

• Among the tiniest particles of all are neutrinos. They are thousands of times lighter than electrons.

Read further > compounds / elements
pg15 (b22; l29); pg17 (c22)

Atomic partners

Atoms usually bond (join) together in groups to form combinations called molecules. A molecule is the smallest particle of a substance that can exist on its own. For example, a molecule of oxygen, the gas we breath so we can live, occurs as a pair of oxygen atoms bonded together. Water, also essential for life, is a molecule of two atoms of hydrogen and one of oxygen joined together.

▸ Particles with opposite electrical charges (positive and negative) attract each other. A proton has a positive electrical charge. An electron has an equal but opposite (negative) electric charge. Atoms contain protons and electrons, which attract each other, holding the atom together.

▲ In a hydrogen atom, one electron zooms around one proton nucleus.

▲ In a helium atom, two electrons zoom around a nucleus of two protons and two neutrons.

Atomic

At the center of an atom is a nucleus (dense cluster) of two kinds of particle: proton and neutron. Even tinier particles, called electrons, zoom around the nucleus (see pg13 [q33]). The various sub-atomic particles are just concentrations of energy that are likely to occur in certain places. Protons have a positive electrical charge, electrons have a negative electrical charge. Neutrons have no charge.

 Electron
Proton
Neutron

▸ In an oxygen atom, eight electrons zip around a nucleus of eight protons and eight neutrons.

▾ A carbon dioxide molecule (waste product when we breathe out) is a chemical compound that consists of one carbon atom and two oxygen atoms. Carbon dioxide has the chemical formula CO_2.

Read further > electricity
pg20 (l9); pg21 (e22)

Check it out!

• http://www.chem4kids.com/files/atom_intro.html
• http://www.pbs.org/wgbh/aso/tryit/atom/

Crystal gazing

Most naturally occurring solids form crystals. Crystals are hard, shiny chunks that form in uniform geometric shapes. Each crystal is made from a regular framework, or lattice, of atoms or molecules. Grains of sugar *(see pg35 [r28])* and salt are crystals. So, too, are most gems, like diamonds and emeralds. Most rocks and metals are built up from crystals, too, although the individual crystals are often far too small to see with the naked eye.

▲ *Diamond, made of carbon atoms linked together in a rigid structure, is the hardest natural material we know of.*

Read further > metals / carbon
pg16 [i14]; pg18 [i13]

BRIGHT SPARKS

• Most of an atom is empty space. The distance from its nucleus to the closest electron is about 5,000 times the size of the nucleus. If the nucleus was 0.3 in wide, the closest electron would be about 164 ft away.

• Protons normally push each other away because they are all positively charged. Inside an atom a powerful force, called a strong nuclear force, holds them togehter and stops the nucleus from flying apart.

Different atoms

Each of nature's 100 or so basic chemicals, or elements, is made up from an atom with a certain number of protons in its nucleus. A uranium atom has 92 protons, more than in any other element found in large amounts in nature. In each atom, the number of protons is usually the same as the number of electrons, which are arranged in rings or "shells" around the nucleus. The way an atom reacts with other atoms (its chemical character) depends on how many electrons are in its outer shell.

Read further > electron shells
pg14 [d2; h9]

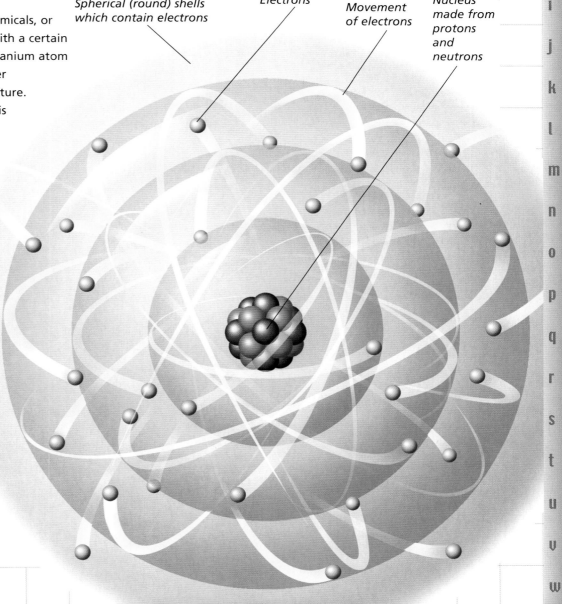

Spherical (round) shells which contain electrons

Electrons

Movement of electrons

Nucleus made from protons and neutrons

 Neutron

Proton

Electron

▶ *In the center of the atom is the nucleus, made up of equal numbers of protons and neutrons. These are bonded by a very strong force, which can be used to create nuclear energy.*

Key substances

A LL THE substances in the universe can be split into smaller pieces until they become the simplest known substances: chemical elements. Examples are gold, carbon, and oxygen. Each element has unique chemical and physical properties because it is made up from its own kind of atoms. All the atoms of an element are the same, with the same number of protons and other parts (*see pg13 [n33]*), and different from the atoms of any other element.

● IT'S A FACT

• The most recently identified elements were not found in nature—they were created by scientists.

• New elements created by scientists are often very unstable and last for only a fraction of a second before they break down. That is why they are not found in nature.

● Arranging the elements

An element's atomic number is the number of protons in its nucleus. Elements can be listed from the lightest, hydrogen (atomic number 1), to heavier elements, such as lawrencium (atomic number 103). Russian chemist Dimitri Mendeleév arranged them in the Periodic Table. The elements in a vertical column, or Group, are similar to each other in chemical and physical features, but get heavier in "jumps" downward. The elements in a horizontal row, or Period, are heavier from left to right by one each time. Each one also becomes less reactive, or able to join with other elements, depending on the number of electrons and gaps for electrons in its outermost shell (*see pg13 [k31]*). The most reactive elements are on the left side, and the least reactive on the right side (*see pg15 [k26]*).

Period or row 1A is a "special case" with just the two lightest elements: hydrogen and helium

▼ Elements also change their characteristics out of step with the Groups/Periods in two subsets: A and B.

Group or column 2A elements (green), called alkaline-earth metals, are fairly soft and reactive

Elements in Groups 3B onward (purple) are mostly hard and shiny, known as transition metals

Read further > atoms / metals
pg13 (i22); pg17 (c22)

Group 1 elements (blue), are soft and react readily, known as alkaline metals

These two rows, (orange and green) lanthanides and actinides, each fit into one position in the main table

H Hydrogen 1																	
Li Lithium 3	Be Beryllium 4															B Boron 5	C Carbon 7
Na Sodium 11	Mg Magnesium 12															Al Aluminum 13	Si Silicon 14
K Potassium 19	Ca Calcium 20	Sc Scandium 21	Ti Titanium 22	V Vanadium 23	Cr Chromium 24	Mn Manganese 25	Fe Iron 26	Co Cobalt 27	Ni Nickel 28	Cu Copper 29	Zn Zinc 30					Ga Gallium 31	Ge Germanium 32
Rb Rubidium 37	Sr Strontium 38	Y Yttrium 39	Zr Zirconium 40	Nb Niobium 41	Mo Molybdenum 42	Tc Technetium 43	Ru Ruthenium 44	Rh Rhodium 45	Pd Palladium 46	Ag Silver 47	Cd Cadmium 48					In Indium 49	Sn Tin 50
Cs Caesium 55	Ba Barium 56		Hf Hafnium 72	Ta Tantalum 73	W Tungsten 74	Re Rhenium 75	Os Osmium 76	Ir Iridium 77	Pt Platanium 78	Au Gold 79	Hg Mercury 80					Tl Thalium 81	Pb Lead 82
Fr Frankium 87	Ra Radium 88		Rf Rutherfordium 104	Db Dubnium 105	Sg Seaborgium 106	Bh Bohrium 107	Hs Hassium 108	Mt Meitnerium 109	Uun Ununnilium 110	Uuu Unununium 111	Uub Ununbium 112						

La Lanthanum 57	Ce Cerium 58	Pr Praseodymium 59	Nd Neodymium 60	Pm Promethium 61	Sm Samarium 62	Eu Europium 63	Gd Gadoloinium 64	Tb Terbium 65	Dy Dysprosium 66	Ho Holmium 67
Ac Actinium 89	Th Thorium 90	Pa Protactinium 91	U Uranium 92	Np Neptunium 93	Pu Plutonium 94	Am Americium 95	Cm Curium 96	Bk Berkelium 97	Cf Californium 98	Es Einsteinium 99

▶▶ ELEMENTS OF THE EARTH see pg59 (c22) ▶▶

BRIGHT SPARKS

• In addition to the atomic number, each element also has an atomic mass. This is the relative "weight" of the atom's whole nucleus—the protons and neutrons added together. Lead's atomic number is 82 but its atomic mass is 207.

• Scientists give each element a symbol. This is usually the first letter of its name, like O for oxygen and C for carbon. If two or more elements begin with the same letter, a second small case letter may be added. So, hydrogen is H and helium, He.

Chemical symbol

Name of element

O
Oxygen
8

Atomic number indicating number of protons in atom's nucleus

Gases most noble

The Group 8 elements down the furthest right of the Periodic Table is a very special Group. It is also called Group 8 or 0, because the atoms of these elements have no electrons missing from their outer shells. With a full outer shell of electrons, their atoms have no need to share electrons with other atoms. They are therefore extremely stable and unreactive. They are also called the noble gases, because they stay noble (apart from) other chemicals. Noble gases, such as argon and krypton, are used in light bulbs just because they are so unreactive and will not burn out the filament—the tiny, thin, coiled wire inside the bulb. Neon is used to make neon lights for the same reason, so it can burn brightly without reacting.

▲ An electric current sent to the lightbulb makes the filament glow to create light. Argon inside the bulb keeps the filament from burning out.

►► Read further > gases
pg11 (q31); pg35 (b22)

He
Helium
2

Group 8 elements (light blue) are known as noble gases and hardly ever react with other elements

N	O	F	Ne
Nitrogen	Oxygen	Flourine	Neon
7	8	9	10

P	S	Cl	Ar
Phosphorus	Sulphur	Chlorine	Argon
15	16	17	18

As	Se	Br	Kr
Arsenic	Selentium	Bromine	Krypton
33	34	35	36

Sb	Te	I	Xe
Antimony	Tellurium	Iodine	Xenon
51	52	53	54

Bi	Po	At	Rn
Bismuth	Polonium	Astatine	Radon
83	84	85	86

Some elements in Groups 3A to 7A (green) are called poor metals

The other elements in Groups 3A to 7A (brown) are called non-metals

Er	Tm	Yb	Lu
Erbium	Thulium	Ytlerbium	Lutetium
68	69	70	71

Fm	Md	No	Lr
Fermium	Mendelevium	Nobelium	Lawrencium
100	101	102	103

Compounds

Pure elements are quite rare in the world. Most substances are made of two or more elements joined together in a compound. A compound is not just a mixture of elements. When the elements combine they are changed chemically to make an entirely new substance. Sodium, for instance, is an element that fizzes violently when dropped in water, while chlorine is a thick, green gas; but they combine to make a compound called sodium chloride, ordinary table salt.

▲ Eggs are a compound of sulphur, carbon, nitrogen, phosphorus, hydrogen, and oxygen.

▼ Citric acid, found in lemon juice, is a compound of hydrogen, oxygen, and carbon mixed with water.

►► Read further > ores /salt
pg16 (i14); pg17 (k31)

Check it out!

- http://www.funbrain.com/periodic/
- http://www.chem4kids.com/files/elem_pertable.html

▶ When food products such as eggs, butter, and sugar are mixed together and cooked, the heat bonds the different compounds together into a new compound.

Chemicals and materials

THE UNIVERSE is made up from millions of different substances that we know about—and probably millions more that have not yet been discovered. Barely 100 of these are pure chemical elements consisting of identical atoms. Most are compounds made from different combinations of these atoms. Many natural substances, like wood, soil, and rocks, are a mixture of two or more compounds. Metals exist naturally as compounds, and pure water is a compound of the elements hydrogen and oxygen. Tap water and sea water are mixtures, for there are always other substances mixed in with them. Some substances, when mixed with water, form an acid.

● Mixed metals

Metals are very rarely pure. Most occur naturally in the ground in compounds called ores, and the metal must be extracted by heating and other processes. Even then, metals usually contain some impurities. Sometimes impurities are added deliberately to create an "alloy," which gives the metal a particular quality, such as resistance to corrosion, or extra strength. Carbon is added to iron to make an incredibly tough alloy called steel: chromium is added to steel to make stainless steel, which does not rust or stain.

◄ Alloys of aluminum and magnesium are very strong and corrosion-resistant. This makes them ideal for producing vehicle chassis and buildings that have to withstand the weather and environmental pollution.

▶▶ **Read further › carbon**
pg18 (d2; i13)

▸ Metals such as steel are used in building tough structures like cars.

Metallic

Three out of every four elements is a metal, such as gold or iron. Most metals are shiny, hard substances that ring when you hit them. They are mostly tough, yet can often be easily shaped—either by hammering or by melting into moulds. This makes them wonderful materials for making everything from spoons to cars and space-rockets. The atom of metals knit together into a strong framework or lattice. Atoms within the lattice share their electrons freely. The freely dancing electrons make metals great conductors of heat and electricity, because the moving electrons pass them on like batons in a relay race.

Read further > conduction
pg29 (c22; r30)

▸ Anybody can float easily in the Dead Sea, Israel. The very high salt content gives greater upward force than fresh water.

Read further > hydrogen
pg14 (d2); pg35 (b22; b34)

Liquids that burn

When some substances dissolve in water they create a special liquid called an acid. A drink that tastes sour, such as lemon juice, is a weak acid. Strong acids, such as sulphuric acid, are highly corrosive, attacking clothes and skin, and dissolving metals. All acids, both weak and strong, contain hydrogen. When mixed with water, the hydrogen atoms lose their one electron, and become ions— electrically charged atoms. It is these ions that make acids sour tasting and corrosive.

▸ The chemical opposite of an acid is a base. Strong bases, such as caustic soda, are so corrosive that they are dangerous so protective gloves and clothing is worn when they are handled. Weak bases, such as baking powder, taste bitter or might have a soapy feel.

Salt of the earth

Table salt is just one of many substances called salt. Many of the minerals that make up the rocks of the Earth's surface are salts. Salts are a special kind of solid made of crystals that can take a variety of shapes. Salt is obtained from sea water in hot countries. Some sea water has a high salt content. The water is held in shallow pools and the salt gathered when all the water has evaporated in the heat. A salt forms when an acid and a base react together. For example, table salt forms when the base sodium hydroxide reacts with hydrochloric acid. Most salts dissolve in water, which makes them very good materials for living things. Salts in the body maintain water balance and keep nerve signals healthy.

Read further > crystals / dissolving
pg13 (b22); pg35 (m22)

Check it out!

• http://www.miamisci.org/ph/phpanel.html

▸▸ NERVOUS SYSTEM see pg172 (m8) ▸▸

a b c d e f g h i j k l m n o p q r s t u v w

1   22   23   24   25   26   27   28   29   30   31   32   33   34   35   36   37   38   39

Carbon chemicals

CARBON IS a very special element. The hardest known substance, diamond, is carbon. Coal and the graphite in pencils are also carbon. Carbon has an ability to form compounds easily because of the structure of its atom. There are more than one million known carbon compounds, from limestone to diesel oil. With four out of the full eight electrons in its outer shell, a carbon atom can form compounds either by gaining electrons or by losing them. This means it will join up with just about anything to make a wide variety of products, from oil-based paints to parachutes.

● **IT'S A FACT**

- Most plastics are made of a group of chemicals called ethenes, which are derived from petroleum.
- Natural diamonds formed deep in the Earth billions of years ago.

● **Carbon**

Pure carbon occurs in four allotropes (forms): diamond, graphite, soot, and charcoal, and in a special manufactured form called fullerene. Graphite can be stretched out into long fibers called carbon fibers.

◀ *When bonded together, carbon fibers make an incredibly light but tough material, ideal for making things like oars used for rowing a boat.*

Diesel

Graphite

Carbon

Diamond

Charcoal

▶▶ **Read further > alloys**
pg16 (i14)

◀ *Carbon and its compounds can be used for many things: diesel fuel to run vehicles; graphite for pencils; diamonds in jewelry; and charcoal burned to make energy.*

● **Check it out!**

- http://www.spinaweb.ie/showcase/1124/content/intro.htm

▶▶ AGE OF THE EARTH see pg65 (b22) ▶▶

▸ *Products such as paints, fabrics, and cosmetics are manufactured from organic compounds.*

▸ *The long, arc shape of this parachute is created by air pushing up against it, which helps slow down the speed at which the forces of gravity pull the parachutist to the ground.*

● Organic chemicals

Carbon has an almost unique ability, not only to form compounds with other elements, but to join together with other carbon atoms to form complex chains and rings. Complex carbon chain and ring molecules are the basic chemicals that are blocks of life. For example, the proteins from which the body is built are all carbon compounds. There is such a huge variety of carbon compounds that there is an entire branch of chemistry, called organic chemistry, devoted to their study.

▶▶ Read further > compounds
pg15 (l29)

● Plastic world

Plastics are among the most amazing of all materials, used for everything from bottles to car bodies. Light and easy to shape into any form, they can be made as soft as silk or as strong as steel. They are entirely manufactured: the trick is to get molecules of carbon compounds—mainly carbon and hydrogen—to link up in long chains called polymers. In some plastics, the chains are tangled together like spaghetti to make them strong yet flexible. These are ideal for making things like parachutes, which need to be strong enough to support weight and yet flexible enough to glide in the air. Chains that are held together rigidly make stiff plastic, used for such things as window frames.

▶▶ Read further > molecules / steel
pg12 (i14); pg16 (i14)

● The carbon cycle

▶▶ Read further > the Sun's energy
pg23 (b22)

Most carbon atoms have existed since the beginning of the Earth and, through a process called the carbon cycle, circulate through animals, plants, and the air. The leafs and stems of every plant are built mostly from a natural material called cellulose. Like plastic, cellulose is a polymer—a long chain of carbon-based molecules. Plants put these chains together from sugar molecules called glucose, which they make with water and carbon dioxide from the air and using energy from the Sun. Animals eat plants, using the carbon compounds taken in.

▸ *When living things decay, fuels burn, and plants and animals break down sugars to release energy. Carbon dioxide is released into the air during this process, completing the carbon cycle.*

● BRIGHT SPARKS

• Plastic's durability makes it hard to dispose of, so scientists have developed kinds that can be degraded (broken down) by light or bacteria. However, the world still faces increasing problems with plastic waste.

• Fullerenes are molecules of between 32 and 600 carbon atoms linked together in a ball shape. The first fullerene was a ball of 60 carbon atoms. It was named Buckminsterfullerene, or the "Bucky Ball," after the architect, R. Buckminster Fuller, who made geodesic domes that the Bucky Ball resembled.

▶▶ PLANTS USING SUN'S ENERGY see pg88 (m2) ▶▶

a b c d e f g h i j k l m n o p q r s t u v w

Electricity and magnetism

IT'S A FACT

• Lightning is the sudden release of a giant charge of static electricity that builds up inside storm clouds.

• The best conductors of electricity are materials that contain a lot of free electrons, such as copper and silver.

ELECTRICITY IS one of the most useful of all forms of energy, providing us with everything from heat and light to the tiny pulses that make computers work. Electricity is closely linked with magnetism—the invisible force between magnetic materials. When electricity moves, magnetism is created. When magnets move, electricity is created. Together, electricity and magnetism form one of the forces that holds the universe together—electromagnetism.

▼ *Pylons carry electric cables from power stations through a distribution grid. Electricity can travel safely, high above ground.*

Cables carry flow of electricity

High pylons hold electric cables safely above ground

BRIGHT SPARKS

• The Earth is a giant magnet. If a magnet is left to move freely, the Earth's magnetic field ensures that it always points with one end aimed at the North Pole and the other at the South Pole.

• Materials that do not conduct electricity very well are called insulators. Plastic and rubber are good insulators.

Electric currents

When a magnet and a coil of wire move near each other, the magnet induces (creates) an electric current in the wire by pushing electrons through it. Power stations do this to make electricity. Flowing water, or a jet of steam, spins coils of wire around powerful magnets. Electric currents are induced in the coils. The electricity then flows through wires to our homes, schools, and workplaces. The wires are either held above ground on top of tall pylons or are laid underground.

▼ *Electricity is made from atoms that move along a wire.*

▶▶ **Read further › currents**
pg21 (m22)

Atom

Electrons can be pushed from one atom to the next and when billions do this every second, electricity flows

Electron

Check it out!

• http://www.kapili.com/index_p4k.html/files/elec_main.html
• http://www.simco.nl/simco/static0.htm
• http://www.mos.org/sln/toe/toe.html
• http://www.factmonster.com/ce6/sci/A0831162.html

▶ *Charged particles such as those generated by a Van de Graaf generator, can make hair stand on end. All the hairs have the same charge (all positive or all negative) and so repel (push apart) each other. They stand on end to get away from each other.*

Static electricity

Electricity is caused by the behavior of electrons, which are electrically charged particles. If a material gains extra electrons it becomes negatively charged. If a material loses electrons it becomes positively charged. When two materials rub together, electrons may rub from one onto the other. They both become electrically charged, one positive and the other negative. This is called static electricity, because the electric charges on the charged material do not move, they are static (stationary).

Read further > protons / electrons
pg12 (o2); pg13 (i22)

Electric currents

Electrons move easily through material called conductors. Metals, such as copper and gold, are used as connectors in electric circuits because they are very good electrical conductors. They have many electrons, which can move easily through wires. When lots of electrons move in the same direction an electric current is generated. These flow around loops, or circuits. Batteries provide the energy to drive these electrons around a closed loop. They produce currents that flow instantly in one direction—direct currrent (DC).

▲ *Power stations generate currents that reverse many times every second. Unlike the currents in batteries, power station currents are called alternating currents (AC).*

Magnetic attraction

Magnets are special pieces of metal, usually iron, that have the power to attract magnetic materials such as iron and steel. Around each magnet is a region or "field" where its effect is felt. The field is strongest at the two ends or "poles" of the magnet, and gets weaker farther away. The magnet's power works in opposite directions at each pole, so one is called a north pole and the other a south pole. While opposite poles on two magnets attract each other, identical poles repel (push each other apart). So north poles attract south poles but repel north poles.

Read further > iron / water
pg17 (c22); pg35 (b34)

▶ *Objects containing iron, such as nails or screwdrivers are affected by magnetic fields.*

Magnetic field

Magnetic lines of force

Electric magnets

When an electric current flows through a wire, it produces a magnetic field around the wire. The magnetic field is stronger when the wire is coiled around a piece of iron. This type of "electric magnet" is called an electromagnet. Unlike a bar magnet, an electromagnet can be switched on and off. The magnetic field is gone when the electric current is switched off.

▶ *An electromagnet can lift a car into the air by attracting the iron-based steel of the car's body.*

Read further > electrical charges
pg12 (o2)

Electromagnetic radiation

L IGHT BEAMS, radio signals, microwaves used for cooking, heat rays from fires, and X-rays used in hospitals are all part of the same family of electromagnetic radiation. They are called electromagnetic waves because they are partially electric and partially magnetic. They travel in straight lines and at the same speed: the speed of light. In the vacuum of space, electromagnetic waves travel at 984.25 million ft/sec. At that speed, the waves could travel around the world in about one-tenth of a second. The difference between electromagnetic waves is the length of each wave.

IT'S A FACT

• Glass lets visible light pass through, but not infra-red (heat) rays. Greenhouses are warm inside because light can enter and warm the contents, and the heat rays produced inside the greenhouse are trapped by glass.

• Nearly all the fuels we use today, including oil and wood, were produced by the action of electromagnetic radiation from the Sun on plants.

BRIGHT SPARKS

• Scientists can track the movements of all sorts of creatures, from whales and polar bears to tigers and elephants, by fitting them with radio collars. A radio collar transmits (sends out) a radio signal that can be received a long way away, even by satellite, so that the animal's position can be marked on a map.

• Weather satellites can take pictures of the world's weather at night by using infra-red cameras.

Energy waves

Electrons emit a huge range or "spectrum" of electromagnetic waves. The light we see, called visible light, is just a small portion in the middle of the spectrum. At one end of the spectrum are waves too long for our eyes to see, including radio waves and microwaves. At the other, end are waves too short for us to see, including ultraviolet light and X-rays.

Gamma rays—dangerous, high-energy rays that can penetrate solids and are created in nuclear bombs

X-rays—longer than gamma rays, are short enough to pass through most body tissue, except bones

Shortest ultraviolet rays in sunshine are very dangerous—in small doses can make skin brown

Visible light—contains all colors of rainbow—violet are shortest wavelengths; red are longest

Infrared light—radiation given out by hot objects

Microwaves—used to heat food quickly

Television broadcasts—use radio waves about 1.6 ft long

Radio waves—between 1,000 ft to 5,000 ft long

◄ *The varying lengths of electromagnetic waves are each useful for different purposes.*

▶▶ Read further › electromagnetism
pg20 (f2)

Check it out!
• http://imagine.gsfc.nasa.gov/docs/
science/know_11/emspectrum.html

▶▶ X-RAYS see pg231 (h25) ▶▶

1 2 3 4 5 6 7 8 9 10 11 12 13 14 15 16 17 18 19 2

Sun

Most of the radiation hitting the Earth comes from the Sun, which puts out huge amounts of energy. Some of the Sun's radiation is waves, such as light and X-rays. Fortunately, Earth's atmosphere only lets through the light and warmth that we need, and shields us from the most harmful rays, such as extreme ultraviolet and X-rays.

Read further › magnetic fields
pg21 (b31)

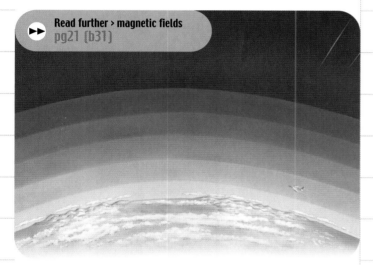

▲ *The Earth's atmosphere is vital, allowing for humans and animals to breathe, while keeping out the most harmful radiation from the Sun.*

Radiation hazard

Some electromagnetic radiation can be dangerous. Even low energy radiation from the Sun can cause harmful diseases, such as skin cancer, after prolonged exposure from sunbathing. But it is short wave, high-energy rays, such as X-rays and gamma rays that are the main hazards. Rays like these damage living tissues by "ionizing" the atoms in them—that is, knocking electrons off. This can cause damage to the biological mechanisms of the body. This is why people who work with X-rays in hospitals are protected behind lead screens.

◄ *Prolonged exposure to ultraviolet (UV) rays can cause serious damage. Suntan lotions containing a block against these UVA and UVB rays help prevent sunburn and diseases like skin cancer.*

Read further › atoms / electrons
pg12 (i22)

Heat pictures

Hot objects emit (give off) electromagnetic waves. We are unable to see them, but thermal cameras can detect them, and make pictures of them. In a thermal picture the hottest things are the brightest and the coldest things are the darkest. Thermal cameras can take photos in total darkness because they do not rely on light. They can be useful in showing how animals behave in the wild at night, without shining bright lights on them.

▸ *Thermal cameras are used to to diagnose illnesses by highlighting different parts of the body according to temperature. The yellow areas show heat, and possibly disease, blue areas show cooler parts of the body.*

▸ *Satellites and spacecraft use radio waves to send pictures and other information to Earth.*

Space waves

Unlike sound waves, which need something to travel through, electromagnetic waves can travel through empty space. This property is very useful. It lets us see distant stars at night—the light from them has to travel through empty space to reach us. It also lets us speak to astronauts in space and communicate with satellites by radio.

Read further › waves
pg27 (m34)

Force and motion

FORCES ARE pushes and pulls. They change the speed, direction, or shape of things. Some forces act only when things touch each other, like kicking a football. Other forces, including gravity and magnetism, act at a distance. Forces always occur in pairs—a force pushing one way always creates an equal force pushing in the opposite direction. These two forces are called action and reaction. When you push against a wall, the wall pushes back equally hard. If it did not, your hand would go through it. The main types of forces in nature are gravitational (gravity), electrical, magnetic, and nuclear.

▲ When sky-divers open their parachute, its air resistance force acts in the opposite direction of gravity, slowing them down.

Rollercoaster ride

A rollercoaster has no motor. It reaches scary speeds through gravity. It is towed up high and released. As it hurtles downhill, the constant pull of gravity makes it go faster and faster. When it reaches the bottom of a slope it is going so fast that it carries on uphill to the top of the next slope. The tendency of a moving body to keep moving is called momentum.

▶▶ Read further › gravity
pg25 (j28)

Falling down forcefully

One of Newton's most startling discoveries was that things do not just fall of their own accord: they fall because they are pulled down by a force called gravity. Gravity is the force of attraction that pulls everything towards the center of the Earth. Every single bit of matter in the universe, no matter how tiny, exerts its own gravitational pull on other matter. The strength of the pull depends on the mass (matter) of the object. More massive objects exert a stronger pull of gravity. The further apart things are, the weaker their pull of gravity on each other.

▶▶ Read further › Newton / black holes
pg25 (q30); pg37 (m22)

Check it out!

• http://www.funderstanding.com/k12/coaster

▶▶ GRAVITY see pg220 (n13) ▶▶

Work, effort, and load

Work, effort, and load are important concepts in physics, especially in relation to machines, which usually move something. Load describes the size of the object moved, measured in kilograms or pounds. Effort describes the force used to move it, measured in newtons or pounds. Work describes just how long the effort is applied—or more specifically, the force used times the distance moved by the load. In the metric system, the unit of work is the joule—the work done when a force of one newton moves something one meter. One joule equals one newton-meter. In the U.S.A. the unit of work is a foot-pound. This is the work done when a force of one lb moves something one ft.

Figure skater being lifted does "work" by moving and holding her body in the right position

Energy is being used as effort to lift figure skater

Figure skater being lifted is affected by force of gravity

▶▶ **Read further › gravity**
pg24 (m12)

▸ *The lifting force of the figure skater overcomes the force of gravity as he lifts the load.*

▶▶ **Read further › energy**
pg26 (d2)

Acceleration and mass

In the 17th century, English scientist Isaac Newton realized that forces work the same way everywhere in the universe, and that their effect can be predicted. A force makes objects accelerate. Just how much they accelerate depends on how strong the force is and how great the object's mass is—how much matter it contains. The bigger the force, the greater the acceleration. More massive objects need a bigger force to give them the same acceleration.

◂ *A heavy cannon ball needs a very strong force to give it the required amount of acceleration.*

BRIGHT SPARKS

• Like all forces, gravity makes things accelerate. Anything falling towards the Earth accelerates, gaining speed at the rate of 32 ft/sec, when near the Earth. This is called acceleration due to gravity, or g.

• Objects resist changes of motion. The more mass (matter) a substance contains, the more it resists changes. The resistance is called inertia.

The Laws of Motion

In the late 17th century, Isaac Newton summed up the link between force and motion with three laws: Law one: an object only accelerates (changes speed or direction) when a force acts on it. Law two: acceleration increases as the force increases, but decreases as the mass increases. Law three: every action (force) is matched by an equal and opposite reaction (opposing force). These three laws apply to everything from kicking a ball to flying a spacecraft.

▶▶ **Read further › Newton**
pg24 (m10)

▾ *Without gravity or air resistance a football, when kicked, would continue on its path.*

Air resistance slows the ball down

Force is applied when the ball is kicked

Gravity pulls the ball down

Air resistance and gravity combine to bring the ball back down to the ground

▶▶ NEWTON see pg220 (l2) ▶▶

Energy and work

ENERGY IS the ability to make something happen. It is not just the light that comes from the Sun, or the heat that comes from a fire. Scientists say that energy is the capacity to do work. It is involved in everything that happens everywhere in the universe, however tiny or gigantic, from grass growing to stars exploding. All substances have energy locked up inside their atoms and molecules. Energy comes in many different forms and it can change from one form to another.

● BRIGHT SPARKS

• Energy can never be created or destroyed; it can only be changed from one form to another. So, all the energy in the universe has always existed no matter what form it is in now.

• Scientists define work as a force multiplied by the distance a load moves when the force acts on it. In the metric system, the unit of energy is called the joule. One joule is the work done when a force of one newton moves an object a distance of one meter, or a meter-newton. The foot-pound is the imperial energy unit used in the U.S.A.

● IT'S A FACT

• All the energy in the universe may eventually turn to heat. This is called the "Heat Death of the Universe" theory.

• Walking needs about five times as much energy as sitting still; running needs about seven times more energy.

● Movement energy

A moving object has a type of energy called kinetic energy. The more massive the object is and the faster it moves, the more kinetic energy it has. When runners start at the beginning of a race, they convert chemical energy in their muscles to kinetic energy. The faster they can change chemical energy into kinetic energy, the faster they run. At the end of the race, they stop producing kinetic energy. Air resistance and friction between their running shoes and the ground slow them down.

►► **Read further › chemical energy**
pg16 [d2]

▼ *For a split second, as sprinters come off the starting blocks, they accelerate faster than an average sports car.*

▸ *At the end of the race, runners quickly lose their kinetic energy and stop.*

🌐 **Check it out!**

• http://www.eia.doe.gov/kids/
• http://www.energyquest.ca.gov

►► SUN see pg42 (k2) ►►

▾ Power stations are giant energy converters: they convert chemical, or nuclear, energy in a fuel into heat.

● Converting energy

The heat generated by power stations is transferred to water. This changes into steam, which is released out of large, concrete chimneys. The kinetic energy of the steam makes a turbine spin. The rotational (spinning) energy of the turbine drives a generator, which changes the rotational energy into electrical energy for us to use.

▶▶ **Read further › chemical energy** pg16 [d2]

▸ When ocean waves crash onto a shore, the energy they carry can move sand and stones, and even make some cliffs collapse.

● Potential energy

Things can have energy because of where they are. This kind of energy is called potential energy. It is stored energy. A crane has to work against gravity to lift an object high off the ground. The object stores the energy needed to lift it. If the crane drops it, its potential energy changes to motion as it hurtles toward the ground.

● Making waves

All waves, including water waves and electromagnetic waves, carry energy. When waves hit something they give up some or all of their energy. If a pebble is thrown into water, the vibration travels outward as a wave. When light waves strike the back of our eyes their energy affects the retina (the light-sensitive part) so we see things. When infrared waves hit something their energy changes into heat. When radio waves hit the antenna of a radio, their energy changes into electric currents that the radio converts to sound.

▶▶ **Read further › gravity** pg24 [m12]

▾ When something is lifted, it stores the energy used to lift it as potential energy.

▶▶ **Read further › gravity / waves** pg24 [m12]; pg31 [o22]

a b c d e f g h i j k l m n o p q r s t u v w

Heat

H EAT IS another name for "internal energy" or energy stored inside a substance. It is a form of energy that moves from one place to another when its temperature varies. You can give extra internal energy to a substance by heating it or working on it. A bicycle pump warms up when you use it because the air inside it is squashed every time you push the handle. The work put into squashing the air gives it more energy, which makes its atoms and molecules move around faster. Every time energy changes from one form to another, some of it turns into heat, which then spreads to its surroundings. That is why computers, television sets, and all sorts of machines often heat up when they are working.

▼ A refrigerator is a heat pump—it pumps heat energy from cold to hot, the opposite of the way it flows in nature.

● **Hot and cold**

Heat always flows from hot to cold in nature, but it can be made to flow in the opposite direction using a refrigerator. Heat from food inside the refrigerator warms a special liquid flowing through pipes in the fridge. The heat makes the liquid evaporate (change from a liquid to a gas). The gas is piped outside the refrigerator, where it is first cooled and then compressed (squashed) to change it back to a liquid. It goes back inside the refrigerator where it gathers more heat from the food and evaporates.

▶▶ **Read further > changing states** pg10 (d2)

● **Expansion and contraction**

When things heat up they expand because their molecules vibrate more and move further apart. When they cool down, they contract because the molecules vibrate less and move closer together. With solids, the expansion and contraction is usually too small to see. For example, a steel bar becomes only 0.0001 percent longer for every degree the temperature rises. But the force of expansion is so powerful that extreme heat can make, for example, railroad tracks buckle.

Iron

Copper

Heating element

▶▶ **Read further > solids** pg11 (b22)

◀ Bimetallic strips used in thermostats to respond to a change in temperature consist of iron and copper bonded firmly together. The strip bends when heated because the copper expands more than the iron.

▶▶ **Read further › radiation**
pg23 (b22)

● Moving heat

Heat spreads in three ways: conduction, convection, and radiation. Conduction is the spread of heat from atom to atom. The atoms in a hot substance move fast and hit each other. These collisions pass energy on to nearby atoms, those atoms pass their energy on to the next atoms, and so on. Convection spreads heat in gases and liquids. When they are heated, their molecules speed up, collide more often and spread farther apart. The gas or liquid becomes lighter than the surrounding, cooler gas, or liquid, and floats upward. Convection currents carry warm air up from a radiator. Radiation spreads heat with invisible infrared (heat) rays.

◄ Hot liquid heats a metal spoon by conduction.

▲ Radiation is one of the ways that heat spreads from a flame.

◄ Air warmed by a radiator gets lighter and rises. Cold air moves in from below to replace it, and this is heated up too.

▶▶ **Read further › temperature**
pg11 (b33)

▼ Double glazed windows are used in most office buildings to slow down the loss of heat energy.

● Stopping the flow

Sometimes it is necessary to stop heat moving and keep it in one place. When a building is heated during winter the heat tries to escape to make the building the same temperature as the air outside. Glass conducts heat faster than walls and roofs, so a lot of heat escapes through windows. Therefore, some buildings have double-glazed windows to help keep the heat in. Double-glazed windows have two panes of glass instead of one, with a small gap between them. The air in the gap is not a good conductor of heat.

 Check it out!
• http://www.powermasters.com
/heat_energy.html

▶▶ HOT–AIR BALLOON see pg189 (b31) ▶▶

a b c d e f g h i j k l m n o p q r s t u v w

Light

LIGHT IS the only kind of electromagnetic radiation which we can see. We are surrounded by light most of the time, but, surprisingly, few things actually radiate light. The Sun is our main source of light (*see pg22 [t5]*). Light, also comes from stars, candles, electric light and even small insects, like glow-worms. But most things are only visible because they reflect light from other sources.

▶▶ **Read further › waves**
pg27 {m34}

IT'S A FACT

• All the colors of the rainbow can be made by mixing just three "primary" colors of light: red, blue, and yellow.

• Light waves are so short that 2,000 of them would easily fit on a pinhead.

● Light and shade

When light rays hit an object, they bounce off, are absorbed, or pass through. Substances, such as clear glass, which let light through without breaking the direction of the rays, are transparent. Substances that jumble the light on the way through, like frosted glass, are translucent. Those that stop the light altogether are opaque.

Clear glass is transparent

● Casting a shadow

Light travels in straight lines. Different substances allow different amounts of light to pass through them. When light hits an opaque object, it does not curve around it. Opaque objects cast two types of shadow: if no light reaches an area, a dark shadow called an umbra is formed. If some light reaches an area, a grey shadow called a penumbra is formed.

▼ *The pillars at Stonehenge are opaque, so when sunlight falls on them, the area behind them receives no light and is left in shadow as light cannot pass through.*

Frosted glass is translucent

China objects are opaque

▶ *Not all light gives off heat. Glow-worms and fireflies attract a mate by making a part of their body glow using chemical reactions inside their bodies.*

Reflection and refraction

When light strikes a surface, some or all of it is reflected. On most surfaces, it is scattered in all directions. On mirrors and other smooth shiny surfaces every ray might bounce off in exactly the same pattern as it came. The result is a perfect reflection of the light source, or a mirror image. When light passes through something transparent, such as water, the rays are bent, or refracted, as the light slows down. This is why swimming pools sometimes look more shallow than they are, and straws appear bent when standing in a glass of water.

◄ *Refraction makes a straw look bent. It is not really bent: the light rays bend when they pass through the water.*

► Read further › solar rays
pg23 (n22)

Colors of light

When we see different colors, we are seeing different wavelengths of light. Sunlight appears colorless but it is called white light, which is actually a mixture of all colors. When it hits raindrops in the sky it can be split up into all the different colors to form a rainbow. They are split because the raindrop refracts (bends) each wavelength of light differently, fanning out the colors in a particular order, from red (the longest waves) at one end, to violet (the shortest) at the other.

► Read further › Sun's rays
pg23 (b22; n22)

◄ *The whole band of color is called the spectrum. The individual colors are created by splitting white light.*

How light travels

Light moves faster than anything in the universe. In space, it travels at nearly one billion ft/sec and takes just eight minutes to reach Earth from the Sun. It travels slightly slower through air, and slower still in water, but still travels very fast. Light always travels in tiny waves. But, these waves are tiny vibrations of energy, nothing like ripples in a pond. Every beam of light is a stream of tiny packets of these vibrations called photons, each with its own wavelength. Photons are particles like electrons, but so small they have no mass at all.

BRIGHT SPARKS

• Fluorescent lights can be made from a tube filled with the gas, neon. When electricity passes through the tube, energy is given to particles in the gas, which transfer it into light—neon light.

• Scientists think the human eye is so sensitive that a single photon falling on the eye can trigger a signal to the brain.

▼ *The waves in the electromagnetic spectrum are all different in lengths, but all make the same form of energy—just at different levels.*

Long radio waves   *Microwaves*   *X-rays*   *Gamma rays*

Shorter radio waves (TV)   *Light waves*   *Short X-rays*

► Read further › light
pg27 (m34)

Check it out!
• http://unmuseum.mus.pa.us/speed.htm

►► SPLITTING WHITE LIGHT see pg220 (l2) ►►

a b c d e f g h i j k l m n o p q r s t u v w

Sound

EVERY SOUND you hear, from a child's cry to the noise of an engine, is created by a vibration. Sometimes you can see the vibration—like a guitar string quickly twanging back and forth. Often, the movement is invisible, but the vibration is always there, and as the sound source moves to and fro, it pushes the air around it back and forth, too. The air is alternately squeezed and stretched to create waves that spread out in every direction. When these sound waves reach you, the sensitive mechanisms in your ears respond to the air vibrations, so you hear sound.

Waves of sound

Sound waves radiate in all directions from the sound source. Sound can travel through liquids, such as water, and many hard solids too. But a vacuum—completely empty space—is completely silent, because there is nothing to transmit the sound waves.

▶▶ Read further > solids / waves
pg10 (d2); pg27 (m34)

Echoes and acoustics

If you shout in a large empty hall, you might hear the sound ringing out momentarily afterward. This is because the sound of your voice bounces back to you off the hard walls. Every smooth, hard surface, such as a wall, bounces sound back, but you only hear echoes in big, empty spaces where the walls are far enough away for there to be a gap between the origin of the sound and its return. Although you may not always hear a distinct echo, sound reflections always affect the quality of the sound you hear. Concert halls must be designed carefully so that the internal surfaces of the hall create the right acoustics—sound vibrations—for the musicians and orchestras playing there.

▸ Whales and dolphins make high-pitched squeaks, clicks, and whistles that bounce off the seabed and surrounding fish or rocks. The echo that returns to the whale or dolphin helps it to find food.

▶▶ Read further > reflection
pg31 (b22)

▶▶ EARS see pg169 (b22) ▶▶

1   2   3   4   5   6   7   8   9   10   11   12   13   14   15   16   17   18   19

◀ *The sound of a jet plane moving through the air is created by sound waves that move slower than light waves. Therefore we see the plane before we hear it, because light waves reach us first.*

Read further › vibrations
pg36 (r2)

Volume and frequency (pitch)

Sounds can be soft or loud, high-pitched or low-pitched. It all depends on the energy and frequency of the sound waves. Big, energetic waves move your eardrums a long way within the ear and sound loud; small, low energy waves seem quieter. Volume is measured in "bels," or tenths of bels, called decibels. The pitch of a sound depends on the frequency of the waves (the number of waves that reach your ears per second). The greater the frequency, the higher the pitch of the sound. Frequency is measured in hertz (Hz), waves per second.

Atomic explosion – 180 dB

◀ *Sounds that are too loud can damage the ears. Sounds of 130 dB or over are painful, and prolonged exposure to sounds of between 90 to 100 dB can defen a person. People who work with loud machinery in factories or workshops have to wear ear protectors to protect their ears from the noise.*

Jet plane taking off – 110 to 140 dB

Express train—80 dB

Whispering—20 to 50 dB

Speed of sound

Sound takes time to travel through air. In a thunderstorm, you hear the thunder just after the flash of lightning that caused it, because light travels faster than sound. Sound travels slightly faster in warm air than cold air. In icy air at 32°F, sound travels only 1084 ft/sec. In milder air at 70°F, sound travels at 3,700 ft/sec. In hot air at 102°F, the speed of sound is 3,900 ft/sec. In liquid, the speed of sound is four times faster, and, in hard solids such as wood and steel it travels even faster.

Read further › light
pg31 (o22)

▾ *When an orchestra stops playing in a concert hall, the sound can be heard for about two seconds afterward. This is called the reverberation time.*

BRIGHT SPARKS

• A supersonic jet plane flies faster than sound. Its speed is given as a Mach number. The Mach number is the speed of the plane divided by the speed of sound in the air the plane is flying through. Mach 1 is the speed of sound, Mach 2 is twice the speed of sound.

• Most sounds contain many frequencies jumbled together—some are louder than others. A guitar and a violin playing the same note will sound different, because they produce a different mix of strong and weak frequencies.

Air and water

AIR AND water are the two most important substances in the world. Without air and water, life on Earth would be impossible. Air not only provides living creatures with the oxygen they need to breathe, but also a place to move around easily. The Earth's blanket of air, called the atmosphere, provides vital protection against the harmful radiation from space and helps to maintain a stable environment where life can flourish.

▼ *Plants need water to grow and survive. Rainforests get a lot of rain annually, and so are abundant with plant life and animals. In an ecosystem, each organism (living thing) is dependent on the other organisms living there.*

IT'S A FACT

• At the temperature called the triple point (32°F), water can exist in all three states (solid, liquid, and gas) at the same time.

• Only two percent of the world's water is permanently frozen in ice caps and glaciers.

BRIGHT SPARKS

• Water is less dense as a solid (ice) than as a liquid, which is why ice floats. Water expands as it freezes, which is why pipes break in cold winters and frost can split rock.

• Carbon dioxide (CO_2) makes up 0.03 percent of the air, but the proportion is continually changing as it is breathed out by animals and taken in by plants as they grow. Extra gas pumped out by industries and vehicles burning oil boosts CO_2 levels dramatically.

Ecosystems

Plants and animals interact with one other in regions called ecosystems. Earth is the only planet in the Solar System with a lot of water. In fact, three-quarters of the Earth is covered in water in the oceans *(see pg10 [r9])*. Earth's atmosphere is also unique—even more transparent than glass—and rich in oxygen, which is the gas upon which all life depends.

▶▶ Read further ⟩ Earth's atmosphere pg23 [b22]

Check it out!
• http://kids.earth.nasa.gov/

What are air and water?

Water is a compound in which two atoms of hydrogen gas (H_2) combine with one atom of oxygen gas (O) to form a colorless, odorless, tasteless liquid (H_2O). Sometimes, though, it may contain dissolved traces of other chemicals. Air, however, is always a mixture—not a compound—containing a variety of gases that are mixed but not chemically linked. More than three-quarters of the air is nitrogen (about 78 percent), and most of the rest is oxygen (about 21 percent). The remaining one percent consists of carbon dioxide, water vapor, and traces of other gases such as neon, helium, ozone, and krypton.

Nitrogen
78.08%

Oxygen
20.94%

Carbon dioxide
0.03%

Argon and other gases
0.95%

Read further › gases
pg11 (q31); pg15 (b29)

◄ *Air is a unique mixture that exists on Earth and nowhere else in the Solar System.*

Read further › attraction
pg21 (b31)

Why is water liquid?

Water is the only substance that can be solid, liquid, or gas at everyday temperatures. As a water molecule consists of two hydrogen atoms and one oxygen atom, the hydrogen atoms at one end of the molecule have a positive electrical charge; the oxygen atom at the other end has a negative charge. Molecules like this are called polar molecules. The positive and negative charges attract each other and hold water molecules together. Without them the molecules break away from each other more easily and water would change to steam at a lower temperature.

What is a solution?

A remarkable property of water is its ability to make solutions with other substances. A solution is formed when a substance is added to a liquid. Instead of just floating in the liquid, the substance breaks up entirely, so that its atoms and molecules completely intermingle with those of the liquid. This happens when coffee is added to water. The substance dissolved is called the solute; the liquid is called the solvent.

▸ *When sugar dissolves in coffee, the sugar is the solute and the coffee is the solvent.*

Read further › crystals / salt
pg17 (k31)

▲ *Ice is slightly less dense than water, which is why icebergs float in water, often partially above the surface depending on the volume (size) of the iceberg.*

◄◄ POSITIVE AND NEGATIVE CHARGES see pg21 (b31) ◄◄

22　23　24　25　26　27　28　29　30　31　32　33　34　35　36　37　38　39

Time

B EFORE THE invention of clocks, people measured time by the natural rhythm of the Earth—by watching the movements of the Sun, Moon and stars in the sky. Now we can see time passing as hands move or figures change on a clock. Modern atomic clocks can measure time with astonishing accuracy. Yet scientists and philosophers still find it hard to agree on what time is. Scientists say time is a dimension (like length and width) and that we move through time just as we can move sideways or backward and forward, or up and down. Time is said to be the fourth dimension: the other three are length, width, and depth. But time only runs one way: a candle cannot be unburned, or your life lived backward.

IT'S A FACT

• All living things have their own "biological" clocks to control their lives and stimulate certain behaviour at specific times.

• The shortest time that can be measured is a pico-second—one trillionth of a second.

Detector counts the atoms

Magnet separates atoms

▸ *Atomic time is measured by how many electromagnetic waves are absorbed by atoms.*

Oven where atoms "boil off"

Microwave source

Frequency divider

Computer adjusts microwaves

Digital display to show time

Atomic time

Just as a guitar string vibrates at a certain pitch or frequency, so do atoms and molecules. Atomic vibrations are so regular that they can be used to make the world's most accurate clocks—atomic clocks. These special clocks, all housed in special laboratories, mostly use the caesium-133 atom *(see pg14 [r2])*. Since 1967, one second has been defined as 9,192,631,770 vibrations of a caesium-133 atom. Atomic clocks are also used to set the world's standard time, called Coordinated Universal Time (UTC), set by the United States National Institute of Standards and Technology (NIST) agency.

▶▶ **Read further › vibrations** pg32 (d2)

Check it out!

• http://www.mrdowling.com/ 601–time.html

Natural clock

Sundials work well in the sunshine, but they do not work at night or in cloudy weather. Other ways of measuring time that did not count on sunshine were invented in the ancient world. A candle burns down steadily, so time can be measured by the changing length of a burning candle. Water or sand running steadily from one container to another can also mark the passing of time. Then, in the 17th century, the great Italian scientist Galileo Galilei noticed that a pendulum (a weight on the end of a wire or rod) of a certain length always swings at the same rate. This discovery made it possible to build accurate clocks by linking the swinging pendulum to pointers (hands) that showed the time on a dial (clock face).

▲ *As the Sun moves from east at the beginning of the day to west at the end of the day, the position of the shadow cast on the sundial moves, showing what time of day it is.*

Read further › shadows pg30 (k2)

BRIGHT SPARKS

• The length of a day on Earth has not always been the same. In the past, days were shorter and in the future, days will be longer, because the Earth is spinning more slowly as time goes on. The average day is 1.6 milliseconds (thousandths of a second) longer every 100 years.

• Einstein showed how the faster things travel, the slower time runs. When *Apollo 11* went to the Moon, an accurate clock on board lost a few seconds, not because of any fault but because time ran more slowly in the speeding space ship.

▼ *Time travel has been the subject of many books and movies. The machine in H.G. Wells' classic novel* The Time Machine *is portrayed on screen as being able to withstand the immense pressure of wormholes.*

Time travel

The brilliant scientist Albert Einstein suggested that time does not exist on its own but is part of something called space-time, which includes the whole universe. When we move around, we are not moving through space while time passes separately. We move through space-time. If time is linked to space, some scientists wonder if we might be able to move through the time part of space-time into the past or future. Objects in space called black holes have such a strong force of gravity that they might be able to bend space-time enough to create pathways called worm-holes that link to other places or times. If wormholes do exist then they are understood to be even smaller than an atom. Some scientists believe it might be possible to enlarge them using an extremely powerful electric field, holding them open long enough to make a tunnel through space-time and thus travel through time.

Read further › gravity pg24 (m12)

►► SPINNING EARTH see pg60 (m2) ►►

a b c d e f g h i j k l m n o p q r s t u v w

What is space?

SPACE IS everything in the universe that lies outside Earth's atmosphere. Looking at the night sky space seems filled with stars. Yet the distances between the stars are unimaginably vast and there is almost nothing between them but clouds of stardust. Much of space is a vast, empty void which is how it gets its name. No one knows how large space is. Much of it is too far away to see but using modern technology astronomers are discovering much more.

ABOVE AND BEYOND

• Since light takes a long time to reach Earth from distant objects in space, we see them not as they are now but as they were when the light left them. We see the bright star Deneb as it was 1800 years ago, during ancient Roman times.

• When we look at the Andromeda Galaxy, we see it as scientists believe it looked over two million years ago, when the first human type creatures evolved in Africa.

The scale of the universe

What we can see of space is only a tiny fraction of what is actually there. With powerful telescopes intensely bright clusters of stars or galaxies, (see pg52 [j17]) called quasars, can be seen from 13 billion light-years away. So, if there are quasars equally far away in all directions the universe must be at least 26 billion light-years across. The light of some stars, when seen through a telescope, may be thousands or even millions of light-years away.

▶▶ Read further › light
pg39 (d22); pg54 (j6)

IT'S A FACT

• It takes light about eight minutes to reach us from the Sun.

• It takes light four years to reach us from Proxima Centauri, the star nearest the Sun.

▲ *Even nearby stars are over 25 trillion mi away; many stars are billions of time farther.*

Check it out!

• http://www.kidsastronomy.com/academy
• http://www.angelfire.com/tx/etetall/index2.html

▶▶ TELESCOPES see pg195 (b22) ▶▶

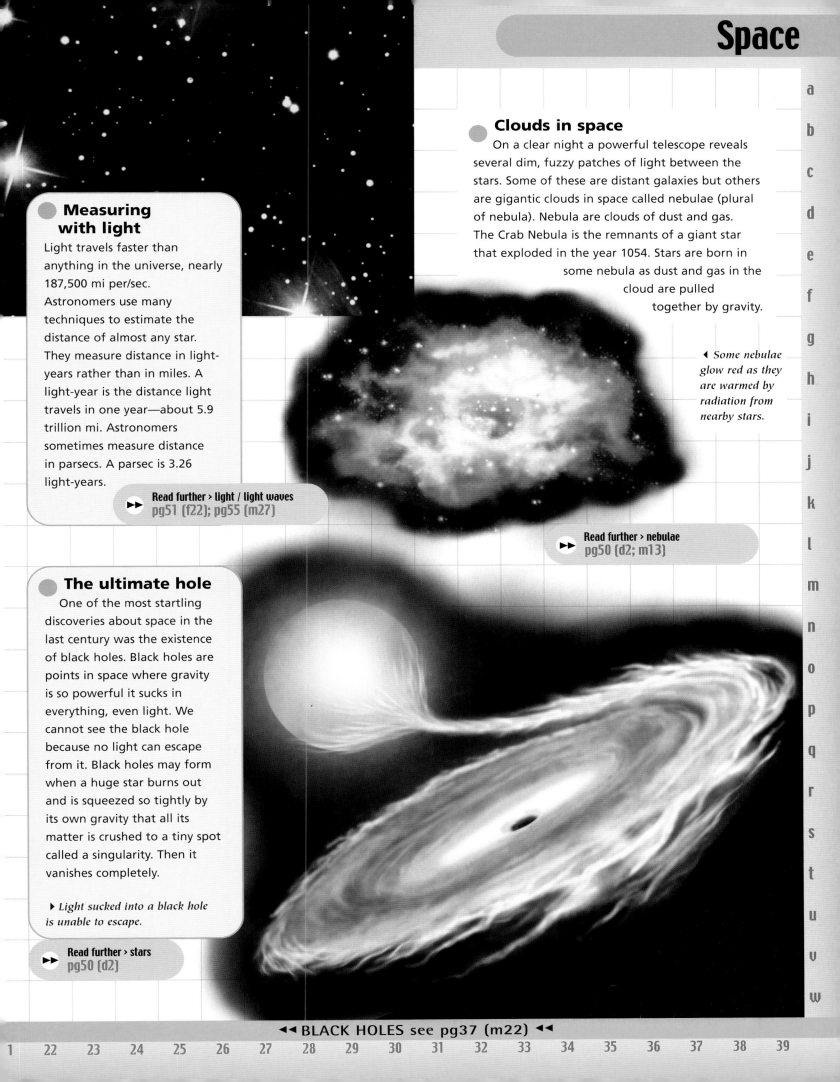

Measuring with light

Light travels faster than anything in the universe, nearly 187,500 mi per/sec. Astronomers use many techniques to estimate the distance of almost any star. They measure distance in light-years rather than in miles. A light-year is the distance light travels in one year—about 5.9 trillion mi. Astronomers sometimes measure distance in parsecs. A parsec is 3.26 light-years.

▶▶ **Read further > light / light waves**
pg51 (f22); pg55 (m27)

Clouds in space

On a clear night a powerful telescope reveals several dim, fuzzy patches of light between the stars. Some of these are distant galaxies but others are gigantic clouds in space called nebulae (plural of nebula). Nebula are clouds of dust and gas. The Crab Nebula is the remnants of a giant star that exploded in the year 1054. Stars are born in some nebula as dust and gas in the cloud are pulled together by gravity.

◀ *Some nebulae glow red as they are warmed by radiation from nearby stars.*

▶▶ **Read further > nebulae**
pg50 (d2; m13)

The ultimate hole

One of the most startling discoveries about space in the last century was the existence of black holes. Black holes are points in space where gravity is so powerful it sucks in everything, even light. We cannot see the black hole because no light can escape from it. Black holes may form when a huge star burns out and is squeezed so tightly by its own gravity that all its matter is crushed to a tiny spot called a singularity. Then it vanishes completely.

▶ *Light sucked into a black hole is unable to escape.*

▶▶ **Read further > stars**
pg50 (d2)

◀◀ BLACK HOLES see pg37 (m22) ◀◀

a b c d e f g h i j k l m n o p q r s t u v w

1 22 23 24 25 26 27 28 29 30 31 32 33 34 35 36 37 38 39

White ball of rock

T HE MOON is the biggest, brightest object in the night sky, shining almost like a night-time sun. Yet it has no light of its own. It is just a big cold ball of rock that shines only because it reflects the light of the Sun. It is Earth's companion in space, about 240,000 mi away, and circles slowly around us once a month. As the Moon moves around, it also rotates (turns) slowly on its axis so that the same face is always toward us. The far side of the Moon is never seen from the Earth's surface.

▼ *After each full Moon, the visible portion of the Moon shrinks again.*

Full Moon   Waning Moon   Half Moon   Old Moon   New Moon

● Walking on the Moon

When astronauts landed on the Moon in 1969, they found a landscape of cliffs and plains, completely covered in many places by a fine white dust. This lunar dust was created long ago when the Moon's surface broke up under the impact of meteorites. Because there is no air, wind, rain, or snow on the Moon, the dust never moves and so the footprints left behind by astronauts will be there for millions of years.

▸ *The Earth seen from the Moon.*

● Phases (changes) of the Moon

All that can be seen of the Moon from Earth is its brightly lit, sunny side *(see pg43 [c27])*. As it circles the Earth, the sunny side of the Moon is seen from different angles so it seems to change shape. At the New Moon, it is positioned directly between the Earth and the Sun so all that can be seen from Earth is just a crescent-shaped glimpse of the moons sunny side. Over the next two weeks more and more of the Moon is revealed until the Full Moon, when it is farthest away from the Sun, all of it becomes visible. During the next two weeks, less and less of the Moon is visible until it returns to a crescent shape, called the Old Moon.

▶▶ **Read further › eclipse** pg43 [b22]

▶▶ EARTH'S ORBIT see pg60 (m2) ▶▶

● Seas and craters

All over the Moon are large, dark patches that people once thought were seas, so they are called *Mare*, from the Latin for sea. Today, scientists know they are vast, dry plains formed by ancient lava from volcanoes that erupted early in the Moon's life. Most of the craters that pit the Moon's surface also date from early in the Moon's life. They were formed by the impact of huge rocks that crashed down from space.

▶▶ **Read further › Moon's surface** pg40 (o2)

▶ *The Moon's surface is pitted with ancient craters that were made by the impact of asteroids.*

● THE MOST MOONS

Planet	Moons
Uranus	21
Saturn	18
Jupiter	16
Neptune	8
Mars	2

Earth and Pluto each have 1 moon

To scale
1 square = 1,875 mi

The Earth and the Moon shown to scale

Moon = 2,188 mi across

Earth = 7,973 mi across

● Moon landing

The Moon is the only other world humans have ever visited. The first men to walk on the Moon were American astronauts, Neil Armstrong and Buzz Aldrin, on the *Apollo 11* space mission. They touched down on the surface on July 20, 1969. The first woman in space was Russian, Valentin Tereshkova.

▼ *Alan Bean from* Apollo 12.

▶▶ **Read further › space travel** pg40 (o2); pg56 (h32)

 Check it out!

- http://kids.msfc.nasa.gov/Earth/Moon/
- http://www.dustbunny.com/afk/howdo/howdo.htm

▶▶ VOLCANOES see pg70 (d2) ▶▶

j
k
l
m
n
o
p
q
r
s
t
u
v
w

Great ball of fire

THE SUN is a star just like all the stars in the night sky. In fact, it is a medium-sized star in the middle of its 10 billion-year life. Yet it is much nearer than any other star— just 90 million mi away. Like all stars it is incredibly hot. Huge pressure inside the Sun creates temperatures of over 27 million°F. This tremendous heat turns the Sun's surface into a raging inferno that burns so brightly that it floods the Earth with light, giving us daylight.

IT'S A FACT

- Each 2.25 sq/in of the Sun's surface burns with the brightness of 1.5 million candles!

- The Sun is 100 times wider than the Earth.

Inside the Sun

The Sun is made mostly of two gases: about three-quarters hydrogen and one-quarter helium. The energy that is generated inside its core takes 10 million years to rise to the surface, passing through several layers including the glowing surface or photosphere—a forest of flames called the chromosphere and a crowning halo of fire called the corona.

▼ The Sun's corona flares out behind the Moon during a solar eclipse.

▶▶ Read further › Sun's heat pg43 (f34)

Photosphere 10,800°F

Chromosphere 18,032°F

Solar flare (18 million°F)

Radiating zone

Core (27 million°F)

▲ Cutaway of the Sun showing its layers.

▶▶ USE OF SUN'S ENERGY see pg205 (j22) ▶▶

1 2 3 4 5 6 7 8 9 10 11 12 13 14 15 16 17 18 19 2

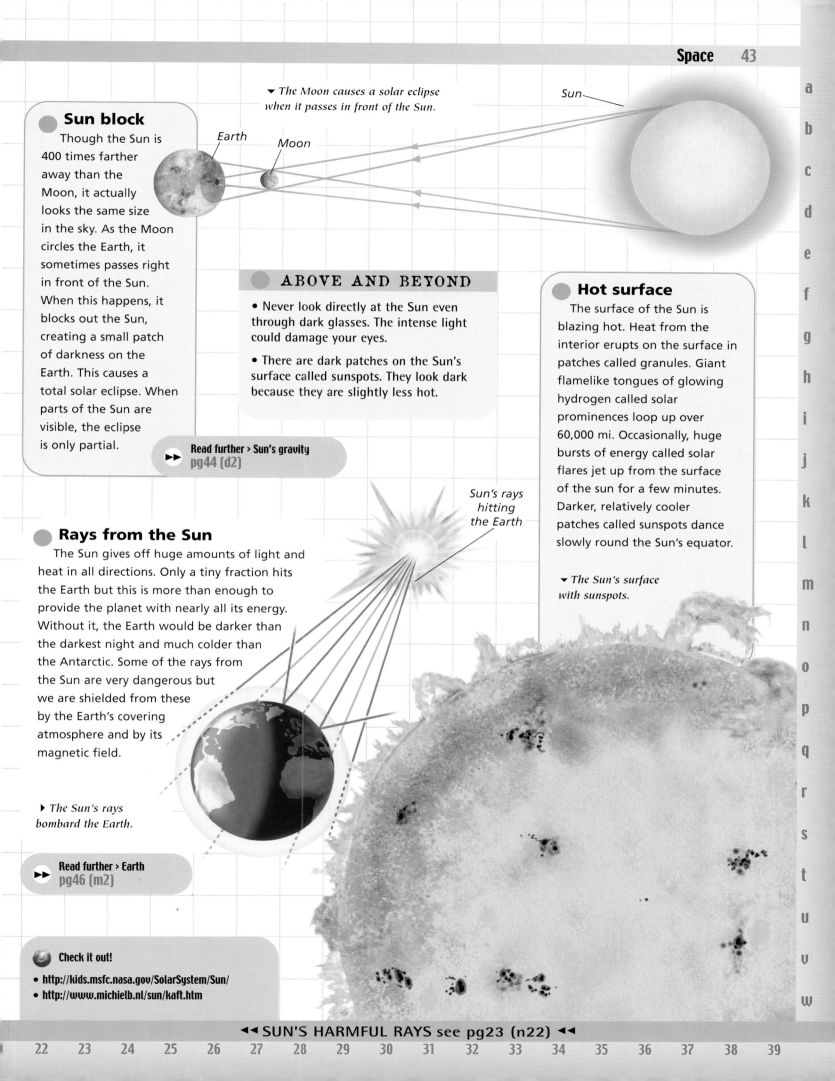

▼ The Moon causes a solar eclipse when it passes in front of the Sun.

Sun—

Earth Moon

Sun block

Though the Sun is 400 times farther away than the Moon, it actually looks the same size in the sky. As the Moon circles the Earth, it sometimes passes right in front of the Sun. When this happens, it blocks out the Sun, creating a small patch of darkness on the Earth. This causes a total solar eclipse. When parts of the Sun are visible, the eclipse is only partial.

▶▶ **Read further › Sun's gravity** pg44 (d2)

ABOVE AND BEYOND

• Never look directly at the Sun even through dark glasses. The intense light could damage your eyes.

• There are dark patches on the Sun's surface called sunspots. They look dark because they are slightly less hot.

Hot surface

The surface of the Sun is blazing hot. Heat from the interior erupts on the surface in patches called granules. Giant flamelike tongues of glowing hydrogen called solar prominences loop up over 60,000 mi. Occasionally, huge bursts of energy called solar flares jet up from the surface of the sun for a few minutes. Darker, relatively cooler patches called sunspots dance slowly round the Sun's equator.

▼ The Sun's surface with sunspots.

Rays from the Sun

The Sun gives off huge amounts of light and heat in all directions. Only a tiny fraction hits the Earth but this is more than enough to provide the planet with nearly all its energy. Without it, the Earth would be darker than the darkest night and much colder than the Antarctic. Some of the rays from the Sun are very dangerous but we are shielded from these by the Earth's covering atmosphere and by its magnetic field.

Sun's rays hitting the Earth

▶ The Sun's rays bombard the Earth.

▶▶ **Read further › Earth** pg46 (m2)

Check it out!

• http://kids.msfc.nasa.gov/SolarSystem/Sun/
• http://www.michielb.nl/sun/kaft.htm

◀◀ **SUN'S HARMFUL RAYS** see pg23 (n22) ◀◀

22 23 24 25 26 27 28 29 30 31 32 33 34 35 36 37 38 39

a b c d e f g h i j k l m n o p q r s t u v w

Circling planets

EARTH IS not alone in space. Including Earth, nine planets circle, or orbit, the Sun. They move around the Sun in the same direction, in eliptical (oval) orbits and are held in place by the pull of the Sun's gravity. Many of the other planets have their own moons and in between the planets are tiny chunks of rock called asteroids. Together, the Sun, Earth, the other planets, their moons, and the asteroids are called the Solar System.

● Solar System

All the nine planets of the Solar System orbit the Sun in the same plane, except for Pluto, the most distant, which cuts across at an angle. The farther a planet is from the Sun, the longer it takes to complete its orbit. Mercury, the nearest planet to the Sun, takes just 88 days, Venus 225 days, and Earth 365 days. Distant Neptune takes 165 years and Pluto, which is even more remote, takes almost 250 years.

▶ *How the planets circle the Sun.*

Read further › solar planets
▶▶ pg47 (b22); pg48 (b22)

▼ *Galaxies such as this form from swirling gas and dust.*

● How it began

By measuring the age of meteorites (rocks that fall to Earth from space), scientists have figured out that the Solar System is about 4.6 billion years old. When it began to form, it was a whirling mass of stardust and gases, but as it spun around quickly, gravity began to pull it tighter together. Eventually, the dense center formed the Sun and dust farther out gathered into lumps and became the planets.

Read further › Big Bang theory
▶▶ pg54 (j6)

▶▶ DISCOVERY OF ORBITING PLANETS see pg277 (b31) ▶▶

◀ After visiting Jupiter, Saturn, Uranus, and Neptune, Voyager 2 is now leaving the Solar System.

Exploring the planets

Until barely 200 years ago, people used to think there were only five other planets in the Solar System—Mercury, Mars, Venus, Jupiter and Saturn—because only these could be seen with the naked eye. Powerful telescopes have revealed three more—first Uranus (1781), then Neptune (1846) and finally Pluto (1930). Now, unmanned space probes have visited all the planets except Pluto and have landed on Mars and Venus.

▶▶ Read further › exploring the Solar System pg57 (b22)

ABOVE AND BEYOND

• The size of the Solar System measures at least 12,500 million mi across. If Earth were the size of a grain of salt, the Solar System would be the size of a sports stadium.

• Over 70 of the known planets outside our Solar System are circling stars visible to the naked eye.

Faraway planets

Scientists guess that about 30 billion other stars in our galaxy have planets circling them just like the Sun. Astronomers are now looking for some of these "extra-solar" planets. The planets are much too far away to see but they can be detected because their gravity makes their star wobble slightly. Astronomers have spotted about 100 "extra solar" planets—most of them as big as Jupiter. One day they hope to spot planets as small as Earth, too. The dense atmosphere on some of the planets may give them a bright color, such as the purple shown in this artwork.

Check it out!

• http://amazing-space.stsci.edu
• http://www.stardate.org/
  resources/ssguide/

▶▶ ASTRONOMERS see pg218 (d2) ▶▶

a b c d e f g h k l m n o p q r s t u v w

22 23 24 25 26 27 28 29 30 31 32 33 34 35 36 37 38 39

Rocky planets

THE FOUR planets nearest to the Sun are, in order, Mercury, Venus, Earth, and Mars. All four are small compared to most of the planets farther out, such as Jupiter. These four planets are sometimes called the "terrestrial" or Earth—like planets. Unlike the giant outer planets they are made mostly of rock and have hard surfaces on which a spacecraft could land. In fact, space probes have landed on both Venus and Mars, the nearest planets to Earth. All the rocky planets have an atmosphere, a layer of gas—although Mercury's barely exists—but otherwise they are very different. Earth, above all, has abundant water and life but each planet has its own unique qualities.

IT'S A FACT

• Mercury is the second smallest planet, after Pluto.

• Mars is about one-tenth of the weight of the Earth.

Earth

Earth is the third planet from the Sun, about 93,750 mi away from it. Earth is sometimes called the 'Goldilocks' planet after the fairy story in which the little girl chooses the porridge that is neither too hot nor too cold. Earth is not so close to the Sun that it is scorching hot nor so far away that it is icy cold. It is also the only planet that has huge amounts of liquid water on its surface. This combination makes it uniquely able to support life.

▶ *Oceans and continents are clearly visible through Earth's atmosphere.*

▶▶ Read further > Earth and Sun pg43 (l22)

Pluto

Besides the four inner planets, there is another rocky planet, Pluto. Pluto is tiny—smaller than our Moon—and very far away, on the outer edge of the Solar System.

◀ *Like Earth, Pluto has one moon.*

▶ *Mars' surface is cracked by a valley called the Vallis Marineris (Mariner Valley).*

▶▶ EARTH see pg58 (d2) ▶▶

1   2   3   4   5   6   7   8   9   10   11   12   13   14   15   16   17   18   19

Mercury

Mercury is the planet nearest to the Sun, often less than 30 million mi away. With almost no atmosphere to protect it, temperatures on the side of mercury facing the Sun soar to 800°F while the dark side plummets to −292°F. Mercury is so close to the Sun it travels around it in just 88 days (compared to 365 days for Earth). Yet it spins very slowly, taking over 58 Earth days. There are fewer than two days in Mercury's year.

The Sun scorches Mercury's surface.

▶▶ **Read further › Mercury**
pg46 (d15)

▲ *Mercury has no moon.*

Venus

Venus is almost exactly the same size as the Earth. It is about 7,000 mi across and weighs about one-fifth less than the Earth, it is unlike the Earth because its atmosphere is thick with poisonous carbon dioxide and clouds of sulphuric acid. This thick atmosphere traps the Sun's heat and makes the surface a scorching desert where temperatures rise to 900°F, making it the hottest planet in the Solar System.

◀ *Venus with its thick, dense atmosphere.*

ABOVE AND BEYOND

• Like Earth, Mars has volcanoes. Olympus Mons on Mars is the biggest volcano in the Solar System, and, at 16,619 ft is three times higher than Mount Everest.

• Venus reflects sunlight so well from its atmosphere that it shines brighter in the night sky than any other star. As it appears just after sunset and just before sunrise, it is known as the evening or morning star.

Mars

Mars is the only planet with daytime temperatures and an atmosphere similar to Earth's except it is mainly carbon dioxide. It is also the only other planet with water on its surface. But Mars' water is frozen solid in ice caps. Most of the planet is a desert, with no oceans or any sign of life— just the iron-rich red rocks and dust which earned it the nickname "the red planet." The Mars Pathfinder mission confirmed this when it landed the robot exploration vehicle *Sojourner* on Mars in 1997. Although Mars appears to be a lifeless planet scientists hope space probes will find traces of microscopic life under its surface.

▶▶ **Read further › Mars**
pg47 (m33); pg56 (b14)

◀ *The* Sojourner *robot on Mars.*

Check it out!

• http://www.spacewander.com/USA/english.html
• http://kids.msfc.nasa.gov/Solar System/Planets/

i j k l m n o p q r s t u v w

▶▶ ORBITING PLANETS see pg219 (b22) ▶▶

Giant balls of gas

OUT BEYOND Mars are four planets bigger than any of the others in the Solar System: Jupiter, Saturn, Uranus, and Neptune. Jupiter and Saturn are really huge. Jupiter is twice as heavy as all the other planets combined and 1,300 times bigger in size than Earth! Saturn is almost as big. Despite this, all these giant planets are mostly gas, not rock. Only a tiny core in the center is rock. The gas around it is squeezed by the huge pressure of its gravity until it often becomes liquid or even solid.

IT'S A FACT

• Neptune has winds of over 1,250 mph.

• Saturn and Jupiter have cores of rock that are twice as hot as the Sun's surface.

Jupiter

Jupiter is by far the biggest planet in the Solar System— over 90,000 mi across—and it takes almost 12 years to orbit around the Sun. Despite its immense bulk, Jupiter spins round faster than any other planet. In fact, it turns all the way around in less than 10 hours, which means the surface is whizing along at almost 28,000 mph. Its surface is covered with colorful clouds of ammonia gas whipped into storm belts by violent winds, lightning flashes, and thunderclaps. One storm, called the Great Red Spot, is 25,000 mi across and has lasted for at least 300 years. Jupiter has a faint ring system and 16 moons.

▶ *Jupiter, with the Great Red Spot clearly visible, bottom left.*

Check it out!

• http://www.spacewander.com/METRIC/metric.html
• http://kids.msfc.nasa.gov/Solar System/Planets/

▶▶ GALILEAN MOONS see pg221 (b22) ▶▶

1 2 3 4 5 6 7 8 9 10 11 12 13 14 15 16 17 18 19

Saturn

Saturn is the second largest planet—a pale butterscotch-colored ball of gas over 75,000 mi across. It is known as the ringed planet, because it has a spectacular halo of rings around it. The rings consist of countless tiny chunks of ice and rock. Barely thicker than a house, the rings stretch out over 105,000 mi into space.

▸ *Saturn is made almost entirely of gas—helium and hydrogen.*

Read further › rock core
pg48 (d15)

Neptune

Neptune is the eighth planet from the Sun and the fourth largest planet in the Solar System. Like Uranus, Neptune is covered in deep oceans of liquid methane that fill the atmosphere with methane and give it a beautiful cobalt-blue color. It is so far from the Sun—about 2.5 billion mi—that it takes 164.79 years to complete its orbit. It has not circled the Sun once since it was discovered in 1846.

▾ *Like Saturn and Uranus, Neptune is circled by rings.*

Read further › wind
pg48 (d15)

Uranus

Uranus is so far from the Sun that its surface is unimaginably cold. Temperatures at the cloud tops on Uranus drop to –378°F! In this bitter cold, even the methane (natural gas) that makes up much of the planet's atmosphere turns to liquid. As with Neptune, Uranus' startling blue color is caused by methane in the atmosphere.

▴ *Uranus is completely covered in deep oceans.*

Read further › Sun
pg42 (d2)

ABOVE AND BEYOND

• Uranus revolves around the Sun with its south pole pointing sunward. As a result, the south pole of Uranus is the hottest place on the planet. Summers here last 42 years!

• Because Jupiter is so massive, its gravity is very strong—its pressure squeezes the planet so hard that it makes it hot.

►► GRAVITY see pg220 (n13) ►►

Glowing lights

LIKE THE Sun, stars are huge, fiery balls of incredibly hot gases. They shine because they are making energy. Deep inside every shining star, huge amounts of pressure squeeze atoms of hydrogen gas together to create nuclear reactions millions of times more powerful than a nuclear bomb. These reactions boost the star's core temperature so much that the surface glows white-hot. A star continues to glow, sending out light, heat, radio waves, and other radiation until all the hydrogen is used up.

1. *A star is born when nuclear reactions begin*

2. *A star burns steadily*

3. *Dust swirling around a new star may form planets*

4. *A nebula formed from cloud and dust*

▲ *The four main stages of a star's formation.*

Star quality

Stars create their energy in the same way as nuclear bombs but they rarely explode. Medium-sized stars burn steadily for billions of years because there is a balance—between the heat energy, which pushes gases outward as they expand, and gravity, which pulls them back in. Only when the star's nuclear fuel burns out is this balance broken and the star shrinks or, on some occasions, explodes.

◄ *A medium-sized star.*

A star's life

Stars are starting up and dying down all over the universe. They begin in giant clouds of gas and dust, where material gathers into clumps called nebulae, each containing evaporating gas globules or EGGs, the beginning of stars. Inside the dark nebulae, EGGs are squeezed by their own gravity until they become hot. When an EGG is hot (at least 5 million°F), nuclear reactions begin and it becomes a star. Medium-sized stars such as our Sun burn for about 10 billion years.

◄ *Stars are born in clouds of dust and gas.*

▶▶ **Read further** › nebulae
pg39 (b32)

▶▶ RADIATION see pg231 (i32) ▶▶

1   2   3   4   5   6   7   8   9   10   11   12   13   14   15   16   17   18   19

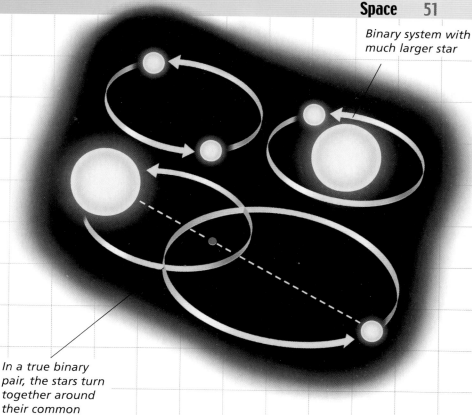

Binary system with much larger star

In a true binary pair, the stars turn together around their common center of gravity

▲ *Binary system with similar sized stars. The stars may be close together or millions of miles apart.*

The brightest stars

The color of a star's light depends on its temperature: blue stars are hottest, red stars are coolest. Astronomers rank the brightness of each star with a number or "magnitude." The brightest stars have the lowest magnitude, which may be minus numbers. Some stars look brighter than others only because they are closer to Earth so astronomers talk of "relative" magnitude—the brightness of a star compared to others and "absolute" magnitude—how bright a star really is.

Increasing brightness

Red giants

Blue stars

Main sequence stars

The Sun

Yellow stars

White dwarfs

Red stars

Increasing temperature

▲ *Graph showing how a star's brightness varies with its temperature. Medium-sized stars fall in a straight line—the main sequence—showing a simple relationship.*

▶▶ **Read further › light-years**
pg39 (d22)

Twin stars

Many stars are in companion pairs called binaries. True binaries are pairs of stars that whirl around together like a pair of dancers held together by their mutual gravity. Sometimes, one star passes in front of the other which then seems to become dim. Some stars look like binaries even though they are nowhere near each other because they are in the same line of sight from the Earth. These are called optical binaries.

HOTTEST STARS

Star	Temperature
• Blue	up to 72,000°F
• Blue-white	19,800°F
• White	13,500°F
• Yellow	10,800°F
• Orange	9,000°F

Check it out!

• http://www.bbc.co.uk/science /space/stars/index.shtml
• http://www.howstuffworks. com/star.htm

▶▶ ASTRONOMERS see pg218 (d33) ▶▶

22 23 24 25 26 27 28 29 30 31 32 33 34 35 36 37 38 39

a b c d e f g h i j k l m n o p q r s t u v w

Star cities

STARS ARE not scattered evenly throughout space.
Instead, they cluster together in groups called galaxies,
with vast stretches of completely empty space between
them. The three galaxies that can be seen with the naked
eye look like faint blurs in the night sky
but though powerful
telescopes show that
they contain billions
of stars. Most galaxies
are too far away to be
seen but astronomers
estimate that there are
about 100 billion in the
universe. An average
galaxy, such as the Milky
Way, contains 100 billion
stars and is about 100,000
light-years across.

▲ Our Milky Way Galaxy
seen edge-on from deep space.

● Star cities

The biggest galaxies are
egg-shaped or elliptical
and may contain as many
as a trillion stars. These
elliptical galaxies probably
formed a very long time ago,
sometime over 10 billion years,
not long after the dawn of the
universe (see pg44 [u16]).
Elliptical galaxies are rarely alone,
and tend to group together into clusters.

▲ Eliptical galaxy clusters can contain
thousands of galaxies of all kinds.

● The Milky Way

On clear nights, far from any
town, when there is no Moon,
a faint, hazy, white band can
be seen stretching right across
the sky. This band is called the
Milky Way. Through binoculars,
it is clear that the Milky Way
consists of countless stars. It is a
vast cluster of over 100 billion
stars. The Milky Way appears to
us as a narrow band, because
we are looking at it edgewise.
If we could look down on it,
we would see that it looks like
a giant spinning wheel, with a
dense bulge at its center
containing mostly older stars.

▶▶ Read further › egg–shaped galaxies
pg53 (k27)

Spiral galaxies

Many galaxies, such as the Milky Way, are spiral shaped, with a dense cluster of stars at the center. They are spiral because they are spinning and billions of stars trail from long arms as they rotate at tremendous speed. Although we feel no movement because we are "glued" to the Earth by gravity. our Sun is being swept round by the galaxy at nearly 62 million mph.

▶ *Spiral galaxies are said to spin like a spinning wheel.*

Read further > Earth
▶▶ pg46 (m2)

ABOVE AND BEYOND

• Spiral galaxies may have a giant black hole at the center which stars sucks in like water spiraling down a plug hole.

• Although the stars make spiral galaxies which look like giant fried eggs, these galaxies are actually shaped more like burgers, because they are mostly made of invisible "dark matter." The stars are just the filling.

Shapeless galaxies

About one in ten galaxies have no obvious shape at all. Some astronomers think these irregular galaxies formed from the debris of a gigantic space collision when two galaxies crashed into each other.

▶ *Irregular galaxies contain many young and newborn stars.*

Check it out!

• http://www.windows.ucar.edu/tour/link=/
the_universe/Galaxy
• http://www.enchantedlearning.com
/subjects/astronomy/solarsystem

Read further > star birth
▶▶ pg50 (m13)

◄◄ BLACK HOLES see pg37 (m22) ◄◄

22 23 24 25 26 27 28 29 30 31 32 33 34 35 36 37 38 39

Big Bang

THE UNIVERSE may not always have existed. Scientists think it began about 13 to 15 billion years ago with the "Big Bang." It is believed that one moment there was just a tiny hot ball containing everything in the universe and then a moment later the universe burst into existence with the biggest explosion of all time, separating into basic forces such as electricity and gravity—so big that everything is still hurtling out from it—even today.

IT'S A FACT

• The farthest galaxies from Earth are hurtling away at almost the speed of light.

• The afterglow of the Big Bang can be detected in microwave radiation which emanates from all over space.

The Big Bang theory

1. At first the entire universe was a hot ball tinier than an atom and much hotter than any star. This swelled much, much faster than the speed of light, growing to the size of a galaxy in just a tiny fraction of a second.

2. As the universe expanded, it began to cool and tiny particles of energy and matter— each of them much smaller than atoms—began to form a thick, soup-like material.

3. After about three minutes, gravity started to pull the particles together. Atoms joined together to make gases such as hydrogen and helium, and the thick "soup" began to clear and thin out. By the end of the third minute, the matter that surrounds us today had been created.

Check it out!

• http://curious.astro.cornell.edu/
cosmology.php
• http://www.amnh.org/rose/
hayden-bigbang.html
• http://cbc4kids.cbc.ca/general/
the-lab/big-bang/

◄◄ ELECTRICITY see pg20 (f2) ◄◄

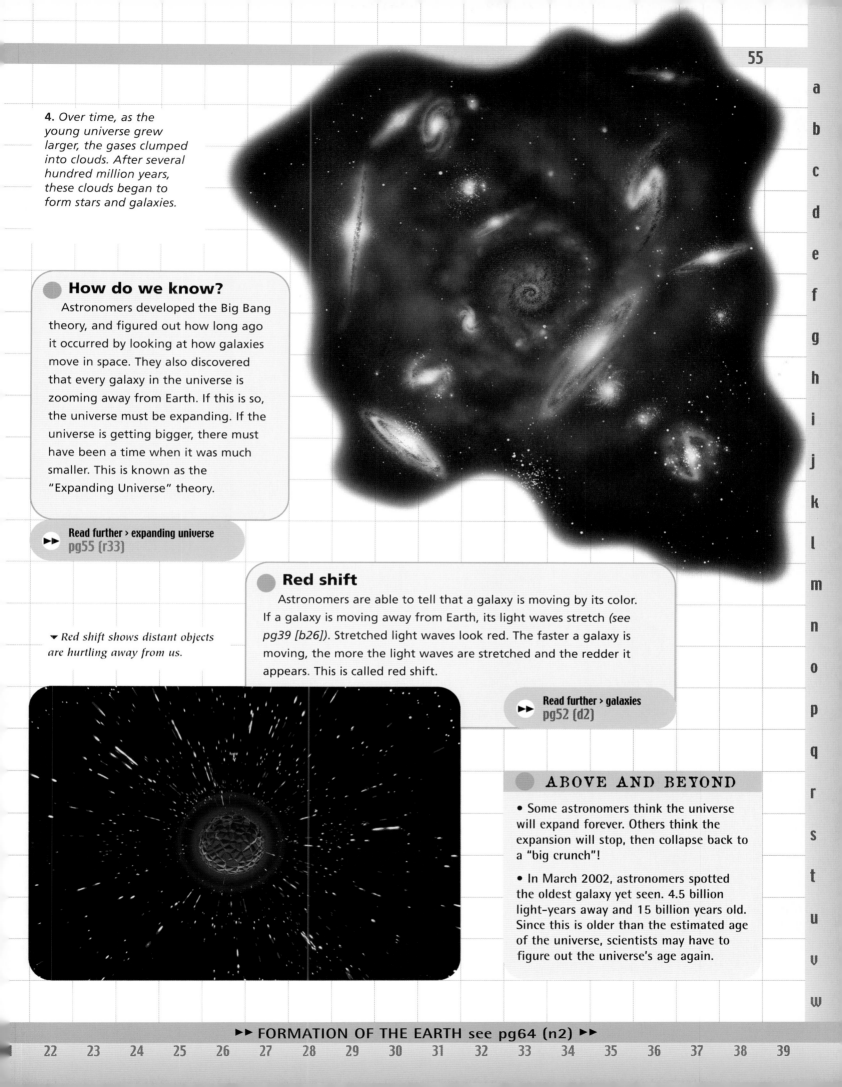

4. *Over time, as the young universe grew larger, the gases clumped into clouds. After several hundred million years, these clouds began to form stars and galaxies.*

How do we know?

Astronomers developed the Big Bang theory, and figured out how long ago it occurred by looking at how galaxies move in space. They also discovered that every galaxy in the universe is zooming away from Earth. If this is so, the universe must be expanding. If the universe is getting bigger, there must have been a time when it was much smaller. This is known as the "Expanding Universe" theory.

▶▶ **Read further › expanding universe**
pg55 (r33)

▼ Red shift shows distant objects are hurtling away from us.

Red shift

Astronomers are able to tell that a galaxy is moving by its color. If a galaxy is moving away from Earth, its light waves stretch *(see pg39 [b26])*. Stretched light waves look red. The faster a galaxy is moving, the more the light waves are stretched and the redder it appears. This is called red shift.

▶▶ **Read further › galaxies**
pg52 (d2)

ABOVE AND BEYOND

• Some astronomers think the universe will expand forever. Others think the expansion will stop, then collapse back to a "big crunch"!

• In March 2002, astronomers spotted the oldest galaxy yet seen. 4.5 billion light-years away and 15 billion years old. Since this is older than the estimated age of the universe, scientists may have to figure out the universe's age again.

a b c d e f g h i j k l m n o p q r s t u v w

Space travel

THE AGE of space travel dawned half a century ago when the tiny Russian satellite *Sputnik 1* was blasted into space in 1957. Since then hundreds of spacecraft have been launched and the boundaries of space exploration are being pushed farther and farther, as spacecraft venture into the Solar System. In 1969, the astronauts of *Apollo 11* set foot on the Moon. In 1976, the *Viking 1* robot space probe landed on Mars. In 1973, *Pioneer 10* reached Jupiter. *Voyagers 1* and *2*, launched in 1977, have flown beyond Pluto, though not yet out of the Solar System.

● ABOVE AND BEYOND

• Mars has already been visited by more space probes *(see pg47 [t29])* than any other planet, though not all were successful. It may become the first planet (beyond Earth) to be visited by humans.

• The first living creature in space was a dog named Laika that went up in the Russian *Sputnik 2* in 1957. Sadly, she could not be brought back to Earth.

Orbiter *goes into orbit around the Earth*

Orbiter *crew place satellite in space*

● Space shuttle

In the early days manned spacecraft could only be used once with just a tiny capsule carrying the astronauts as they fell back to Earth. Now astronauts are carried up into orbit above the Earth by a shuttle craft which can take off and land again and again, like an airplane. The Russian version was a one-off named the Buran or "snowstorm"; the American shuttle is known as the shuttle orbiter.

Orbiter *positions itself to re-enter Earth's atmosphere*

Main fuel tank falls away 80 mi up

Shuttle being transported to launch pad

Solid fuel rocket burners fall away 28 mi up

Orbiter *lands like a glider*

▶▶ **Read further ▸ space shuttle**
pg57 [h32]

● IT'S A FACT

• It will take NASA's *New Horizons* space probe ten years to reach Pluto—due to be launched in 2006.

• The first man in space was Russian cosmonaut, Yuri Gagarin, in April 1961.

● Check it out!

• http://galileo.jpl.nasa.gov/
• http://www.nasa.gov/kids/kids_spacetravel.html
• http://kidsastronomy.about.com/cs/missions/index.htm

Robot explorers

Humans have only been to the Moon but robot spacecraft have now visited all the planets in our Solar System except for Pluto. Among the most successful probes was NASA's *Galileo* mission, which reached Jupiter in December 1995. The probe orbited the planet and descended into its atmosphere, relaying stunning pictures of the planet's surface and its moons. NASA's next space probe is due to explore Pluto.

◀ *The Galileo space probe orbiting Jupiter.*

Read further > space probe / Jupiter
pg46 (n22); pg48 (l2)

Rocket launch

Powerful rockets are needed to boost a spacecraft to the speed it needs to break away from Earth's gravity. But once it is out in space, these rockets are no longer needed, so spacecraft are launched by a series of rockets or stages that drop away once their task is done and their fuel is spent.

▶ *The stages in a rocket launch.*

Read further > rocket launch
pg56 (k11)

Living in space

Space stations are spacecraft that remain in space, as they continually orbit the Earth. They provide a home in space for astronauts and scientists—and the occasional high-paying tourist. They are built up in space bit by bit in a series of missions. The current space station, the International Space Station, will be the biggest yet, 99 mi long, providing as much living space as two jumbo jets.

Read further > space station
pg41 (l29)

▼ *The International Space Station.*

▶▶ SPACE PROBES see pg213 (c33) ▶▶

The jewel planet

THE EARTH is one of nine planets in the Solar System that orbit the Sun. Like some of the other planets, it is a big ball of rock, wrapped around with a thin layer of gases, called the atmosphere *(see pg78 [i18])*. Yet the Earth is different from the other planets in crucial ways. From a distance, it looks like a blue-and-green jewel hanging in space. It is partly blue because, uniquely among the planets, the Earth has huge amounts of water in oceans *(see pg77 [q25])*. It is partly green because, unlike any other planets, Earth's water supports life.

▶▶ **Read further › tectonic plates**
pg72 (d2); pg73 (b22)

Continents (see pg66 [r16])

● Inside the Earth

The Earth is not a solid ball. Vibrations from earthquakes *(see pg72 [k13])* and volcanic explosions *(see pg70 [o11])* have revealed a complex internal structure. Around the outside is a thin rocky shell, or crust, between 4 and 25 mi thick. Beneath the crust is a thick mantle of rock so hot that it flows like treacle, only very, very much slowly. The mantle is about 6,813 mi thick. Beneath it, there is a core of metal (mostly iron and nickel). The outer core is so hot it is always molten; the inner core at the very center of the Earth is solid because pressures are so great it cannot melt, despite top temperatures of over 12,600°F.

Crust

Mantle

Outer core

Inner core

● View from above

From space, it is clear just how much of the Earth is covered by oceans—nearly three-quarters of its surface *(see pg77 [q25])*. Emerging above the oceans are seven masses of land *(see pg66 [s16])*. These are the continents of North and South America, Oceania, Antarctica, Africa, Asia, and Europe, plus many thousands of islands, of all different sizes—some no bigger than a small rock.

◀◀ SOLAR SYSTEM see pg44 (d2) ◀◀

IT'S A FACT

• The center of the Earth is 3986 mi below the surface.

• The Earth weighs about 6000 trillion trillion tons.

◄ *Seen from space, swirls of cloud, the oceans, and continents are visible on the Earth.*

Oceans
(see pg77 [d29])

Atmosphere
(see pg78 [i18])

Read further › Earth's crust
pg58 (o2)

Composition of the Earth

Most of the Earth is made from just four chemical elements: iron, oxygen, silicon, and magnesium. Much of its rocky crust is made from combinations of two of these elements; oxygen and silicon, known as silicates. But there are small quantities of many other elements, such as aluminum and calcium. The various ways these elements combine mean that the Earth's crust contains many different materials.

Sulphur 2.7%

Nickel 2.7%

Calcium 0.6%

Aluminum 0.4%

Magnesium 13%

Others 0.6%

Silicon 17%

Iron 35%

Oxygen 28%

Read further › early Earth / age of the Earth / radioactive dating
pg64 (h16; n2); pg65 (b22)

Space rock

The Earth has not always existed—it formed gradually over time *(see pg64 [p10])*. Radioactive dating (the study of atoms and their radioactive rays) has shown that the oldest meteorites—large rocks from space—that crashed down into the Earth are about 4.5 billion years old. From this, scientists have worked out that this is probably how old the Earth is. Meteorites are made from rock and iron, just like the Earth, and originated around the same time. In fact, the Earth was probably created by the collision of masses of meteorites.

◄ *A meteorite crashing into the Earth. The meteorite penetrates the Earth's atmosphere and hits the ground.*

DOWN TO EARTH

• The Earth is not perfectly round. It bulges at the Equator (the middle), making it slightly tangerine-shaped.

• The diameter of the Earth at the Equator is 7,972 mi, but only 7,945 mi at the North and South Poles.

Check it out!

• http://www.enchantedlearning.com/subjects/astronomy/planets/earth/Inside.shtml
• http://sse.jpl.nasa.gov/features/planets/earth/earth.html
• http://stardate.org/resources/ssguide/earth.html

◄◄ CHEMICAL ELEMENTS see pg14 (h9) ◄◄

Spinning globe

THOUGH IT seems perfectly still, the Earth is actually spinning around at an average speed of over 994 mph. It is also hurtling through the darkness of space on its journey around the Sun at over 62,140 mph. We are unaware of this rapid movement because we are firmly standing on the ground through gravity. But, as the Earth spins and whirls through space, the view of the Sun from different places on the Earth is constantly changing, bringing not only day and night but the four seasons, too.

IT'S A FACT

• During each orbit of the Sun, the Earth travels a distance of more than 583,669,454 mi.

• The Earth's distance from the Sun is about 93 million mi.

• Climate is affected by sunspots—dark patches on the Sun.

Earth lit having turned toward the Sun

◄ *This satellite picture shows half the Earth is exposed to the Sun at any time. Radiation from the Sun is the Earth's main source of energy. This provides huge amounts of both heat and light, without which there would be no life on Earth.*

Day and night

At any one time, half the Earth is facing toward the Sun and is brightly lit, while the other half is facing away from the Sun and is in darkness. As the Earth turns while the Sun stays still, the dark and sunlit halves move around the world, bringing day and night to different parts of Earth. Because the Earth turns eastwards, we see the Sun rising in the east as the Earth turns our part of the world toward it, and setting in the west as it turns us away from the Sun. The Earth turns completely around once every 24 hours, which is why there are 24 hours in every day.

Earth in darkness having turned away from the Sun

Check it out!

• http://www.enchantedlearning.com/subjects/astronomy/planets/earth/Seasons.shtml

• http://www.hexadyne.com/Educational/Science/4seasons.html

• http://kids.msfc.nasa.gov/News/2000/News-AutumnalEquinox.asp

DOWN TO EARTH

• As the Earth spins around every 24 hours, places near the poles barely move at all, while places at the Equator whizz around at over 994 mph.

• The Earth takes 0.242 of a day longer than a calendar year to complete its orbit. To make up for this, an extra day is added to the end of February every four years. This is called a leap year.

Yearly journey

Read further › Sun's heat
pg63 (c31)

The Earth's orbit around the Sun takes 365.242 days, which is why there are 365 days in a calendar year. Since the orbit is not a perfect circle but an ellipse (oval), the Earth is closer to the Sun at some points than others. Its closest point, called the perihelion, occurs on January 3; its furthest point, called the aphelion, occurs on July 4.

▼ The world's 24 time zones.

Time around the world

As the Earth rotates, the Sun rises in one place and sets in another. So that noon is always at the middle of the day, the world is divided into 24 time zones, one for each hour of the day. You put your clock forward one hour for each zone you pass through as you travel east; or behind one hour for each time zone as you travel west. So at noon in London, it is 7 a.m. in New York and 8 p.m. in Tokyo.

Read further › time zones
pg60 (m2)

All the seasons

The Earth does not spin upright, but tilted at an angle, which always remains the same. When the Earth is on one side of the Sun, and the northern hemisphere (the world north of the Equator) is tilted toward it, so it receives more sun, bringing summer. At the same time, the southern hemisphere is tilted away from the Sun, bringing winter. When Earth is on the other side of the Sun and the northern hemisphere is tilted away, winter occurs. In between, as the Earth moves around the Sun, neither hemisphere is tilted more toward it, and then we have spring and the fall.

Northern hemisphere is tilted away from the Sun—winter

Southern hemisphere is tilted toward the Sun—summer

Read further › climate patterns
pg62 (p2); pg63 (b22)

◄◄ TIME see pg36 (d2) ◄◄

a b c d e f g h i j k l m n o p q r s t u v w

Warm and cold

THE NEARER a place is to the Equator, the weather, or climate, tends to be warmer. At the Equator, the Sun climbs high in the sky so its rays are hot. Away from the Equator, the Sun does not climb as high, so its rays give less heat. At the North and South Poles, the Sun is so low at times that, it gives very little warmth at all. The effect is to give the world three broad climate bands on either side of the Equator: the warm tropics, the cold polar regions, and a moderate "temperate" zone in between.

Temperate grassland (prairie and steppe)

Cool conifer forest (taiga)

North Pole

Equator

South Pole

Temperate deciduous woodland

Dry temperate

Tropical grassland

Mountainous

● Climate patterns

The warmth of a region's climate depends on how close it is to the Equator. But oceans and mountain ranges have a very large influence too, so the pattern of climate is complicated, with many local variations. Coastal areas tend to be damper and cooler, for instance, while continental interiors, far inland, tend to be drier and more extreme, with hot summers and cold winters. Antarctica has the coldest climate. It is so cold that almost nothing grows and no one lives there.

Tropical forest

Desert

Polar and tundra

🌐 Check it out!

• http://www.panda.org/climate
• http://www.exploratorium.edu/climate
• http://www.worldweather.org

● DOWN TO EARTH

• One of the most pleasant climates in the world is Quito, Ecuador. It rarely drops below 45°F at night, nor rises above 72°F during the day, and 4 in of rain falls reliably each month of the wet season.

• Only seven percent of the world has a truly temperate climate, yet well over half the world's population lives in these temperate zones.

▶▶ GRASSLANDS AND DESERT see pg100 (d2) ▶▶

1 2 3 4 5 6 7 8 9 10 11 12 13 14 15 16 17 18 19

Warm tropics

The tropics are very warm, with temperatures averaging over 80°F all year round. But the tropical climate is varied. Some tropical places are warm and dry, including hot deserts such as the Sahara; some are warm and wet; yet others have marked wet and dry seasons. Where it is wet in the tropics, it tends to be very wet, since the warm air picks up huge amounts of moisture. Large thunderclouds usually build up in the morning heat, then they unleash torrents of rain during the afternoon *(see pg81 [q29])*. Steamy rainforests flourish in this hot, wet climate.

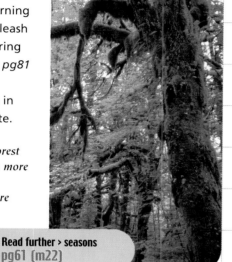

▸ *The Amazon rainforest of South America has more species of plants and animals than anywhere else on Earth.*

Read further › seasons
pg61 (m22)

Read further › ozone layer / atmosphere / pressure
pg63 (n22); pg78 (l2); pg79 (j22)

Global warming

When heat from the Sun reaches the Earth, some of it penetrates the atmosphere and reaches the ground. Much of this heat is reflected back into space. Certain gases in the air trap heat reflected from the ground, like panes of glass in a greenhouse. In the past, this natural "greenhouse effect" has kept the Earth comfortably warm. But the gases pumped into the air from burning coal and oil in homes, factories, and cars, for example, have trapped much more heat than before. Scientists believe this is causing global warming of the climate, which could have devastating effects.

Heat trapped inside the atmosphere by greenhouse gases

Rays turned away by the atmosphere

Rays from the Sun

Heat reaching the Earth's surface

Trashing the Earth

In recent years, human activity is making an increasing threat to the Earth's fragile resources, damaging everything from the atmosphere to animal life. Car exhaust and industrial pollutants are choking the air and turning rain acidic. Gases from supersonic jets and refrigerators are punching a hole in the world's protective ozone layer. Farming chemicals poison the rivers. Unique species of animals and plants are vanishing forever. Forests are being cut down, vast areas of countryside are being buried under concrete, and beautiful marine environments are gradually being destroyed.

▸ *Danger to the world's climate caused by human activity.*

Read further › global warming
pg63 (c31); pg78 (l2); pg79 (j22)

▸▸ JET see pg189 (h22) ▸▸

22   23   24   25   26   27   28   29   30   31   32   33   34   35   36   37   38   39

Earth story

T HE STORY of the Earth began about 4.6 billion years ago when dust whirling around the newborn Sun started to clump into lumps of rock called planetesimals. Then, pulled together by their mutual gravity, the planetesimals clumped together to form the Earth and other planets. Soon after this, a giant rock crashed into the Earth so violently that the rock melted, splashed off, and cooled to become the Moon. The Earth was so shaken by this impact all the elements separated. Dense metals, iron and nickel, collapsed to the center to form its core, lighter materials formed the Earth's rocky crust.

DOWN TO EARTH

• Fossils indicate to geologists whether the rock in which they are found is relatively old or young.

• Radioactive dating works because after rocks form, certain atoms break down at a steady rate, sending out rays or radioactivity. By assessing how many atoms in the rock have changed, geologists can figure its age out.

Early Earth

A mass of erupting volcanoes and smoke appeared when the Earth was formed. Streams of lava (molten rock) turned the Earth's surface into churning, red-hot oceans. Huge gas bubbles rose from Earth's interior and belched out through the volcanoes, forming a thick, cloudy, and highly poisonous, atmosphere. Eventually, as the Earth began to cool, a crust formed on the Earth as the lava oceans cooled and hardened.

▼ The steam and gas that billowed from volcanoes made up Earth's poisonous atmosphere.

In the beginning

When the Earth first formed, it was little more than a red-hot ball. But, during half a billion years, it gradually cooled down, and slowly, a hard crust of rock began to form. An atmosphere containing poisonous gases, such as methane, hydrogen, and ammonia, soon wrapped around the planet, rising from fierce volcanic activity on the surface (see pg70 [p11]). After about one billion years, the air began to clear, water vapor that had gathered in the clouds fell as rain, to create the oceans by flooding basins in the Earth's crust, and formed continents.

▶▶ Read further > volcanoes
pg70 (n2)

▶▶ Read further > volcanoes / oceans
pg70 (n2); pg76 (d2)

Ages of the Earth

►► Read further › Inside the Earth
pg58 (o2)

Layers of rock tend to form one on top of another, so the oldest is usually at the bottom. The order of layers, from top to bottom, is known as the geological column. Even if the layers have been disturbed, it is often possible to work out the order in which they were formed. Because different plants and animals lived at different times in the Earth's past, experts can date a layer of rock by the fossils it contains. Using these clues, they have built up a picture of each of the successive rock layers. This way, they have divided the last 590 million years of the Earth's history into 12 units of time, called Periods, representing many millions of years each.

Quaternary Period: 0–2 mya
Many mammals die out; humans evolve

Tertiary Period: 2–65 mya
First large mammals appear; birds thrive; grasslands spread

Cretaceous Period: 65–144 mya
Dinosaurs die out; first flowering plants

Jurassic Period: 144–213 mya
Age of the dinosaurs; some dinosaurs evolve into birds

Triassic Period: 213–248 mya
Mammals and seed-bearing plants appear

Permian Period: 248–286 mya
Conifers appear, but many animals die out as deserts spread

Carboniferous Period: 286–360 mya
Reptiles evolve; vast areas of swampy fern forests

Devonian Period: 360–408 mya
Insects and amphibians evolve; ferns and mosses as big as trees

Silurian Period: 408–438 mya
Plants appear on land and fish in rivers

Ordovician Period: 438–505 mya
Sahara is covered in ice; fish-like creatures evolve in the sea

Cambrian Period: 505–590 mya
No life on land but shellfish thrive in the oceans

Precambrian Time: Before 590 mya
First micro-organisms appear and give atmosphere the oxygen that larger animals need to breathe

▲ *Timeline showing the Earth's formation millions of years ago (mya) plus layers of rock built up through the ages.*

IT'S A FACT

• If all Earth's history was crammed into the hours of one day, humans would appear less than two minutes before midnight!

• The oxygen most animals need to breathe was put into the air by minute plants in the sea, called cyanobacteria, over billions of years.

Fossil record

The first signs of life on Earth, probably tiny bacteria, appeared almost four billion years ago. But, the first animals with shells and bones emerged less than 600 million years ago. Some life has been preserved as fossils—over time their hard remains turned to stone. With the help of fossils, like the ammonite shellfish, geologists have built up a detailed picture of Earth's history.

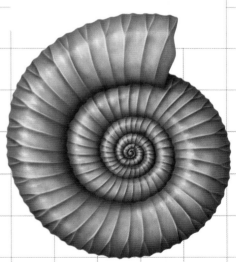

▲ *The ammonite's body was covered by a spiral shell. The body rotted and the shell became a fossil.*

Check it out!

• http://www.kidscosmos.org/kid-stuff/kids-basalt-history.html

►► SHELLFISH see pg124 (f2) ►►

Moving continents

SLOWLY, SLOWLY, the Earth's surface is shifting beneath our feet all the time. Look at a map of the world and you will see, for example, that the west coast of Africa looks as if it would slot into the east coast of South America like two pieces of a jigsaw puzzle. The reason is that 220 million years ago— just before the age of the dinosaurs—they were actually joined together. In fact, all the world's continents were joined together then, in one huge landmass geologists call Pangaea. Pangaea gradually split up into today's continents as plate movements caused earthquakes. The continents drifted to where they are today (continental drift), and are still moving!

● IT'S A FACT

• New York is moving about 1 in farther from London each year.

• On average, continents move at the same rate as fingernails grow, about 0.25 in every month.

• Some tectonic plates have moved so far that they have traveled half way around the globe.

▶▶ Read further › earthquakes pg73 (b22)

220 million years ago (mya) there was just one giant land mass, called Pangaea (meaning "all Earth"), and one giant ocean, known as Panthalassa. But a long arm of the ocean, the Tethys Sea, stretched into the heart of Pangaea

200 mya Pangaea split so that it was on both sides of the Tethys Sea. To the north was Laurasia, including North America, Europe, and most of Asia. To the south was Gondwanaland, including South America, Africa, Australia, Antarctica, and India

135 mya the South Atlantic Ocean opened up between the continents of Africa and South America. India then broke off from Africa and drifted toward Asia. Europe and North America were still joined at this time

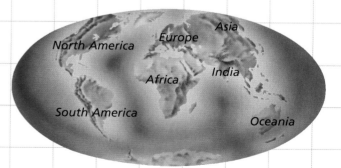

Today North America and Europe are widely separated, having split 60 million years ago. India has crunched into Asia, Australia is moving into the tropics, and Antarctica has moved to the South Pole

The world's biggest plates

It is not just the continents that are moving—so are the ocean beds. In fact, the whole of the Earth's surface is on the move. Its rigid outer shell of rock is split into about 20 giant slabs called tectonic plates: nine huge ones and about 12 smaller ones. These plates are constantly moving, slipping past one another, jostling one way or another. The continents are embedded in these plates like raisins in a cookie, and move along with the plates.

Key

——— *Plate boundaries pulling apart*
– – – *Plate boundaries pushing together*
········· *Plate boundaries sliding past each other*

▲ *The jagged boundaries between the plates of the Earth's surface.*

Read further > fault lines
pg69 (o22)

Plates pushing together

In some places, tectonic plates are crunching together. Where this happens, one of the plates—typically the plate carrying a continent—rides over the other and crushes it down to the Earth's interior. This process is called subduction. Where one plate dives beneath the other, there is often a deep trench in the ocean's floor *(see pg76 [q10])*.

▼ *One plate being pushed under another.*

Read further > where plates meet / ocean shelf
pg71 (b22); pg76 (h15)

Check it out!
• http://kids.earth.nasa.gov/archive/pangaea/
• http://www.enchantedlearning.com/subjects/
dinosaurs/glossary/Contdrift.shtml

DOWN TO EARTH

• One sign that continents have moved is the discovery of fossils of tropical ferns in the Arctic and tropical reptiles in Antarctica!

• Many of the same dinosaurs were found in both Europe and North America. This is because the continents were joined together until after dinosaurs died out, about 65 million years ago.

Plates moving apart

In some places, usually in the mid-ocean on the seabed, tectonic plates move apart, or diverge. As they do so, hot molten magma *(see pg70 [w11])* from the Earth's interior wells up through the gap and solidifies on its exposed edges. This makes the seabed grow wider and wider. The floor of the Pacific Ocean is becoming wider by about 8 in every year.

▼ *Two plates moving apart (diverging) under the ocean.*

Read further > where plates diverge
pg68 (b14); pg72 (d2); pg76 (h15)

Mountain high

MOUNTAINS LOOK solid and unchanging, but they are being built up, then worn away by the weather, all the time. The world's highest mountains were actually formed quite recently in the Earth's history. The Himalayas, for example, were built up in the last 40 million years, and are still growing, even today. The most ancient mountain ranges have been worn flat, or reduced to hills, like New York's Adirondacks, which are now over one billion years old.

● Neat folds

A few mountains, such as Washington's Mount St Helens, are volcanoes—tall cones built up by successive eruptions of lava and ash. Most, however, are thrown up by the immense power of the Earth's crust moving. Some are huge slabs called fault blocks, or "horst," caused by powerful earthquakes. But all the world's great mountain ranges, such as the Andes and Rockies, were made by the crumpling of rock layers as tectonic plates pushed against each other. Such mountains are called fold mountains.

▸ *Three types of mountain range.*

Volcanic peak

Fold mountain

Fault block mountain

▶▶ **Read further › formation of volcanoes** pg71 (b22)

To scale

Each square = 3,280 ft

The highest mountains—measured from sea level to summit—in each continent, to scale

Jayakusuma (Oceania)	Elbrus (Europe)	Kilimanjaro (Africa)	Mt McKinley (North America)	Aconcagua (South America)	Mount Everest (Asia)
16,502 ft	18,510 ft	19,340 ft	20,321 ft	22,834 ft	29,098 ft

◀◀ VOLCANOES ON MARS pg47 (m33) ◀◀

1 2 3 4 5 6 7 8 9 10 11 12 13 14 15 16 17 18 19

IT'S A FACT

• If you traveled from London to Paris and back again eight times, you would cover the same distance as the length of the Andes mountain range.

• The largest recorded volcanic eruption happened in 1550 BC in Santorini, Greece.

Folding rock

Read further > folds
pg68 (b14)

Most rocks form in flat layers called strata. Some rocks are sedimentary and form from sand and mud settling on the seabed. Others are volcanic, such as the large basalt plateaus at the center of many continents. Fold mountains build up where the movement of the Earth's crust tilts, crumples, and squeezes, lifting these flat layers.

Strike—the direction of the folding movement

Dip—how steep of an individual fold is

The Himalayas

Himalayan mountains

The Himalayas were crushed up by the collision of India against Asia. India has been plowing relentlessly north into Asia for the last 40 million years. As it does so, layer upon layer of rock in Asia's southern edge has crumpled, like the bow wave of a boat pushing through water or sludgy mud. While India continues moving, the Himalayas will keep on crumpling up in front of it.

Asian plate

Folded rock layers

India moving north

Read further > faults
pg73 (b22)

Read further > Earth moving
pg67 (j22)

Round the block

As the Earth's crust moves during earthquakes (see pg72 [m13]), huge blocks of rock can slip or "fault." Sometimes, they move only a bit of an inch. Occasionally, they move over many feet. But over millions of years, successive movements can shove a block up or down huge distances. In California's Sierra Nevada faulting has created a steep slope 10,991 ft high and hundreds of miles long.

▸ *Geologists describe fault movements using these terms.*

▲ All 14 of the world's peaks over 8000 m are in the Himalayas – in Nepal, China and Kashmir.

Throw

Heave

Fault plane—the surface of the slipping block

WORLD'S HIGHEST

Mountains	Height
• Everest	29,078 ft
• K2	28,248 ft
• Kanchenjunga	28,208 ft
• Lhotse	27,923 ft
• Makalu	27,824 ft

Check it out!

• http://www.eduscapes.com/42explore/mountain.htm

• http://www.americanparknetwork.com/parkinfo/rm/geology/index.html

▶▶ BOATS pg186 (o16) ▶▶

Fiery mountains

VOLCANOES ARE places where hot molten rock, magma, wells up to the surface from deep within the Earth's interior. Sometimes, the magma flows out over the ground as red-hot liquid rock or lava. At other times, the volcano becomes clogged up with a thick plug of magma, then suddenly erupts in a gigantic explosion that sends up jets of steam and hurls fiery fragments of magma high into the air. Successive eruptions can build up such a huge cone of ash and lava around the volcano that it becomes a mountain (*see pg68 [i8]*).

DOWN TO EARTH

• The eruption of Mount Tambora, Java in 1815, sent up so much ash that the Sun was blocked throughout the world, making cool, wet summers for two years.

• One of the most gigantic eruptions in history occurred in Yellowstone, U.S.A. 2.2 million years ago. It poured out enough magma to build today's biggest volcano six times over.

IT'S A FACT

• The biggest recent eruption in the U.S.A. was from Mount St. Helens in 1980.

• The eruption of the volcanic island of Krakatoa, near Java, in 1883, could be heard a quarter of the way around the world!

All fired up

The biggest volcanic eruptions are powered by a combination of steam and carbon dioxide gas. They remain dissolved in the magma inside the volcano because of the extreme pressure. But, as the plug of magma breaks, the pressure is suddenly released, creating an explosion big enough to send chunks of rock the size of houses many thousands of feet up into the air.

Eruptions begin with a build-up of pressure in the magma chamber beneath the volcano

As the steam and gas jet out, they carry clouds of ash with them along with larger fragments of the broken plug of magma, called volcanic bombs or tephra

Bubbles of steam and gas form and swell rapidly inside the magma, and burst out like the froth from a violently shaken bottle of fizz

With the volcanic plug out of the way, magma surges up and out of the volcano, and flows down as lava

◀ *Magma chamber inside a volcano.*

◀◀ CARBON DIOXIDE see pg12 (q15) ◀◀

1 2 3 4 5 6 7 8 9 10 11 12 13 14 15 16 17 18 19

Types of volcano

Read further > tectonic plates
pg67 (b22); pg73 (b22)

Most volcanoes occur near cracks between the giant tectonic plates that make up the Earth's surface, but they vary in shapes and sizes. Spectacular, violently erupting volcanic cones, or "cone" volcanoes, develop where the plates are pushing together *(see pg67 [q26])*. Here, magma is trapped below ground, making it so acidic—and so thick and sticky—that it clogs the volcano up and then it erupts sporadically and dramatically. Where plates are pulling apart, the magma is less acid and more runny. It reaches the surface easily and floods out steadily as lava to form a gentle slope that looks like an upturned shield, known as a "shield" volcano.

Cone volcano

Shield volcano

▸ *Volcanoes in the Pacific spray out fiery lava fountains.*

Rock soup

The lava that gushes from the Hawaiian volcanoes in the Pacific is very runny. Because of this, the explosive gases leak out, and so the lava rarely bursts out in a huge explosion. Instead, it tends to spray out frequently in fiery fountains, or well out in slower streams of molten rock.

Read further > volcanic eruptions
pg70 (n2)

Boiling fountains

Even if magma does not erupt in a volcano, its tremendous heat can produce other effects. Rainwater trickling into the ground, for instance, may be heated under pressure, then burst on to the ground's surface in a tremendous shot of steam called a geyser. A mix of hot water and mud may bubble up to the surface to create areas of boiling mud called mudpots. Sometimes, hot fumes of toxic gases escape through cracks in the rock to emerge like smoke from a chimney in "fumaroles."

Mudpot

Fumarole

▾ *Geyser blowing superheated steam.*

Read further > black smokers
pg77 (l31)

Check it out!
- http://volcano.und.nodak.edu/vwdocs/kids/kids.html
- http://www.fema.gov/kids/volcano.htm

Top notch

When a volcano erupts, it can completely empty the magma chamber as lava, ash, and other debris are blown out. This leaves the top of the cone unsupported, so it collapses into the volcanic vent. This creates a huge pit, or crater, at the summit of the volcano. Once the volcano stops erupting, the crater may gradually fill with water to form a lake, such as Oregon's famous Crater Lake.

Read further > lakes
p75 (c34)

Shaky ground

THE GROUND sometimes trembles when a heavy truck passes by. But major earthquakes that make the ground shudder violently are set off by the movement of tectonic plates—the giant slabs of rock that make up the Earth's surface (*see pg67 [c34]*). Tectonic plates are moving all the time, radiating minor tremors as they grind past each other. But every now and then they get jammed. Then the pressure builds up until they suddenly lurch on again, sending out vibrations, called shock waves, in all directions, creating major earthquakes that can bring down mountains and destroy cities.

▼ *Earthquakes occur where slabs of the Earth's surface are moving in opposite directions.*

Epicenter

Hypocenter (focus)

Radiating shock waves

● Shock waves

In an earthquake, shock waves radiate out in circles from its origin or epicenter. Shock waves vibrate throughout the ground, but it is on the surface that they do the most damage. Damage is most severe at its epicenter where the shock waves are strongest. But they can often be felt up to thousands of miles away.

🌐 Check it out!

• http://www.fema.gov/kids/quake.htm
• http://earthquake.usgs.gov/4kids/
• http://www.yahooligans.com/Science_and _Nature/The_Earth/Geology/Plat_ Tectonics/earthquakes/

▲ *Devastation to buildings caused by a Taiwanese earthquake in 1999.*

● DOWN TO EARTH

• Most earthquakes last less than a minute. The longest recorded one, in Alaska on March 21 1964, lasted 4 minutes.

• Typically, tectonic plates slide only 1 to 1.5 in past each other each year. In a slip that triggers a major earthquake, they can move 3 feet or more.

• In most earthquakes a few minor tremors (preshocks) are followed by an intense shock lasting 1 or 2 minutes.

◄◄ WAVES see pg31 (o22) ◄◄

1   2   3   4   5   6   7   8   9   10   11   12   13   14   15   16   17   18   19   2

a
b
c
d
e
f
g
h
i
j
k
l
m
n
o
p
q
r
s
t
u
v
w

Earthquake zones

Places near the edges of tectonic plates, such as south-east Europe and the Pacific coast, are at very high risk of earthquake. In these earthquake zones, minor quakes are frequent, and a quiet period may often be the build-up to a really big one. People in California, U.S.A. are constantly threatened by the movement of the San Andreas fault, where two great tectonic plates grind past each other *(see pg67 [c34])*. When the San Andreas fault juddered in 1906, it set off earthquakes that destroyed San Francisco.

▶▶ **Read further > earthquake devastation**
pg72 (m2)

▼ Earthquakes and volcanoes occur in the same regions, where tectonic plates meet.

Measuring earthquakes

Seismologists (scientists who study earthquakes) measure the strength of the shock waves with a device called a seismometer. They grade the severity of a quake on the Richter scale, from one (slight tremor) to over nine (devastating quake). The Richter scale shows the size of an earthquake—its absolute magnitude—but not its effects. So experts also rate an earthquake on the Mercalli scale, which assesses the damage on a scale of one (barely noticeable) to twelve (total destruction), written in Roman numerals, I to XII.

A seismometer records earthquake vibrations as up and down lines on paper or displays them on a computer screen

MERCALLI SCALE

III – light fittings shake

VI – windows shatter

VIII – chimneys fall down

X – major structural damage to bridges

Tidal waves

The world's most awesome waves are called tidal waves or tsunami (pronounced "soon-ami") which are caused by earthquakes *(see pg72 [t10])*. Under the ocean earthquakes or a landslide into the ocean can send out a giant pulse of water racing along the seabed as fast as a jet plane. When the pulse reaches shallow water, a huge wave of many many feet high rears up, swamping everything in its path.

As the pulse moves into shallow water it rears into a giant wave and swamps coastal regions

A shift in the seabed sends out a pulse of water

▶▶ **Read further > tectonic plates**
pg69 (o22)

Water on the land

THE AMOUNT of water in the world remains constant, but it is continually moving around the Earth and its atmosphere in a process called the water cycle. Rain falling from clouds gathers in rivers, lakes, and oceans. Heat from the Sun causes the water to evaporate (become water vapor). As the water vapor rises into the atmosphere, it cools and condenses (changes back into water), and forms clouds. When the water in the clouds becomes too heavy, it falls back to Earth as rain and returns to the rivers. Some of the rain soaks into the ground and is used by plants. Plants return unused water as it evaporates from their leafs (transpiration).

● Water, water everywhere

There is a huge amount of water in the world—over 126 million cubic mi—but 97 percent is salt water in the ocean. The other 3 percent is fresh water, but most of this is frozen in ice sheets at the poles, or deep underground. Only a very tiny portion moves round in the water cycle, but this precious water keeps rivers flowing and provides us with water to drink and plants with the water they need for growth.

1. Water evaporates from the sea and lakes and the water vapor rises into the air

2. Water is taken up from the ground by plants and transpires from their leafs

3. As the water vapor rises, it cools and condenses into droplets of water and ice crystals to form clouds

4. When the water is too heavy to be held by the clouds, they drop their moisture as rain

5. Falling rain gathers into rivers and runs directly down to the sea, or seeps into the ground, where it may be taken up by plants

To scale

Each square = 621 mi

The longest rivers in each continent. *The Amazon and the Nile can be measured from various points, thus their official lengths sometimes change*

Darling (Oceania)
1,702 mi

Volga (Europe)
2,193 mi

Mississippi-Missouri (North America)
3,740 mi

Yangtze (Asia)
3,914 mi

Nile (Africa)
4,149 mi

Amazon (South America)
4,194 mi

◀◀ ICEBERG see pg35 (b34) ◀◀

1   2   3   4   5   6   7   8   9   10   11   12   13   14   15   16   17   18   19

▶▶ **Read further › lakes**
pg71 (k34)

IT'S A FACT

• The world's shortest recorded river is the North Fork Foe River, Montana, U.S.A. at 58 ft long.

• Lake Superior is the largest freshwater lake in the world, bigger than Ireland. It is 348 mi long, with a surface area of 31,699 sq mi.

Lake
Superior

Lake
Michigan

Lake
Huron

Lake
Ontario

Lake
Erie

● Great lakes

Many of the largest lakes in North America and Europe were created barely 10,000 years ago, during the last ice age. Lakes of water melting from the ice-filled hollows were gouged out both by the glaciers themselves and by the huge floods of water released when the glaciers melted. The Great Lakes were probably created this way, including Lake Superior.

● Rivers run down

Whenever there is enough rain or melting snow to keep them flowing, rivers run down to the sea or into lakes. In wetter parts of the world, they are kept flowing even when it is not raining or snowing, from underground water. In fact, a lot of rain does not flow straight over the land, but seeps into the ground, then bubbles out again lower down in places called springs.

▶ *Lake Miramar
in Argentina.*

▶▶ **Read further › seas and oceans**
pg76 (d2)

*Most rivers start as tiny brooks
high in the hills, tumbling
over rocks and rapids*

*As they flow on down,
brooks grow into big streams
as they are joined by other
streams called tributaries*

*Farther down,
streams broaden
into rivers that flow
through deep, meandering
channels of sediment, washed
down from higher up*

● Deltas

A river slows down as it flows into the sea, so it can no longer carry the load of silt it has collected along the way. Often, the silt is dumped in a fan-shape, or delta, and the river splits into branches called distributaries. Where there is a strong coastal current, the head of the delta is swept into a curving or "arcuate" form such as the Nile in Africa. Where the sea current is weak, the distributaries spread out in a ragged "bird's foot" shape like the Mississippi delta.

◀ *An arcuate delta.*

DOWN TO EARTH

• Oxbow lakes form when a river meanders, cutting off patches of water before linking back up (braiding).

• Lake Baikal in Russia is the world's deepest lake. At 5,719 ft, it holds 20 percent of the world's fresh water.

Check it out!

• http://www.amrivers.org/kids/riverstory.htm

• http://www.geography4kids.com/files/water_hydrosphere.html

▶▶ ELEMENTS pg215 (j31) ▶▶

a b c d e f g h i j k l m n o p q r s t u v w

22 23 24 25 26 27 28 29 30 31 32 33 34 35 36 37 38 39

Ocean deep

THERE ARE five great oceans: the Pacific, the Atlantic, the Indian, the Arctic, and the Southern Ocean around Antarctica. There are also many seas, including the Mediterranean and the Red Sea. Until recently, we did not know much more about the ocean floors than we did about the surface of Mars. Now, surveys made with sound equipment and computerized underwater craft have revealed a hugely varied landscape on the ocean bed, with high mountains, wide plains, and deep valleys.

IT'S A FACT

• The West Wind Drift (an ocean current) around Antarctica moves 2,000 times as much water as the Amazon does each year.

• Oceans are, on average, about 6,562 ft deep.

• One of the tides in the Pacific Ocean reaches 30 ft inland, along the coast of Korea.

Into the abyss

Around the edge of the ocean is a shelf of shallow water called the continental shelf. At the edge of the shelf, the ocean bed plunges steeply to the deep ocean floor, known as the "abyssal plain." This plain is vast, but not completely flat. In the Pacific, especially, it is dotted with huge mountains, called seamounts. The world's longest mountain range, the mid-ocean ridge, runs down through the Atlantic and into the Indian Ocean.

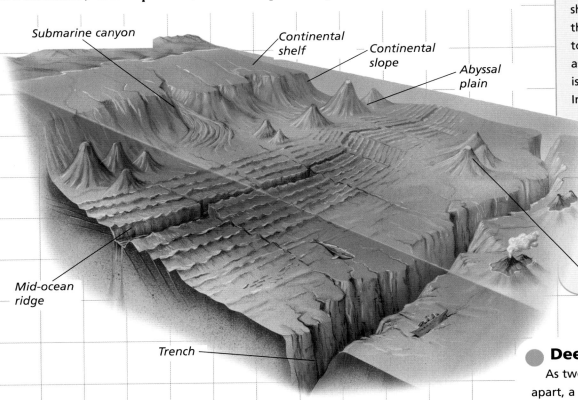

Submarine canyon

Continental shelf

Continental slope

Abyssal plain

Mid-ocean ridge

Trench

Seamount

Deep dive

As two giant tectonic plates move apart, a deep gash opens in the ocean floor—an ocean trench. The deepest point on the Earth's surface is the Challenger Deep in the Marianas Trench in the west Pacific, 33,759 ft deep. In 1960, the *Trieste*, an underwater craft or bathyscaphe, dived almost to the bottom of the trench.

▶ The bathyscaphe called Trieste *that visited the ocean floor in 1961.*

►► UNDERWATER EXPLORERS see pg187 (b25) ►►

One high tide bulge occurs at places in the ocean nearest to the Moon, as water is pulled toward the Moon

The sea moves or "flows" upward and inland as the tide rises

Another high tide bulge occurs in places farthest from the Moon, because the solid Earth, too, is pulled toward the Moon, leaving the ocean waters behind

The sea ebbs, sinking and retreating, as the tide drops

Rising and falling

All around the world, the sea rises and falls slightly twice every day in "tides." As the ocean rises, it flows farther up seashores. As it falls back, it slowly retreats or "ebbs." Tides are caused by the pull of the Moon's gravity on the oceans' waters as the Earth spins around. High tides move around the Earth in two bulges on opposite sides of the world. Spring tides (high tides) happen twice a month. They occur as the Moon and Sun line up, combining their gravitational pull.

▶▶ **Read further › spinning Earth**
pg60 [d2]

DOWN TO EARTH

• The most extreme spring tides are in the Bay of Fundy, Canada, where the sea rises and falls up to 49 ft.

• The Dead Sea is the lowest sea on Earth, at 1,312 ft below sea level.

▶▶ **Read further › geysers**
pg71 [L22]

Undersea chimneys

In deep valleys in the mid-ocean ridges, there are amazing natural chimneys on the seabed. Called black smokers or hydrothermal vents, these chimneys are volcanic features (see pg71 [q30]) that billow black fumes of hot gases and water. Seawater seeping into cracks in the seafloor is heated by hot volcanic magma (see pg70 [w11]). The heated water dissolves minerals from seabed rock and spews from the vents in scalding, mineral-rich black plumes.

▸ Plumes from black smokers.

Calm waters

The Pacific is the world's largest ocean. It is twice as big as the Atlantic and covers an area of 69.8 million sq mi—one-third of the world. The Pacific is peppered with thousands of islands—many are the peaks of undersea volcanoes and most are only about 3.2 ft above sea level. The word "pacific" means calm.

▾ On average, the Pacific Ocean is 13,779 ft deep.

▶▶ **Read further › undersea volcanoes**
pg77 [L31]

◀◀ GRAVITY see pg24 (m12) ◀◀

Swirling air

THE ATMOSPHERE that surrounds the Earth is barely thicker on the Earth than the peel is on an orange. Yet, without it, the Earth would be as lifeless as the Moon. The atmosphere absorbs the Sun's warmth, yet shields Earth from its most harmful rays. It gives us clean, fresh, water to drink (*see pg74 [j11]*). It provides us with the air that we, and most other animals, need to breathe. Our weather is also a result of changes in the Earth's atmosphere. These changes are caused by worldwide and local variations of the heat of the Sun.

Atmospheric layers

The atmosphere may look invisible but it has a number of distinct layers or "spheres." At the bottom is the troposphere—only 6.2 mi thick, but containing over 70 percent of the atmosphere's gases by weight. Above that, the gases get thinner and thinner with each layer, until, at about 497 mi up, they are so thin or "rarified" it is hard to tell where the atmosphere ends and where empty space begins.

IT'S A FACT

• The world's windiest place is George V island in Antarctica, where winds often blow at 199 mph.

• Temperatures drop to nearly –76°F at the top of the troposphere.

🌐 Check it out!

• http://www.enchantedlearning.com/subjects/ astronomy/planets/earth/Atmosphere.shtml
• http://www.windpower.org/en/kids/choose/wind/ tropos.htm

DOWN TO EARTH

• The impact of particles from the Sun on the gases of the upper atmosphere creates shimmering curtains of light called auroras in the night sky over polar regions.

• The atmosphere is a mixture of gases: 78 percent nitrogen, 21 percent oxygen, and one percent argon and carbon dioxide, plus traces of neon, krypton, xenon, helium, nitrous oxide, and methane.

Exosphere:
311–497 mi
Contains hardly any gas; low-level satellites orbit here

Thermosphere:
50–311 mi
Becomes roasted by the Sun to up to 3,272°F, but is so thin in gases that it contains little real heat

Mesosphere:
31–50 mi
Is too thin to soak up much heat, but is thick enough to stop meteorites that burn up leaving fiery trails in the sky

Stratosphere:
6–31 mi
Contains the ozone layer and becomes hotter higher up; little water and no weather; airliners cruise here in the still air

Troposphere:
0–6 mi
Contains three-quarters of the atmosphere's gases and nearly all its water; temperatures drop by about 44°F every mile further

◄◄ ATMOSPHERE see pg35 (b22) ◄◄

1   2   3   4   5   6   7   8   9   10   11   12   13   14   15   16   17   18   19

Cirrus

Cumulonimbus

Cirrostratus

Nimbostratus

Stratus

Cumulus

▲ _The main classes of cloud were named in the 1800s_
by Luke Howard, a British weather scientist.

Clouds

Clouds are made of tiny drops of water _(see pg74 [h13])_ and ice crystals so light they float in the air. There is a large variety of clouds, but only two main shapes: fluffy, heaped "cumulus" that form clouds when air moisture billows upward; and flat "stratus" clouds that form when a layer of air cools down enough for its water content to condense. Both types of cloud take different forms at different heights in the sky.

Read further › evaporation
pg74 (d13)

Read further › global warming / air pressure
pg63 (c31); pg81 (o22)

Hot and cold

Winds blow because the Sun warms some places more than others, creating differences in air pressure (density) that pushes air around. In warm places, air expands and rises, lowering the pressure. In cool spots, the air is heavy and sinks, raising the pressure. Winds blow from zones where pressure is high, called anticyclones, to zones where it is low, called cyclones or depressions. The bigger the difference in pressure, the stronger the wind.

Read further › twisters / hurricanes
pg81 (m2); pg82 (b22)

World winds

Winds often blow from the same, or prevailing, direction in each of three belts around the world. In polar regions, cool, sinking air drives the prevailing winds away from the poles. In the tropics, warm air rising over the Equator draws winds in from either side. In the mid-latitudes in between, winds are driven away from the tropics by cool air sinking. Yet, none of these winds blows directly north to south, because the world is spinning. So, winds veer off to the left in the southern hemisphere and the right in the northern hemisphere.

▼ _Northern hemisphere._   ▼ _Southern hemisphere._

Winds spiral clockwise from high pressure zones and counterclockwise into low pressure zones.

Winds spiral in the opposite direction

Tropics—dry trade winds blow from the south-east or north-east toward the Equator, depending on the time of year

Mid-latitudes—warm, moist, westerly winds (winds from the west) are common

Polar regions—cold, easterly winds blow for much of the year

a b c d e f g h i j k l m n o p q r s t u v w

Stormy Weather

WHEN STORMS rage, winds blow hard, and rains pour down from thick gray clouds. Some storms, such as summer thunderstorms, are over in a few minutes, while tropical hurricanes can blow for over a day. But all storms share the same cause—a powerful combination of heat and lots of moisture. Summer thunderstorms occur when the hot morning sun steams water off the ground to pile up into towering thunderclouds that unleash torrents of rain. Hurricanes occur when these huge thunderclouds mushroom over warm oceans and join together into one giant, spiraling storm system.

● Twister

Tornadoes occur when a funnel of violently spinning air forms beneath a thundercloud and finally touches ground. At the center is an area of low pressure that sucks up everything in its path like a giant vacuum cleaner, while the terrifying winds reach speeds of over 249 mph, tossing people, cars, and buildings in the air like toys. From March to July every year, about 700 of these storms whirl across the Midwest of America in an area known as Tornado Alley.

Minneapolis
Sioux Falls   Chicago
Denver   Kansas City
            St. Louis
Wichita
        U. S. A.
Amarillo   Oklahoma City
        Dallas
            New Orleans
    Houston
MEXICO

▶▶ **Read further > winds**
pg79 (m30)

◀ *Tornado Alley in the U.S.A. Midwest, where tornadoes are also known as twisters.*

● Electric sky

Thunderclouds are built up by strong updrafts on warm, humid days, or along a cold front. These clouds are so big that raindrops grow to huge sizes within them. Whirlwinds within the clouds hurl the drops together so violently that the clouds become charged with static electricity. Eventually, the charge is released in a massive flash of lightning.

▶ *A thundercloud unleashes forks of lightning.*

Check it out!
- http://www.fema.gov/kids/hurr.htm
- http://dailynews.yahoo.com/fc3/ yahooligans/wild_weather
- http://www.ucar.edu/ 40th/webweather/

◀◀ HEAT see pg28 (d2) ◀◀

1   2   3   4   5   6   7   8   9   10   11   12   13   14   15   16   17   18   19

Hurricane force

Hurricanes are huge tropical storms that develop over the eastern Atlantic Ocean, then veer westward toward the east coast of the Americas. By this time, the storm is spiraling around a tight center or "eye" around which rains pour and winds gust at up to 199 mph. Each hurricane is given a name and tracked by satellite to give people plenty of warning that one is on its way— but when it arrives, dragging with it a huge surge of seawater *(see pg73 [q38])*, the impact is devastating.

▶▶ **Read further › sea water**
pg77 (r22)

▶ *Satellite view showing the eye of a hurricane.*

WORLD'S WORST

Worst weather	Disaster
• Most thunder	Tororo, Uganda, Africa averages 250 thundery days a year
• Worst hailstorm	a hailstorm in 1888 battered 246 people in India to death
• Worst hurricane	Hurricane Flora in 1963 killed 6,000 people in the Caribbean

IT'S A FACT

• Hurricanes can be 487 mi across, and take 18 hours or more to pass.

• There are about 45 hurricanes every year.

Frontal storms

Between the tropics and the polar regions, in most of North America, the stormiest weather is often linked to moving depressions (low pressure zones). Depressions are mostly cold air, but a wedge of warm air intrudes into them causing the worst weather to occur along the boundaries of this wedge, called fronts, where the warm air meets the cold air. As a depression moves past, these fronts bring a distinct sequence of weather.

▶▶ **Read further › air pressure**
pg79 (j22)

First to arrive is the warm front, where warm air rides up gently over the cold air, bringing steady rain over long periods

After the warm front passes, there is a brief respite, then the cold front arrives. Here the cold air sharply undercuts the warm air, piling up thunderclouds and unleashing short, but heavy, rain showers and heavy winds

◀◀ STORMS ON JUPITER pg48 (l2) ◀◀

22 23 24 25 26 27 28 29 30 31 32 33 34 35 36 37 38 39

The plant kingdom

THERE ARE millions of different kinds of living things on the Earth, so scientists group them to make it easier to study them. One of the largest groups is the plant kingdom, with more than 400,000 different kinds of plants. Some plants are so small, you need a microscope to see them clearly, while the tallest trees can reach over 328 ft tall. Plants also vary as to how long they live. Some live only a few hours, while others can live for thousands of years.

▸ *There are many different kinds, or groups, of plants and other plant-based living things. The main groups are shown here.*

Flowering plants

Broadleaf trees and bushes, flowers and herbs

Gingkos

Conifers

Cycads

Ferns

Club mosses

Horsetails

Mosses

Liverworts

Fungi

Lichens

Algae and seaweeds

Microscopic plants

● Plants with flowers

More than 250,000 types of plants grow flowers. They are known as the flowering plant group. Monocotyledons and dicotyledons are the two types of flowering plants *(see pg90 [d2])*. Many flowers have brightly colored petals *(see pg92 [p9])* that attract insects to pollinate them. Other types use methods such as self-pollination *(see pg93 [i27])*, or wind pollination *(see pg93 [u34])*. The flowers make seeds that grow into new plants.

▶▶ Read further › monocotyledons and dicotyledons / insect pollination
pg90 [d2; j14]; pg92 [k10]; pg93 [b29; d2]

▶▶ INSECTS see pg121 (b32) ▶▶

1 2 3 4 5 6 7 8 9 10 11 12 13 14 15 16 17 18 19

IT'S A FACT

- The plant with the largest flower is the rafflesia, which grows up to 3 ft across.

- The welwitschia plant of the southern African scrub has two leafs, each many feet long, and last for hundreds of years.

Plants with cones

Conifers are trees that have scaly, or needle-like, leafs they keep all year around. They do not have flowers but grow two types of cone—one makes a yellow dust called pollen *(see pg93 [u34])*, the other makes seeds when it receives the pollen. The cones that contain the seeds are made of a woody material that has slits in it. When the seeds are ready to drop, the slits open and the seeds fall out.

▲ *Cones grow near the tips of conifer branches.*

Read further > pollen
pg92 [d2]

Shady plants

Mosses, ferns, and liverworts are plants that grow in damp, shady places. They do not make seeds or have vessels to carry water. Mosses grow stalks with swollen tips. The tips make spores, which float away in the air. When a spore lands in damp soil it grows into a new moss plant. Ferns' spores form button-like swellings on the underside of their fronds (which resemble feathery leafs).

Read further > forest floor
pg99 [h22]

▲ *Ferns on a forest floor grow close together, making thick vegetation.*

Plants in the sea

Seaweeds grow mostly on rocky shores or underwater close to the coast. They hold on to the rocks to prevent being washed away. The part that holds the seaweed to a rock is called a holdfast, and looks like a root. It grips the rock tightly like a sucker. Seaweeds have tough, leathery fronds (leafs) to stand up to the pounding of the waves. Their bodies are flexible so that they can move with the water currents and not break.

▸ *Seaweeds like kelp belong to the plant group called algae.*

Read further > roots / underwater plants
pg85 [b22]; pg89 [b34]

BIGGEST PLANTS

Type	Plant	Length/weight
• Tallest grass	Bamboo	82 ft
• Tallest cactus	Saguaro	59 ft
• Biggest fern	Norfolk Island tree fern	66 ft
• Biggest seed	Coco-de-mer palm	66 lbs
• Longest leaf	Raffia palm	66 ft

▶▶ UNDERWATER LIFE see pg124 (f2) ▶▶

a b c d e f g h i j k l m n o p q r s t u v w

Plant parts

T HERE ARE four main parts on a flowering plant: the roots; the stem; the leafs; and the flower. Each plays a vital part in keeping the plant alive. The roots grow into the ground, so the plant does not blow away; the stem contains small tubes that carry water to all the parts of the plant; the leafs use the energy from sunlight to make food; *(see pg88 [j14])* and the flower makes seeds from which new plants grow.

Stigma (female) at the top of the carpel is sticky to attract pollen

Stigma

Anther   Stamen

Anther (male) makes pollen

Stem contains many tiny tubes, running from root to stem tip. This supports leafs and flowers, and channels water and minerals up from roots

To scale
1 square = 8 in across

Rafflesia = 40 in

Leafs use sunlight in a process called photosynthesis to make food—the plant's fuel

Roots grow down into soil or water. They hold the plant in place, preventing it from being blown away and allowing it to draw up water and minerals

Check it out!
- http://www.nhm.ac.uk/science/projects/fff/

Read further › photosynthesis
pg88 [d2; m2]

►► NAMING OF PLANT PARTS pg223 (m22) ►►

1 2 3 4 5 6 7 8 9 10 11 12 13 14 15 16 17 18 19

a b c d e f g h i j k l m n o p q r s t u v w

● Roots

There are two kinds of roots: fiberous roots and taproots. Grass plants *(see pg101 [e25])* have many long, thin fiberous roots that spread out in the soil in every direction. The carrot has a taproot—this root has a swollen part below the stem, used to store food for the plant. Side roots grow out from a taproot.

Taproot

▶▶ **Read further > root hairs** pg87 [i22]

GREEN FINGERS

• The leafs of the water hyacinth swell up with air to help the plant float.

• Trees that grow in the Arctic, where cold, strong, winds blow, have stems that grow across the ground and cannot even rise one inch above it.

● Multi-colored leafs

Leafs have a green substance, or pigment, called chlorophyll. This soaks up the energy in sunlight like a sponge soaks up water. This energy is used to make food. Variegated leafs have more than one color. They may have white marks where there is no chlorophyll, or they may have other pigments, such as carotene, that hides the chlorophyll in the leaf, giving it different colors.

● How stems stay upright

The stem must hold up the leafs so they can reach sunlight and make food. It must also hold up the flowers so they can collect pollen and make seeds. Many stems have tough fibers inside that help hold them up. The water that moves through the stem also gives support. If a plant needs water, its stem bends over, or wilts. Trees have thick stems—trunks—made of very strong wood. Plants, such as the strangler fig and dodder, have stems that grow on the stems of other—host—plants. Such parasitic plants use the stems of other plants for support. The dodder and strangler fig suck food out of the plant stems that they climb.

◀ *The strangler fig twists its way around a tree trunk as it grows.*

▶▶ **Read further > seeds** pg94 [d2]

▼ *Canadian maple leafs change to bright colors in the fall because other pigments dominate, hiding the chlorophyll in the leaf.*

IT'S A FACT

• The stem of the bamboo plant can grow over 12 in a day.

• The titan arum can grow a flower that is 8 ft high.

• The mistletoe has roots that grow onto its host, like on an oak tree.

▶▶ **Read further > chlorophyll / leafs** pg88 [m2]; pg89 [b22]

Thirsty work

ALL LIVING things need water to stay alive. Nearly three-quarters of a plant is made up of water, and if it loses too much it simply dies. Plants need water to make food, too, so if a plant cannot get enough water it is in danger of starving to death. The water inside many plants helps hold up the stem and the leafs so they can reach sunlight to make food. If they need water, the stem collapses and the leafs cannot get the sunlight the plant needs to make food.

Water escapes from leafs as water vapor

● Moving water without energy

Plants do not use any energy sucking up water or pumping it to their leafs. Water passes into the roots of a plant from the soil. Inside the root, the water is pulled through the plant to the leafs in tiny tubes or xylem *(see pg87 [n35])*; dissolved food from the leafs to other parts of the plant is carried by phloem *(see pg87 [o34])*. Water that evaporates (transpiration) through holes in the leafs is replaced with more water as it moves up the stem.

▶▶ Read further › roots / stems
pg85 (b22; b34)

Water flows up inside stem through tube-like channels called xylem

● IT'S A FACT

• The tip of a root is covered with a cap of slimy cells. The root cap protects the root tips from being worn away as they grow through the ground.

• Air holes in a leaf open during the day and close at night.

▸ *The path of water in a rose plant. Water input, flow, and loss in a plant is called translocation.*

Roots spread out in soil to collect water

Water enters plant through its roots

Bugs, grubs, and caterpillars feed on leafs

Thicker tubes (xylem) carry water to leaf

Leaf pores (stomata) where water escapes

Thinner tubes (phloem) carry sap away from leaf

Air spaces in leaf

▲ Microscopic view of holes in a leaf.

● How water escapes

Inside the leaf are air spaces. When water reaches the air holes, most of it evaporates and forms a gas called water vapor. When the water vapor evaporates, it passes through holes called stomata on the underside of the leaf. More water is drawn up the plant to take its place. If the air outside the leaf is hot and dry, water vapor escapes quickly so the plant needs plenty of water to keep up the supply.

● Hairy roots

Near the tip of each root are tiny, delicate hairs. They grow out a short way into the soil and collect water. The water moves along the hair and into the root where it enters a water tube. As the tip of the root grows through the soil, the hairs farther back die and new hairs grow at the root tip.

Base of stem

Main root

Secondary root

Branching root tip

◀ Roots grow thick to take in large amounts of water.

Read further › fibrous and taproots pg85 (b22)

● GREEN FINGERS

• Leafs are covered in a layer of wax to prevent too much water from being lost or gained.

• The leafs of underwater plants take in water through their surfaces.

● Water carriers

If you break open a celery stalk, you will see fibers sticking out of the end. These fibers are made from groups of tubes *(see pg89 [f30])* that carry water through the plant. Groups of tubes like these are called vessels. Inside the vessels are coils of cellulose. These help keep the tubes open so that water can always pass along them.

Read further › water storage pg101 (b30)

Xylem vessels (tubes) carry water

Growing layer

Phloem vessels (tubes) carry sap

Strong fibers

▶ Stems have many tubes, or vessels, for carrying food and water.

● Check it out!

• http://www.ars.usda.gov/is/kids

Making food

● **IT'S A FACT**

• During photosynthesis, the oxygen in the air, on which we depend for life, is continually replenished by plants.

• Photosynthesis occurs in leafs in two special kinds of cell: palisade and spongy cells.

Unlike animals, plants are able to make their own food. Plants get energy to make food from sunlight. Certain chemicals are needed to make food and the plants get them from the water in the ground and the air around them. When food is made, some of the energy from the sunlight is stored in it. The plants use this energy to keep them alive and growing. The whole process is called photosynthesis, which, in Greek, means "building with light."

Sun's rays carry light energy to leaf

Carbon dioxide is taken from air into leafs

Oxygen is given off from leafs

● Using sunlight

Most plant leafs contain a green chemical called chlorophyll. This traps some of the energy in sunlight. During photosynthesis, plants spread out their leafs to make a large area of the chlorophyll in which the sunlight shines. Once the energy is trapped, it is used to split up water into two chemicals called hydrogen and oxygen. The plant then uses more energy to join the hydrogen with carbon dioxide in the air to make food substances called carbohydrates, mainly sugars and starches. It emits the oxygen into the air.

▶▶ **Read further > chlorophyll**
pg85 (n22)

▸ *Photosynthesis occuring in a tulip plant—changing simple chemicals into food using sunlight.*

Stem

● GREEN FINGERS

• Huge numbers of algae in the oceans make most of the oxygen we breathe, even for those people who live far from the coast.

• Carbohydrates are foods that contain the chemicals carbon, hydrogen, and oxygen.

• Two important minerals that plants take from the soil are made from chemicals called nitrogen and phosphorus. Plants use them to make protein foods.

Roots

Bulb

🌐 **Check it out!**

• **http://www.alienexplorer.com/ ecology/topic3.htm**

◀◀ CHEMICALS see pg16 (d2) ◀◀

Cells in a leaf

Plants are made from tiny blocks of living matter called cells. There are different kinds of cells. The surface of the leaf is made from flat cells, which are transparent to let the sunlight shine through. Inside the leaf are cells that contain the chlorophyll. It is these cells that trap sunlight and make food. On the underside of the leaf are pairs of banana-shaped cells, which form the holes through which water vapor and carbon dioxide pass.

Read further › water vapour
pg87 (b34)

Waterproof wax coat

Upper layer of leaf

Leaf veins containing tiny tubes

Palisade cells

Leaf pores (stomata)

Spongy cells

Lower layer of leaf

◀ *All leafs have veins that carry water.*

▶ *Canadian pondweed oxygenates in water.*

Blowing bubbles

The oxygen made when sunlight breaks up water forms a gas inside the leaf. In plants that grow in the air, the oxygen simply mixes with other air gases and passes out through holes in the leaf invisibly. In water plants, oxygen form bubbles of gas that escape from the leafs when the plant makes food (photosynthesizes).

Read further › seaweed
pg83 (k30)

Finding light

Unlike other living things, plants cannot move around to find sunlight but they can grow toward it. Sometimes when plants sprout from their seeds, they are surrounded by other plants that keep them in the shade. Fortunately, the plant stems have tips that are sensitive to light, and they help the plant grow in the right direction.

▲ *While a poppy is growing toward sunlight, the plant uses food that is stored in its bulb.*

Read further › shady plants / bulbs
pg83 (b28); pg99 (i32; h22)

Deadly meat-eaters

Carnivorous plants, such as this pitcher plant, feed on living creatures, including insects and small mammals. The plant attracts the prey with a smell of rotting meat. Once inside the plant's vase-shaped leafs, called pitchers, the victim is dissolved by chemicals known as enzymes.

▶ *The pitcher plant digests and absorbs the bodies of its prey.*

Read further › feeding
pg88 (m2)

▶▶ CARNIVORES see pg130 (d2) ▶▶

a b c d e f g h i j k l m n o p q r s t u v w

Flowering plants

THE FLOWERING plant group contains more than 250,000 different species, including flowers, herbs, grasses, vegetables, and trees (but not conifers, which are gymnosperms—they make their seeds in cones). Flowering plants are divided into two main groups: monocotyledons, which have one cotyledon (food store), such as grasses, rushes, lilies, and orchids; and dicotyledons, which have two cotyledons—most flowers are formed like this.

A plant that lives for one year *(see pg96 [m13])* produces a flower at the end of its life. Most plants that live for many years flower yearly. The flower is the part in which seeds are made. Inside each seed is a new plant.

● **IT'S A FACT**

• The Puya raimondii plant lives for 150 years, then grows its first flower and dies.

• Some flowers that grow in the Arctic turn to face the sun all day so they absorb as much light as possible and keep warm.

• Bougainvillea (a tropical plant) does not have colorful flowers but colorful leafs.

● **Inside a flower**

Flowers come in all different shapes and sizes but most have the same parts. The young flower develops inside a bud, protected by green, leaf-like, sepals. As it opens, it displays its outermost parts, the ring of petals, which are usually large and colorful to attract insects. Within the petals is a ring of male parts called stamens. Each has a long, thin stalk—the filament—topped by a brush- or bag-like anther, which contains the male reproductive cells inside the pollen grains. At the center of the flower are the female parts, known as the carpel. This has a sticky pad, the stigma, at the top of a long stalk, the style, which widens at its base into an ovary. Inside the ovary are the female reproductive cells in their ovules (eggs).

▶▶ **Read further › stamens pg93 (n30)**

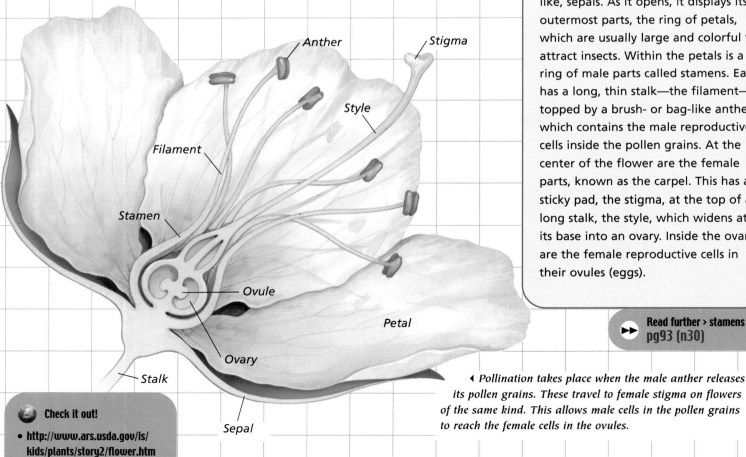

Anther *Stigma*

Style

Filament

Stamen

Ovule

Petal

Ovary

Stalk

Sepal

◀ *Pollination takes place when the male anther releases its pollen grains. These travel to female stigma on flowers of the same kind. This allows male cells in the pollen grains to reach the female cells in the ovules.*

● **Check it out!**

• http://www.ars.usda.gov/is/kids/plants/story2/flower.htm

Catkins

Some trees grow groups of flowers called catkins that hang down from a twig. Stamens hang outside the flowers in a catkin. They make pollen that is blown away by the wind. The wind rocks the catkins and stamens to make the plant release its pollen. The willow and hazel trees grow catkins early in the year before they sprout leafs. The oak grows catkins later in the spring after it has sprouted leafs.

▸ *The alder produces long, slim male catkins, and on the same tree, shorter, rounder female catkins.*

Read further > wind pollination
pg93 (n30)

Flowerheads

Some plants grow a large number of small flowers packed tightly together. The small flowers are called florets and they form a disk called a flowerhead. Many plants, such as the daisy and the dandelion, form many flowerheads that fool us into thinking that they are large flowers.

▾ *The wild daisy looks like a single bloom but it actually consists of many flowers. The flowers around the edge have a single petal.*

Read further > petals
pg90 (j14)

GREEN FINGERS

• Many flowers contain both the male reproductive organs (stamens) and the female reproductive organs (ovaries), but some plants have only one or the other.

• Grass flowers do not have petals. The flowers grow together at the top of a stalk.

• The name "daisy" comes from "day's eye" since these eye-like flowers open by day and close up at night.

Flower buds

A flower forms inside a bud (see pg84 [e15]). Flowers are very delicate when they are growing so the bud has a tough protective covering made from small leafs called sepals. When the flower blooms, the sepals bend backward and may fall off. The sepals of the tomato stay on the plant right through until the fruit is formed. They form the dark, spidery, top of a tomato.

◂ *The sepals of the Iceland poppy protect the bud while it is growing.*

▴ *The sepals form the dark, spidery, top of a tomato.*

Pollination

BEFORE A flower can make seeds, it must be pollinated. Pollen consists of fine yellow particles that are made by the stamens. The pollen has to be transferred to the stigma of another flower of the same type. The process by which pollen is moved from one flower to another is called pollination. There are several ways in which pollen can travel: it can be carried by insects or other animals, by wind, or by water. Flowers that are pollinated by animals have bright colors to attract insects while wind-pollinated flowers are often dull.

IT'S A FACT

• Some people are allergic to pollen. When grass plants release their pollen, these people suffer from a condition called hay fever. This can cause many different reactions such as runny eyes and sneezing.

• Bees collect pollen on their back legs to feed to their young.

Attracting insects

To attract insects, some flowers have brightly colored petals and a powerful scent. Near the base of the petals the flower makes a sugary juice called nectar for insects to drink. As insects search for the nectar, they pick up sticky pollen with their bodies from the stamens or anther *(see pg84 [i17])*. When they visit another flower they transfer the pollen from their bodies to another plant's sticky stigma.

▶▶ Read further > stamens pg90 (j14)

◀ *Brightly colored flower petals attract insects, such as this bee, to land on flowers, so encouraging insects to pollinate them.*

GREEN FINGERS

• A flower can only use pollen that has come from the same type of plant.

• Self-pollination occurs when the pollen moves from the stamen to the stigma in the same flower.

• Cross-pollination occurs when the pollen moves between plants of the same kind.

▶▶ INSECT POLLINATION see pg139 (j31) ▶▶

1 2 3 4 5 6 7 8 9 10 11 12 13 14 15 16 17 18 19

Bee orchids

Some plants, such as the bee orchid, can pollinate themselves if no insect visits them. The bee orchid's petals are shaped to look and smell like a female bee to attract male bees. But if no bees come along, the orchid can bend over to pollinate itself.

Spiky pollen

Flowers that are pollinated by insects make a small amount of spiky pollen. The spikes help the pollen stick to the hairs on the bodies of passing insects. The spikes hold the pollen in place as the insect flies between flowers. When the insect brushes against a sticky stigma, the pollen is pulled off.

▼ *The bee orchid's stamens bend over and release pollen grains straight onto its own stigma.*

Read further › stigma
pg90 (j14)

▸ *Spiky pollen sticks to the legs of this Emperor butterfly.*

Stamen

Pollen

▸ *Magnified pollen grain.*

Stigma

Flowers higher on the stem are smaller

Blowing in the wind

Wind-pollinated flowers, such as grass flowers, have no need of bright colors or scents so they are dull and have no smell. The stamens hang out of the flowers so that the wind can blow the pollen away. Later, the flowers put out stigmas to collect any pollen being carried in the air. The catkins (long, dangling flowers) of trees, such as the willow and hazel, are wind pollinated.

Petals look and smell like a female bee

▸ *The lily's stamens are bent like hooks but the stigma and style are straight.*

Check it out!
• http://www.cnps.org/kidstuff/ pollin.htm

Read further › catkins
pg91 (b22)

▶▶ **BUTTERFLIES see pg120 (k2)** ▶▶

22 23 24 25 26 27 28 29 30 31 32 33 34 35 36 37 38 39

a b c d e f g h i j k l m n o p q r s t u v w

Germination

INSIDE A seed is a tiny plant, or embryo, waiting to grow. The seed also contains a store of food to help the plant grow. When the seed leafs the parent plant, it is usually dry. This protects the seed from mold and keeps it light in weight. A lightweight seed is able to travel further and land on ground where there is room for it to grow. When the seed settles in the soil, it takes in water, swells up, and breaks open so that the new plant can grow out. This process of sprouting is called germination.

Speeding up sprouting

When tiny plants start to grow, they change stored food in the seeds into substances that build their root, stem, and leafs. The speed at which these changes take place is determined by heat. If the seeds are kept in warm conditions such as a greenhouse, the changes take place quickly and the seeds soon sprout. Seeds in cool conditions take longer to sprout. Some seeds, such as those of the ironbark tree, need to be scorched by wildfire before they will germinate.

Read further > food
pg88 (m2)

▸ Gardeners try to mix seeds that flower at different times so the garden is always full of color.

Seed needs

Not all seeds germinate in the same way. Coconut palm trees grow on tropical beaches and the coconuts fall and germinate on the beach. They can also fall into the sea, sometimes traveling for 1,200 mi in different ocean currents before washing up on another warm beach, where they may sprout and grow into another coconut palm.

▸ Coconuts are the fruit of the coconut palm tree. The seed has a hollow center that contains a sweet-tasting milk. The seed is contained in a brown, woody shell called a husk.

Check it out!
• http://www.bbc.co.uk/nature/plants/calendar/apr.shtml

IT'S A FACT

• A seed does not always sprout as soon as it forms. It may spend some time before germination, being inactive or dormant.

• The young plant that grows out of a seed is called a seedling.

• The first parts of a seedling that grow are the tips of the shoot and root.

Stages in sprouting

An embryo inside a seed contains a food store (cotyledon), which is protected by the tough, outer casing (testa). The cotyledon then moves to the tiny plant and nourishes it, making the plant grow. As the plant increases in size, the seed case breaks open. The root is the first part to appear and it grows downward. Later, the tiny shoots appear and grow upward. In the bean seed shown here the food store stays underground and the shoot makes new leafs above ground.

Keeping growing

When a new plant has used up the food store in its seed, it must find another source of food. The root obtains water and minerals, growing strong enough to hold the plant in place. The shoot grows toward the light so that the first leafs can make food.

▸ *Plants can even get all their needs—sunlight and water—in a crack in a sidewalk as rainwater carrying minerals seeps in.*

▶▶ **Read further › sunlight** pg89 (m22)

GREEN FINGERS

• In the sunflower seed, the food store rises up through the soil on the tip of the shoot to become the first pair of leafs.

• If you plant a seed upside down, the root will still grow downward and the shoot will still grow upward. They always grow from the seed in the right direction.

▶▶ **Read further › cotyledons** pg90 (d2)

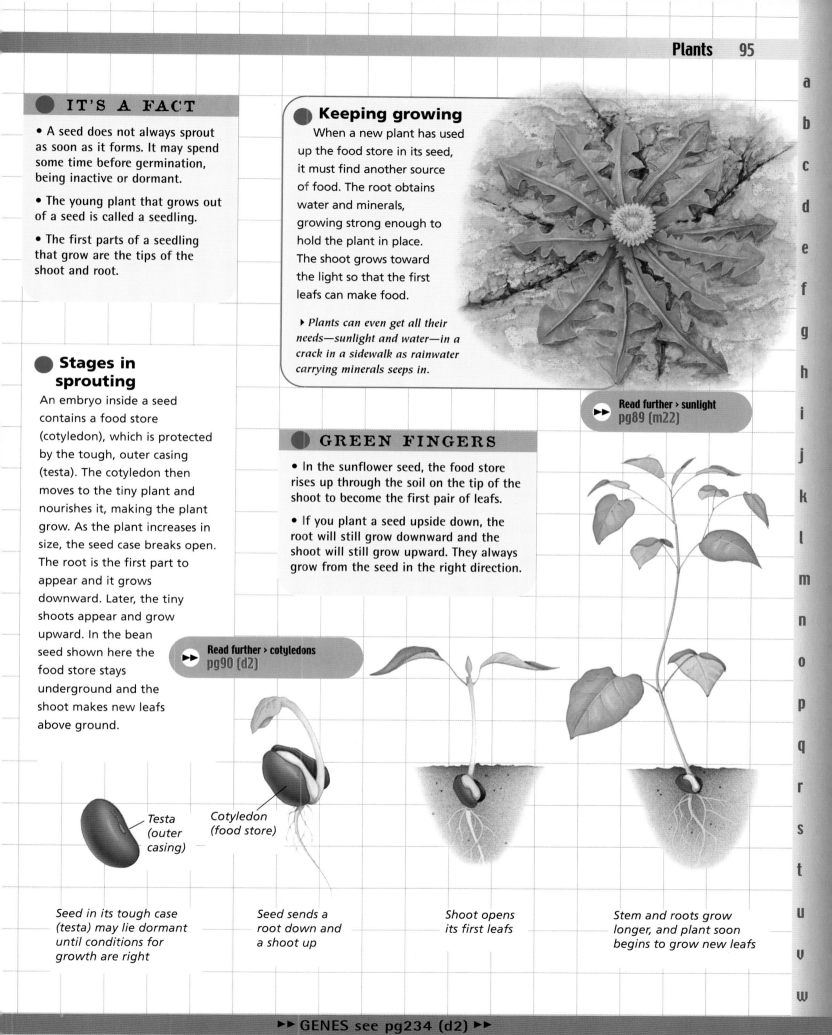

Testa (outer casing)

Cotyledon (food store)

Seed in its tough case (testa) may lie dormant until conditions for growth are right

Seed sends a root down and a shoot up

Shoot opens its first leafs

Stem and roots grow longer, and plant soon begins to grow new leafs

▶▶ GENES see pg234 (d2) ▶▶

Cycles of life

E
VERY PLANT has a life cycle. It begins when the seed first germinates, then it grows and forms flowers that are pollinated, which in turn produce their own seeds. Then the cycle begins all over again. Some plants complete their life cycle in a few weeks— ephemeral plants; others repeat their cycles for hundreds of years— perennial plants. Plants that complete their cycle in one year are annuals. Those that complete their cycle in two years are biennial.

▸ *Annual plants complete their life cycles, from seed to flower to seed again, in one year. In temperate (dry) lands, most of the growth occurs during spring, with pollination in early summer and seed production and growth during spring.*

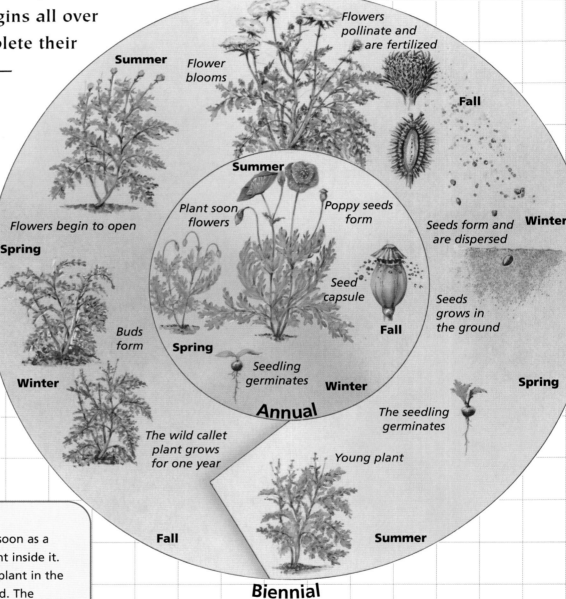

Flowers pollinate and are fertilized

Summer   *Flower blooms*

Fall

Summer

Flowers begin to open

Plant soon flowers   *Poppy seeds form*   *Seeds form and are dispersed*   **Winter**

Spring

Seed capsule   *Seeds grows in the ground*

Buds form   **Fall**

Spring

Winter   *Seedling germinates*   **Winter**   *The seedling germinates*   **Spring**

Annual

The wild callet plant grows for one year   *Young plant*

Fall   **Summer**

Biennial

Annuals

Annual plants live one year. As soon as a seed forms, it has a tiny living plant inside it. The seed may fall from its parent plant in the fall and lie all winter in the ground. The following spring the tiny plant bursts out of the seed and grows steadily for a few months. Finally, it makes flowers, and after its seeds have formed and spread, the plant dies.

▸▸ **Read further › seeds** pg95 (b22)

▲ *Biennial plants take two years to grow from seed to a mature plant. The partially-grown plant must be able to survive the harsh conditions of the cold or dry season, then continue its development the year after to flower and make seeds.*

▸▸ EARLY GROWTH IN HUMANS pg175 (b34) ▸▸

1   2   3   4   5   6   7   8   9   10   11   12   13   14   15   16   17   18   19

Ephemerals

The seed of the shepherd's purse plant sprouts soon after it lands in the soil. Such plants that grow quickly, flower, set seeds, and die in a few weeks are called ephemeral plants. There are many life cycles of the shepherd's purse, one after the other throughout the year. This means that shepherd's purse seeds are being spread around at regular intervals so there is a better chance that some may find a place to grow.

Read further > wind pollination
pg93 (n30)

▲ *Daffodils are perennials— they have bulbs and bloom every year.*

Perennials

When a perennial plant has finished flowering, it may lose some of its parts that are above ground (the flower) but the roots live on underground during the winter. The new shoots sprout the following spring. Perennials, such as tulips and daffodils, have a thick underground food store, called a bulb, that stays alive during the winter when the rest of the plant has died away.

Read further > exploding flowers
pg101 (o30)

Biennials

Biennials have life cycles of two years. In the first year, or growth season, the seed sprouts and the plant grows. During this time the leafs make plenty of food, which is stored in the plant. In the second growth season biennial plants use the stored food to help them grow again, bloom with flowers and produce seeds before dying.

Read further > biennial roots
pg85 (b22)

▲ *In the first year of their life, beetroots develop leafs and a fleshy, red root—they are harvested before the next year.*

GREEN FINGERS

• Ephemerals (short-lived plants), such as chickweed and groundsel, can take over a bare patch of soil quickly and become weeds (plants growing in the wrong place).

• A potato plant grows underground stems, which swell up with stored food to form tubers, called potatoes. Each stem can grow into another plant the following year.

Check it out!
• http://www.alienexplorer.com/ecology/Ecology.html
• http://www.bbc.co.uk/nature/plants

▶▶ FOOD FOR GROWTH IN HUMANS pg164 (d2) ▶▶

22 23 24 25 26 27 28 29 30 31 32 33 34 35 36 37 38 39

a b c d e f g h i j k l m n o p q r s t u v w

Forest life

Whe HEN TREES grow together in large groups they form forests. There are three main types of forest: coniferous, temperate, and tropical rainforests with broad-leafed trees. Each kind of forest grows in different places around the world, depending on weather conditions. When trees grow close together, such as in a rainforest, the leafs on the branches stop most of the light reaching the forest floor. Plants that live on the ground have adapted to the shade beneath the trees.

Emergent layer

Canopy

Understorey

Undergrowth

Forest floor

IT'S A FACT

• The trees in a tropical rainforest are broadleaf evergreen trees.

• The trees in a temperate forest are broadleaf deciduous trees.

• The main trees in a coniferous forest are fir, larch, scots pine, and spruce.

Tropical rainforests

Rainforests are found in the hot, wet, weather conditions around the Equator—the part of the Earth nearest the Sun. The trees in a rainforest are mostly broadleaf, evergreen trees. Most of the trees grow up to 90 ft above the ground and their branches lock together to form a canopy. Many small plants, called epiphytic plants, like orchids, ferns, and bromeliads, live on the branches of rainforest trees. They have short roots to hold them in place and gather the water they need in cups made from their leafs.

▶▶ **Read further › roots** pg85 (b22)

◀◀ EQUATOR see pg62 (p2) ◀◀

| 1 | 2 | 3 | 4 | 5 | 6 | 7 | 8 | 9 | 10 | 11 | 12 | 13 | 14 | 15 | 16 | 17 | 18 | 19 |

▼ *Coniferous forests grow for hundreds of miles in northern parts of North America, Europe, and Asia, usually high up on mountainsides.*

Temperate forests

Temperate forests grow where summers are warm and winters are cool. They are found in parts of North America, Europe, China, Australia, and Japan. Trees in temperate forests lose their leafs in winter. Therefore, in spring, before new leafs grow, light reaches the forest floor, giving flowering plants a chance to flower.

▲ *Bluebells bloom on the forest floor before the trees grow new leafs in spring.*

Read further › mosses
pg83 (b28)

Coniferous forests

Coniferous forests grow where the summers are short and warm but the winters are long and cold. As the trees grow very close together and they keep their leafs all year round, very little sunlight reaches the forest floor so only small plants like mosses can grow. The soil of coniferous forests usually freezes once a year, making it difficult for plants to obtain water.

Read further › sunlight
pg89 (m22)

GREEN FINGERS

• One 57-acre area of Malaysian rainforest has 375 species of tree with trunks thicker than 3 ft.

• The floor of a coniferous forest is covered in a thick layer of dead leafs because they take a long time to rot into the cold, dark conditions.

• Rainforest trees are covered with epiphytes—plants whose roots never reach the soil but take water from the air.

Can forests survive?

Forests provide people with large amounts of wood. Every second, an area of rainforest the size of a football field is cut down (logged) for timber. Within the next 100 years all the rainforests could be destroyed. Planting more trees and recycling paper materials are two ways that can help rainforests survive.

▸ *Logging can destroy whole hillsides in as little as a day.*

Read further › rainforests
pg98 (o2)

▶▶ HABITAT DESTRUCTION see pg148 (o2) ▶▶

Grasslands and desert

GRASSLAND FORMS where there is not enough rain for trees to grow. There is usually a long, dry, season and a short season, when it rains, or even snows. In the dry season, plants and seeds may lie dormant (asleep), but when rain falls the grassland briefly blooms with green leafs and brightly colored flowers. In hot countries, during the dry season, plants face threat of fire, but the fire does not destroy the roots so the grass grows back. A desert is a place where very little rain falls: there may be nine months without rain, then three months with a little rainfall. Deserts can be very hot in the day and very cold at night, so it is hard for plants to thrive without the mineral-rich soil and water that they need to live.

Read further > rainforests
pg98 (o29)

IT'S A FACT

• The continent with the largest area of desert is Asia.

• The world's biggest desert is the Sahara in north Africa. It is 3,106 mi across at its widest point and up to 1,398 mi from north to south.

The savannah

The savannah is a huge area of grassland that covers most of Africa. It covers a much larger area than rainforests or deserts. The tallest grass on the savannah is elephant grass, which reaches 10 ft in height. Some trees, such as the acacia and the baobab, store water and have fire-resistant trunks. They grow in small numbers on the grassy plains.

▼ Acacia trees provide a small amount of shady protection for herds of zebra in the blazing sun and drying winds of the African savannah.

Check it out!

• http://hort.purdue.edu/ext/
prairie_wildflowers.html

▼ *Prairies contain a wide variety of grass, including cottonwood, switch grass, needle grass, panicgrass, asters, Idaho fescue, and big bluestem grass.*

Cacti

The largest group of plants in most deserts are the succulents. Cacti are a particular type of succulent that grow mostly in North and South American deserts. Down the sides of the cactus are grooves that fill out when it takes in water. Cacti do not have broad leafs to make food, because they would lose too much water; instead they use their thick, green, fleshy stems as leafs to store water, and convert sunlight into food. A waxy layer on the stem reduces water evaporation.

Prairies and steppes

Large areas of temperate grassland in North America are called prairies—in Russia they are called steppes. Prairies do not have enough rain all year round for trees to grow naturally but hundreds of grasses, crops, and shrubs thrive.

▶▶ **Read further › forests**
pg99 (h22)

GREEN FINGERS

• Joshua trees, native to North American deserts, can grow to about 30 ft high.

• A large cactus can take in 1 ton of water in a day after it has rained.

• The biggest cactus is the saguaro of southern Arizona, southeast California and northwest Mexico. It can grow up to 66 ft tall and 3 ft thick.

▶▶ **Read further › path of water**
pg86 (m2)

▲ *Needle-like spikes on the cactus stem stop animals from biting into the plant to get water.*

Plants like pebbles

Pebble plants grow in deserts in southern Africa. They develop thick, round leafs, colored like stones and pebbles, to camouflage and protect them from animals that might eat them.

▶▶ **Read further › desert plants**
pg101 (b30)

Exploding seedheads

Some plants cannot store water, so they die when the desert dries up. Their seedheads, packed with seeds, stand on dry stalks until the next rain. When the water soaks into the flowerhead it makes various parts of the plant twist and turn so that the flowerhead explodes, so sending out its seeds. The seeds take in water and sprout quickly to make new plants.

▶▶ **Read further › flowerheads**
pg91 (b34)

▶ *After rain, cactus flowers bloom briefly, adding splashes of color in the desert.*

▶▶ PLANT–EATING ANIMALS see pg132 (d2) ▶▶

a b c d e f g h i j k l m n o p q r s t u v w

All kinds of animals

THE WORLD is full of animals. They live on top of the highest mountains, at the bottom of the deepest oceans, in tropical rainforests, and in the cold, icy wastes of the polar regions. Some animals are so weird and so different from those we have at home or see on farms or at the zoo that we might wonder whether they are animals at all. The study of animals is vitally important—to save wildlife and conserve the wonder and beauty of the natural world for the future, and to improve our farming and food supplies for an increasing world population.

▶▶ **Read further > adapting**
pg105 (d22)

● What is an animal?

Animals come in many different shapes and sizes, and live in a wide variety of habitats. So what defining features do they share that make them all animals? Like plants, their bodies are made of many microscopic parts called cells. However, unlike most plants, they take food into their bodies by eating it and breaking it down, rather than by building it up from simple minerals. They sense, or detect, features of their surroundings such as light or sound. Most animals can move around at some stage in their lives.

▼ *Different parts of the world have their own distinctive types of animal, which adapt, survive, and reproduce in various habitats.*

● IT'S A FACT

• The biggest animals are 1 million million times bigger than the smallest ones.

• More than 999 out of every 1000 kinds of animals that ever lived, such as dinosaurs, died out long ago.

• The total number of kinds, or species, of animals is probably more than 10 million.

▶▶ ANIMAL SENSES see pg136 (d2) ▶▶

KINGDOMS OF LIFE	Very simple microbes	Simple microbes	Fungi	Plants	Animals

Porifera
e.g. sponges

Nematodes
e.g. roundworms

Mollusks
e.g. mussels

Chordates
e.g. vertabrates and sea squirts

Sea squirts and other chordates
e.g. lancelets

PHYLA (MAJOR GROUPS)

Cnidarians
e.g. jellyfish and sea anemones

Annelids
e.g. earthworms

Echinoderms
e.g. starfish

Vertebrates
e.g. animals with a backbone

SUBPHYLA

Platyhelminthes
e.g. flatworms

Many other types of worm
e.g. flatworms

Jawless fish
e.g. lampreys and hagfish

Cartilage fish
e.g. sharks

Arthropods
e.g. insects and crustaceans

Bony fish
e.g. lionfish

Amphibians
e.g frog

CLASSES (NEXT MAIN GROUPS)

Crustaceans
e.g. crabs

Reptiles
e.g. lizards

Birds
e.g. thrush

Arachnids
e.g. spiders

Chilopods
e.g. centipedes

Insects
e.g. butterflies

Diplopods
e.g. millipedes

Mammals
e.g. bears

▲ *The science of grouping animals is called taxonomy. It is important in many ways, for example when deciding which creatures today are the closest relatives of long-dead dinosaurs.*

Animal species

Larger groups of animals are divided into smaller groups, until a single kind or type is reached—the species. Examples of different species within larger groups are the red fox, tiger, golden eagle, housefly, and giant squid *(see pg105 [f35])*. A species is not defined by its appearance, color, or size, but by breeding. If animals can breed together they are members of the same species. If they cannot breed together they are from different species.

►► **Read further › golden eagle**
pg110 (g14)

▲ *Red foxes can breed with each other, which means they are all members of the same species: Vulpes vulpes.*

The animal kingdom

The living world is divided into groups called kingdoms. The animal kingdom has more members than all the other kingdoms put together. Zoologists (scientists who study animals) divide the kingdom into main groups called phyla (singular is phylum), by comparing important body features. This means the phyla are unequal in size. For example, the spoonworm phylum has 150 different kinds, which live on the seabed, while the arthropod phylum has millions of kinds including insects, crabs, spiders, centipedes, and millipedes. Vertebrates are a major group, which includes mammals, fish, birds, reptiles, and amphibians: all other animals are invertebrates.

►► **Read further › insects**
pg118 (d2)

Check it out!
• http://www.worldalmanacfor kids.com/explore/animals5.html

Mammals 1

MAMMALS ARE the most familiar class of animals, because human beings are mammals. Typical mammals have a body covering of fur or hair, are warm-blooded (their body temperature stays at the same high level despite changes in the climate) and feed their babies on milk made by the mother in body parts called mammary glands. However, there are exceptions. The biggest mammals of all, such as whales in the ocean and elephants on land, have almost no hair or fur. And some mammals go into a long winter sleep called hibernation, when their body temperatures fall to just above freezing.

Insect eaters

The insectivores (insect eaters) are mostly smallish mammals such as moles, shrews, and hedgehogs. They have small, sharp teeth, and eat insects, grubs, slugs, worms, and similar juicy creatures. There are about 365 species, including the rat-like tenrecs from Africa, and the rare, long-nosed solenodons that live on some Caribbean islands.

Bears

The eight kinds of bears are members of the small mammal family, ursidae. Their foods vary greatly. Most bears eat large amounts of plant foods, such as leafs, fruits, berries, and nuts, as well as meat. The giant panda eats almost nothing but bamboo. Yet the diet of the polar bear of the far north consists almost entirely of meat. It rivals the brown or grizzly bear as the biggest land predator, weighing over half a ton and standing 10 ft tall.

▶ *Polar bears are almost pure white, while their close cousins, the American grizzly bears, are mostly black.*

▲ *There are 12 species of hedgehogs and most have sharp spines like this European hedgehog—but the desert hedgehog has coarse fur.*

▶▶ Read further › insects / worms
pg118 (d2); pg125 (b33)

▶▶ Read further › biggest predator
pg105 (e22)

▶▶ Read further › mollusks
pg124 (n2)

Life in the water

Cetaceans are porpoises, whales, and dolphins that live in tropical seas and rivers. They are hairless mammals whose bodies have adapted fully to life in the water. Their front limbs are flippers, their back limbs are missing and their tails have wide flaps on either side, called flukes, for swimming. There are about 83 species of cetaceans and they are all carnivorous—they eat other animals. These great whales consume vast amounts of krill—tiny, shrimp-like creatures, while sperm whales prey on large fish and seals.

▲ *The world's biggest predator, the 50-ton sperm whale, attacks the largest invertebrate animal, the giant squid.*

Meat-eating mammals

Any animal that eats mainly meat is known as a carnivore. Confusingly, there is also a group of mammals officially called the Carnivora. It includes dogs, foxes, jackals, bears, raccoons, weasels and stoats, civets and linsangs, hyaenas and cats.

▶▶ Read further › sharp teeth
pg117 (b22)

▲ *Hyaenas have sharp senses to track their victims, fierce claws, and long, sharp teeth—canines—to stab and rip prey.*

Bats

Bats are the second-largest mammal group, with almost 1,000 species. Most bats are small, live in tropical rainforests, and fly at night to catch gnats, moths, and similar flying insects. The flying foxes or fruit bats, with about 175 species, are bigger and eat plant foods such as fruits, seeds, and sap. A bat's front limbs are actually wings that have a thin, stretchy membrane or layer, attached to very long finger bones.

▶▶ Read further › flying insects
pg118 (h16)

▶ *Fruit bats rest with their wings wrapped around their bodies.*

ANIMAL FACTS

• The biggest mammal, and the biggest animal of all, is the blue whale. It is 98 ft in length and weighs more than 100 tons.

• The smallest mammals are shrews on the ground and bats in the air. The pygmy shrew has a head and body smaller than the human thumb. The hog-nosed bat's wings are each about as long as a human finger.

• The longest-lived mammals include the rare, seldom-seen, beaked whales—some may be more than 150 years old.

▶▶ CARNIVORE TEETH see pg130 (l15) ▶▶

22   23   24   25   26   27   28   29   30   31   32   33   34   35   36   37   38   39

a b c d e f g h i j k l m n o p q r s t u v w

Mammals 2

IT'S A FACT

• There are more than 1,650 species of rodents: this is the largest group of mammals.

• The rabbit and hare group, lagomorphs, has 80 species.

• The ungulates or hoofed mammals number about 245 species.

MOST MAMMALS are herbivores—plant eaters. The largest plant-eating group, rodents, make up 40 percent of the mammal group. They include rats, mice, squirrels, beavers, porcupines, and guinea pigs, and their cousins from South America, known as cavies. Rabbits and hares look like rodents because of their long front teeth but they belong to a different mammal order known as lagomorphs. Another large plant-eating order is the ungulates or hoofed mammals. These are divided into two types: the odd-toed ungulates—with one or three toes—such as horses, zebras, asses, tapirs, rhinos, and the even-toed ungulates—with two or four toes—such as pigs, peccaries, hippos, camels, deer, giraffes, antelopes, gazelles, cattle, sheep, and goats.

Rodents

Rodents live all over the world, in almost every land habitat. One species, the beaver, can swim underwater for almost 0.6 mi, holding its breath and keeping its nostrils and ears shut. The rodent's special feature is its front teeth, called incisors. These are very long with straight, sharp edges like chisels. Their incisors keep growing throughout their life, so rodents can gnaw hard foods like nuts and roots, without wearing away their teeth.

▲ Beavers gnaw through tree trunks in minutes with their long, ever-growing incisor teeth.

▶ Most ungulates, like zebra, can run fast. They are able to outrun most predators from a young age.

Read further > underwater
pg109 (m31); pg111 (s31)

Odd-toed ungulates

Horses, zebras, rhinos, and tapirs are called odd-toed ungulates because they have an odd number of toes per foot, each capped with a hard hoof. Horses and zebras have just one toe per foot and their legs are long and slim for running in open habitats such as grasslands. They are grazing animals, and feed mainly on grass that they chew with their powerful jaws and molars.

Read further > ungulates
pg107 (b22)

◄◄ TREES see pg98 (d2) ◄◄

1 2 3 4 5 6 7 8 9 10 11 12 13 14 15 16 17 18 19

Even-toed ungulates

The buffalo is an even-toed ungulate or "cloven hoofed" mammal. Herds on the North American prairies were almost wiped out by European settlers in the 1500s but have since recovered some of their numbers. European buffalo, bison, are slightly smaller and live in thick forests, mainly in Poland and Belarussia, Europe.

 Read further › biggest mammal
pg105 (r32)

▸ *Bison are among the biggest hoofed mammals. A large male American bison can weigh almost 1 ton.*

◂ *Dromedary (one-humped) camels have broad feet to keep them steady on desert sand and long eyelashes to protect their eyes in sand storms.*

Humps store fat

▸ *Bactrian (two-humped) camels have thick fur that helps to keep out the cold of the Mongolian high grasslands.*

Trunk and tusk

Elephants are the largest land mammals. A large, male African savannah elephant can stand 13 ft tall and weigh more than 8 tons. All elephants are plant-eaters. They may look like hoofed mammals, but they have their own order, called proboscidea.

▾ *Elephant tusks are greatly enlarged upper incisor teeth and the trunks are a very long combination of upper lip and nose.*

 Read further › herbivores
pg109 (e31)

Camel humps

Both species of camel—the one-humped dromedary of Africa, the Middle East and Australia, and the two-humped Bactrian of Central Asia—have been domesticated (bred by people) for milk, meat, hides, and carrying. The camel group also includes the camel's South American relations—the guanaco and vicuna in the wild, and their domesticated descendants, the llama and alpaca.

ANIMAL FACTS

• The Sumatran rhinoceros, which has red colored hair, is a relative of the wooly rhinoceros of the last ice age.

• For many years it was believed there were only two types of elephant: African and Asian. But there are three.

• There are two species of African elephant: the African savannah elephant, large with curved tusks, prefers open country; the African forest elephant, slightly smaller with straighter tusks, likes thick woodland. Being different species, they cannot breed with one another.

 Check it out!

• http://www.enchantedlearning.com/subjects/ mammals/classification/ Ungulates.shtml

◂◂ SAVANNAH see pg100 (i15) ◂◂

22 23 24 25 26 27 28 29 30 31 32 33 34 35 36 37 38 39

a b c d e f g h i j k l m n o p q r s t u v w

Mammals 3

SOME GROUPS of mammals have many members while others have very few. The marsupial group consists of about 290 species, including kangaroos and Virginia possums, while the tubulidentata has only one living species—the aardvark of Africa. There are only four species of dugongs and manatees, also known as sirenians or "sea cows." These bulky plant eaters of shallow coastal waters have front limbs like paddles and flipper-shaped tails. Another group, the monotremes, or egg-laying mammals, has just five species, including the duck-billed platypus and echidnas.

IT'S A FACT

• The primate group includes lemurs, monkeys, and humans. They number about 350 species.

• There are only two species of colugos, or flying lemurs, which live in Southeast Asian tropical forests and eat mostly plants.

▼ The Virginia possum may have 18 babies in one litter. After growing in her pouch for 6-8 weeks, they ride clinging to her back.

Cows of the sea

Sirenians are the only sea mammals that mainly eat plants, although they may occasionally eat small fish for added nutrients. Their diet of seagrass, seaweeds, and other aquatic vegetation is low in nourishment, so a sirenian may need to consume up to one-quarter of its body weight every day. Their closest mammal cousins are probably not seals or whales, but elephants and hoofed mammals.

▲ Manatees weigh more than half a ton. They have round, spoon-like tails to help them move through the water.

Read further > hoofed mammals pg107 [b22]

Marsupials

Marsupials live mainly in Australia, with some species found in South America and Southeast Asia. Only one kind, the Virginia possum, has spread to North America. Many smaller marsupials resemble other types of mammals—there are marsupial mice and rats, shrews and cats, and even marsupial anteaters and moles.

Read further > marsupials pg107 [e31]

Check it out!

• http://www.enchantedlearning.com/subjects/mammals/classification/Ungulates.shtml

▶▶ ELEPHANTS see pg146 (q2) ▶▶

1 2 3 4 5 6 7 8 9 10 11 12 13 14 15 16 17 18 19

Powerful digger

The aardvark emerges at night and may travel more than 12 mi in search of ant nests and termite mounds. It has a variety of common names, such as earth-pig, African anteater and ant-bear. Its closest mammal relation is probably the hoofed mammal group, ungulates. The aardvark's teeth are among the most unusual of any mammal: it has no front incisors or canines but molars that grow continuously. In mammals, the number and type of teeth are important for figuring out which of the groups are most closely related.

▶▶ **Read further › ungulates** pg106 (n13)

▲ *The aardvark has a long, sensitive snout to sniff out food in the dark. The nostrils are surrounded by fine hairs to keep out dust as the aardvark digs into its prey's nest.*

ANIMAL FACTS

• The primate mammals include the lesser apes—nine species of gibbons—all in Southeast Asia. They swing through trees, using their very long, powerful arms, and hook-like hands. The largest gibbon, the siamang, is one of the loudest mammals, almost as loud as the South American howler monkey—the noisiest of all land animals.

• The largest meat-eating marsupial, the Tasmanian devil, has a fierce and aggressive reputation, but it rarely gets into fights with others of its kind. It eats many small animals, from insects to possums. Some people keep Tasmanian devils as tame, friendly pets.

▶ *A baby kangaroo is called a joey. It is as small as a grape when it is born. After six months in the pouch, it is ready to leave for short periods of time.*

Bounding along

Marsupials are pouched mammals because in most types, the female has a pocket-like pouch of skin on her front. Her baby is born at a tiny, undeveloped stage and crawls into the pouch, where it feeds on her milk and grows for many weeks. Kangaroos and wallabies are large plant eaters native to Australia. They bound along on their two enormous back legs, using their thick tail for balance.

▶▶ **Read further › Australian emu** pg111 (g22)

▲ *Kangaroos often play fight with each other in groups.*

Egg-laying mammals

One of the most extraordinary mammals is the platypus of Australia. It has a duck-like beak or bill, a flat tail, and webbed feet like a beaver. It is one of the few mammals that does not give birth to babies, but lays eggs in a deep burrow. The eggs hatch after about ten days and the mother then feeds her babies on milk, like other mammals. The four species of echidnas or "spiny anteaters" of Australia and Southeast Asia are also egg-layers.

▶▶ **Read further › beaver** pg106 (p2)

▶ *The platypus feeds on small creatures in streams and pools. Its beak is very sensitive to touch so it can feed at night, just by feel.*

▶▶ MEAT EATERS see pg130 (n2) ▶▶

a b c d e f g h i j k l m n o p q r s t u v w

Birds

BIRDS ARE the only creatures with feathers. These protect the bird and form a large, light wing surface for flying. Feathers also help regulate a bird's body heat—like mammals, birds are warm blooded. Some birds have feathers for camouflage (blending into the surroundings), while others have brightly colored feathers to warn off predators or attract a mate. All birds have a beak, which is made of a strong, horn-like substance. The beak is shaped to eat certain foods. All birds have scaly legs with clawed toes, and breed by laying eggs, usually in a nest made by the parents.

IT'S A FACT

• There are about 9,000 species of birds—this is twice as many species as mammals.

• There are 18 species in the penguin group, and 65 in the pelican group—including darters, cormorants, tropic birds, gannets, and boobies.

• The owl group contains 205 species.

Birds of prey

Some of the largest and fiercest birds are raptors, or birds of prey. There are more than 300 species including eagles, condors, vultures, hawks, buzzards, kites, falcons, harriers, and kestrels. They have powerful toes with sharp claws, called talons, to seize prey, and a pointed, hooked beak to tear off lumps of flesh. Most have big eyes and hunt by sight.

▶▶ Read further › seizing prey
pg105 (e22)

◀ Most parent birds, such as the golden eagle, care for their chicks (babies) and bring them food. These larger birds look after their chicks for longer. A young eagle does not leave its nest for about ten weeks.

BIRDS

Widest wingspan	Width
• Wandering albatross	12 ft
• Marabou stork	10.5 ft
• Andean condor	10 ft
• Swan	9 ft

Check it out!

• http://www.enchantedlearning.com/subjects/birds/Allaboutbirds.html
• http://www.idahoptv.dialogue4kids/birdsofprey/bird.html

◀ *Ostriches are the fastest two-legged runners. They cannot fly but their wings have other uses, such as flapping at enemies, courtship displays, and shading their eggs from the hot sun.*

▶▶ **Read further › fast runners** pg106 (n13)

Flightless birds

More than 50 species of birds cannot fly, including kiwi from New Zealand and some of the water-birds called rails. The biggest flightless birds are the African ostrich, Australian emu, and South American rhea. These birds have powerful legs with two toes per foot. The ostrich can run very fast for about half an hour non stop, reaching speeds of 47 mph. Ostriches eat many foods, like seeds, fruits, and insects.

▶ *A tawny owl returns to its nest with a meal. It feeds mostly on mice, voles, young rats, and large insects.*

Night hunter

As darkness falls, birds of prey such as hawks rest while owls come out of tree holes, cliff crevices, or quiet buildings. These nocturnal (night-time) hunters catch a range of prey, from beetles and mice, to young rabbits and squirrels. Owls can see well in the dark with their huge eyes. They also have the best hearing of almost any bird—their ears are hidden under their head feathers.

▶▶ **Read further › eyes** pg119 (q22)

Seabirds

Hundreds of kinds of birds live on, over, or near the sea. Gannets are sea birds that dive onto prey from as high as 99 ft. They breed in noisy, crowded colonies. To feed, they dive to snatch squid, fish, and other sea creatures from the surface of the water with their long, hook-tipped bill. The most impressive sea bird is the wandering albatross, which can stay in the air for weeks, soaring on strong winds.

▶▶ **Read further › fish defense** pg117 (m34)

▾ *When they dive for food, some types of penguin can stay underwater for up to 20 minutes without surfacing for air.*

◀ *The gannet's strong skull helps cushion the impact of its high-speed dive into water.*

Flying underwater

Penguins flap their flipper-shaped wings to speed through water chasing their prey. All penguins live along coasts and shores in the southern hemisphere, with some breeding on icebergs or the frozen land of Antarctica. They feed in the sea on creatures such as small fish and squid, and shrimp-like krill.

▶▶ **Read further › squid** pg124 (n2)

Reptiles

MOST OF the 8,000 or so species of reptile have scaly skin, lay eggs, and are "cold-blooded." This means, unlike mammals and birds, they cannot generate heat inside their bodies. So most reptiles inhabit warm areas, basking in the sun. In scrublands and deserts, reptiles sleep through long droughts. Reptiles live in all habitats except at the coldest poles—and turtles and sea-snakes live in oceans. The major reptile groups are crocodilians, turtles and tortoises, snakes and lizards, and amphisbenids—tropical worm-like creatures that live mostly underground.

● Deadly predators

There are 23 kinds of crocodilians—crocodiles, alligators, caimans, and one species of gharial. Crocodilians are powerful hunters, they lurk in swamps, lakes, and rivers waiting for prey. Crocodiles are found in Asia, Africa, and Australia, while alligators and caimans are usually found in North, Central, and South America. They make good hunters because they can approach prey through water in stealth, with only their eyes and nostrils above the surface as they move.

▼ *The gharial has a long, thin snout and slim jaws for catching fish.*

►► **Read further › eggs**
pg115 (j22)

▼ *The alligator's snout is broad for seizing large prey.*

▲ *Crocodile snouts are designed to kill large prey. The alligator's snout is broad for seizing large prey.*

▼ *The black caiman's snout tapers at the end so it can catch small prey.*

►► CROCODILE PREY see pg131 (o30) ►►

● Smooth but not slippery

Snakes range from the 3 ft python and the 440 lb anaconda, which constrict or squeeze their prey to death, to tiny thread-snakes smaller than a pencil. All hunt living prey but fewer than 50 types are deadly poisonous to humans. These include adders, vipers, mambas, and cobras. The king cobra is the longest poisonous snake: it is 16 ft long. Its main prey is other snakes.

▲ The puff adder, found in Africa, is highly venomous and is responsible for the most snake attacks on humans.

►► Read further › rodents
pg106 (p2)

◄ A cobra's jaws are so loose and pliable, it can swallow prey bigger than its own head, like a small rodent.

● Slow but safe

Tortoises are chelonians that live on land. Most eat plants but a few also consume small animals. Some survive in the driest deserts, where they burrow into the soil to escape heat and drought. The desert tortoise lays its eggs in a hole or under a rock or log. When these hatch some weeks later, the babies must take care of themselves.

►► Read further › eggs
pg109 (m31)

▲ The desert tortoise has especially large front legs, wide feet, and stout claws, to burrow into the dry soil and avoid the hottest part of the day.

● Ocean wanderers

About 290 kinds of turtles and tortoises make up the reptile group called chelonians. Their main feature is the shell, made of a domed upper part, the carapace, and a flatter underside, the plastron. The carapace and plastron are formed from up to 60 curved bony plates, covered by another layer of horny plates. Some have hard, bony shells to protect against land predators; others have a streamlined carapace for swimming easily through water.

►► Read further › chelonians
pg113 (b33)

▼ Female sea turtles come on to the beach only to lay eggs in a hole on the beach. Males never touch dry land once they have hatched.

▶ The frilled lizard of Australia grows up to 28 in long and its frill can be extended to a width of 10 in.

● Variety of lizards

Lizards are the most wide-ranging and varied of reptiles. The Galapagos iguana dives under the water to eat seaweed, the Nile monitor lizard is powerful enough to catch small antelopes, and the chameleon flicks out a sticky-tipped tongue as long as its body to grab flies. Most lizards have a long tail and four legs, but some, such as slow-worms and skinks, have no limbs at all.

►► Read further › worms
pg125 (b22)

►► COBRA see pg138 (i12) ►►

Amphibians

THE NAME "amphibian" means "both lives," because most amphibians live on land and breed in water. Many of the 5,000 species live in water when young and breathe using gills like fish. As they grow older, a lot of amphibians spend more time on land, lose their gills, and breathe with their lungs. In a change of shape known as metamorphosis, amphibians develop from eggs, to larva or tadpole, to fully grown adults. The three main groups of amphibians are frogs and toads, newts and salamanders, and the smallest group, called caecilians, which are worm-like creatures.

IT'S A FACT

• The flying frog has huge feet with webbed toes that it spreads like parachutes to glide.

• The female Suriname toad carries her eggs in pouches of skin on her back.

• The biggest frog or toad is the goliath frog of West Africa. It is almost as large as a soccer ball.

Frogs and toads

Many frogs and toads have skin that makes a horrible-tasting or poisonous fluid, so predators, such as snakes and spiders, usually avoid them. Many predators build up a resistance to the milder toxins, so, in turn, the frog's skin has evolved to produce a stronger poison. Toads are usually larger than frogs, have lumpier skin, and waddle instead of leaping.

◄ The colors of poison-dart frogs warn predators of their poisonous skin.

►► Read further > defense
pg117 [m33]

Salamanders

Giant salamanders are the largest of all the amphibians. Some species are exceptional in size: the Japanese giant salamander can grow to 4 ft; the Chinese giant salamander can grow up to 5 ft. Like newts, salamanders retain their tails into adulthood. Salamanders have a powerful bite and feed on shellfish, freshwater fish, worms and insects.

►► Read further > poisonous animals
pg113 [b22]

ANIMAL FACTS

• A type of salamander, the rare axolotl, lives in a few lakes in Mexico. It keeps its larval shape and gills all through its life. However, its reproductive organs develop, so it can breed even though it looks too young.

• Amphibians are cold-blooded and in cold regions they survive long winters in a state of inactivity known as torpor. The spring peeper frog of North America can be frozen solid for weeks, then thaw out without hurting it because it has a natural "anti-freeze" substance in its blood and other bodily fluids.

Check it out!

• http://www.yahooligans.com/content/animals/amphibians
• http://www.fonz.org/animals/af-amphibians.htm

▲ The hellbender of North America grows to 32 in long.

►► GILLS see pg135 (j22) ►►

1   2   3   4   5   6   7   8   9   10   11   12   13   14   15   16   17   18   19

a
b
c
d
e
f
g
h
i
j
k
l
m
n
o
p
q
r
s
t
u
v
w

● Newts

Newts are a type of salamander that tend to stay in water for long periods, even when air-breathing adults. Like salamanders, newts do not need to feed often as they do not use a lot of energy. However, like all amphibians, when newts do feed they flick out their long tongues to grab prey, such as worms, slugs, snails, grubs, flies, and other insects and small fish.

▸ *The Eastern newt is red, orange, or brown with black spots. It lives on land up to four years of its early life. It then returns to the water to develop into an adult.*

Read further › insects
pg119 (b24)

● Worm-like amphibians

Caecilians, also known as gymnophiones, live mostly in the damp tropics among soil and leafs on the forest floor or in pools and swamps. They have no legs, very small eyes, and resemble large earthworms, growing up to 24 in long. Like other amphibians they are predators and feed on soil creatures, including earthworms.

▲ *Caecilians burrow powerfully, pushing soil with their broad snouts.*

Read further › earthworms
pg125 (b22)

● Life cycle

The life cycle of the common frog begins when the female lays a clump of gelatinous covered eggs (spawn) in fresh water. The eggs are then fertilized by the male's sperm. The eggs hatch into larvae or tadpoles. Tadpoles have gills, a long tail but no legs, and eat water plants. Gradually they metamorphose into adults. Their legs grow, their tails shrink, and their lungs develop to breathe air.

Read further › eggs hatching
pg113 (b33)

Frog spawn (eggs) float on the surface of water

Adult toad

Froglet loses tail and grows into adult frog

Tadpoles hatch from eggs

Tadpoles grow legs and change into froglets

Adult newt

◂ *The common frog's life cycle is like those of toads and newts. Frogs lay eggs in a clump. Toads lay eggs in long strings or "necklaces." Newts lay eggs singly.*

▸▸ FROGS BREEDING see pg147 (l22) ▸▸

Fish

A TYPICAL FISH lives in water, has a long, slim body, large eyes, a finned tail that swishes from side to side for swimming, body fins to control its movements, a covering of scales, and feather-like gills on either side of its head that take in oxygen from the water. However, many fish lack one or more of these features. Eels are long and thin like snakes, usually scaleless, lungfish can breathe out of water, and many catfish have leathery skin or bony plates instead of scales.

● ANIMAL FACTS

• The biggest hunting fish is the great white shark or white pointer. The biggest grow to about 30 ft in length and weigh up to 3 tons.

• At 39 to 46 ft in length and weighing more than 10 tons, the whale shark is the biggest fish. But it is not a fierce hunter like the great white shark. It filters small plants and animals (plankton) from seawater, using comb-like rakers on the insides of its gills.

►► Read further › predators
pg110 (g14); pg112 (o2)

● IT'S A FACT

• The smallest fish, the dwarf goby, is as long as the word "fish" and lives in streams and pools on the Philippine Islands.

• One of the longest fish is the eel-shaped oarfish of open oceans that grows to more than 26 ft—one is caught about every ten years.

▼ The 20 ft tiger shark prefers warm-blooded victims such as monk seals. However, it will eat almost anything, from sea turtles to rotting, leftover food, thrown from ships.

● Ocean killers

There are about 330 species of sharks. As well as eating plankton, which includes plant matter, all sharks eat meat, either catching victims or scavenging from dead animals. Unlike most fish, a shark's skeleton is made of cartilage (gristle) not bone. A shark also has unusual scales called denticles that are tiny and tooth-shaped. Much larger denticles form the shark's teeth, which are always being worn away or broken off and replaced by new ones.

● Check it out!

• http://www.iwrc-online.
  org/kids/Facts/Fish/fish.htm
• http://www.kidzone.ws/sharks
• http://www.fishid.com/
  facts.htm

►► CATFISH see pg137 (c32) ►►

1   2   3   4   5   6   7   8   9   10   11   12   13   14   15   16   17   18   19

a b c d e f g h i j k l m n o p q r s t u v w

● Fish food

Different types of fish eat a huge variety of food. Piranhas have razor-sharp teeth and gather around a large animal in the water to tear off chunks of flesh. In fresh water, the pike lurks in weeds and then rushes out to grab a victim in its huge mouth. Carp sift through mud for worms and other creatures. On coral reefs, butterfly fish and parrot fish eat tiny plants and animals growing on the rocks.

▼ *Piranhas live in South American rivers and swamps. They feed on other fish, insects, even fruit, but as a ferocious predatory group they can attack and kill small mammals and even humans.*

►► **Read further > teeth**
pg106 (p2)

● "Dino"-fish

Coelacanths lived during the age of dinosaurs, about 250 million years ago, and were thought to be extinct. However, in the 1930s, a coelacanth was discovered in the Indian Ocean off southern Africa. Another type was found in the 1990s in the Celebes Sea off Southeast Asia. Fish like these may have developed their fins into legs to become the first amphibian, more than 350 million years ago.

▼ *Coelacanths have fleshy, muscular bases to their fins that they use to "walk" over rocks.*

◄ *The stonefish is the world's most poisonous fish. It produces a deadly venom from dorsal spines along its side.*

● Bottom of the sea

Below about 1,640 ft the sea is completely dark, so that colorful bodies are useless. Most deep-sea fish, such as the gulper eel, viperfish, and deep-sea anglerfish, are black. Some have tiny eyes and some have no eyes at all. Others have huge eyes to detect what little light there is.

►► **Read further > color**
pg121 (i32)

▼ *Deep-sea lantern-fish make their own light with rows of glowing spots.*

▶ *Deep-sea anglerfish have a blob of flesh that dangles in front of them. This attracts smaller fish that think it might be edible.*

● Defense

Some fish defend themselves with poisons, which they can jab into enemies using their stiff, sharp, fin spines. The lionfish, or dragonfish, of Southeast Asia has large, lacy-looking fins and bright colors to warn predators of its venom. In contrast, the stonefish is camouflaged as a piece of rock for protection.

►► **Read further > poison**
pg119 (b35); pg123 (e33)

▼ *The lionfish's organs are luminous (light reflects through).*

►► EXPLORING OCEAN DEPTHS see pg187 (b25) ►►

Insects 1

ARTHROPODS ARE invertebrate animals (lacking a backbone) with a hard outer body shell, and limbs with joints, rather than flexible tentacles. Insects are the biggest group of arthropods and the most numerous animals on Earth. More than one million species have been discovered. A typical adult insect has three body parts: head, thorax, and abdomen. The head has the antennae or feelers, large eyes, and mouthparts; the thorax bears the wings (usually four) and six legs; the abdomen contains digestive and reproductive parts. Insects live in every land and freshwater habitat, from frozen polar regions and icy mountaintops to scrub, deserts, rivers, and deep lakes. However, no insects dwell in the ocean.

ANIMAL FACTS

• Most insects have short lives of a few months, but some survive for many years. The periodic cicada is a type of bug. It dwells as a young form, or nymph, in the soil, eating roots and other bits of plants, for up to 17 years.

• Cicadas are also the noisiest insects, and for their size, they make the loudest sounds of any animals. Only the males "sing." They vibrate thin, flexible patches of body casing, like drum skins, on either side of the abdomen.

IT'S A FACT

• Some cave crickets and cockroaches have antennae (feelers) that are ten times as long as their bodies, since they cannot see in total darkness underground and so must feel their way.

• About three in every ten species of insect are beetles.

Fast and fierce

Dragonflies are among the biggest, fastest and most ferocious insects. They catch smaller insects, such as gnats, in mid-air, using their dangling legs like a scoop or basket, and then take the victim back to a favorite perch to eat. Each dragonfly has its own area or territory, which usually includes water, such as a pond or stream. It "buzzes" rival dragonflies who come too near, chasing them off their territory.

◂ Dragonflies have four wings and hunt using their huge eyes, which are larger than any other insect.

Read further › legs
pg111 (g22)

Thorax

Abdomen

Set of four wings enables dragonfly to fly fast

Head

Check it out!

• http://www.iwrc-online.org/kids/Facts/Insects/insects 2.htm
• http://www.yahooligans.com/science_and_nature/living_things/animals/invertebrates/arthropods/insects/

►► STICK INSECT REPRODUCTION see pg147 (b30) ►►

1   2   3   4   5   6   7   8   9   10   11   12   13   14   15   16   17   18   19

Insect cities

Termites are sometimes called "white ants" but they are a separate group of insects—isopterans—with 2,800 species that live mostly in the tropics. They build huge mounds of hardened mud, with a nest deep inside, that may hold more than five million termites. They feed mainly on bits of wood, plants, and decaying matter.

◀ A termite mound keeps its occupants cool, dark, damp, and protected.

▶▶ Read further › nests
pg110 (r11)

▼ *The female praying mantis eats the male immediately after they have mated.*

▲ *The female mosquito, about 0.8 in long, feeds on animal and human blood.*

▶▶ Read further › sucking
pg121 (b22)

Insect pests

Mosquitos, a type of fly, have needle-like mouthparts to pierce human skin and suck blood. This causes an itchy spot on the skin and sometimes spreads serious diseases such as malaria, which can be fatal. Fleas have huge rear legs for jumping, no wings and suck blood in the same way as mosquitos. Many flies, cockroaches, and similar insects feed in dirt and decay and spread germs carried on their bodies, legs, and mouthparts.

▼ *Great green bush crickets are also known as katydids. Most species mimic (take the appearance of) leafs or bark.*

Insect eyes

▶▶ Read further › senses
pg105 (h32)

Almost all of the 2,000 kinds of mantises (mantids) are fierce hunters. They grab prey with their front legs, which fold at the end like spiky scissors. An insect's eye is made of many separate parts, ommatidia, each detecting a tiny part of the scene. Mantids have huge eyes—each with more than 20,000 ommatidia. Mantids' wings are folded along their backs, ready to flash color at their enemies.

Great leapers

Most grasshoppers and locusts, and some crickets, eat plant food. They all have two small leathery wings, like flaps, and two very large wings for flying. They can also leap great distances using their long, powerful back legs. Males "sing" by rubbing their back legs on one of their wing veins (hard tubes that support the wings), which has a row of "teeth" like a tiny comb.

▶▶ Read further › teeth / fangs
pg123 (e33)

▶▶ HUMAN SKIN see pg154 (i11) ▶▶

a b c d e f g h i j k l m n o p q r s t u v w

Insects 2

NEARLY ALL insects hatch from eggs, laid by the female. Only a few insect mothers, such as the earwig, care for their eggs or young. With some insects, such as grasshoppers and dragonflies, the young—nymphs—resemble their parents, although they are smaller and without wings. Nymphs gradually develop into adults by molting (shedding their body shells) regularly. As their bodies go through little change, this type of development is incomplete metamorphosis. Other insects, such as butterflies, moths, beetles, bees, wasps, and ants, have greater changes in body shape and experience a complete metamorphosis.

Complete metamorphosis

A butterfly's eggs hatch into small, wiggly young, called larvae or caterpillars. The young eat huge amounts of food and shed their skins several times as they grow. They develop a hard body case and become inactive pupae, or chrysalises. After a time the pupa's casing splits and the adult insect emerges. Most caterpillars eat mostly leafs, while butterflies sip nectar from flowers.

Female butterfly lay tiny eggs, usually under leafs

Caterpillar hatch from eggs and eat leafs

Caterpillar becomes pupa

Adult butterfly emerges

Pupa's case splits open

▶▶ Read further > flowers
pg121 (i32)

ANIMAL FACTS

• Many species of beetles have larvae (grubs) called "worms," because they are long, legless and wriggly. They include mealworms and woodworms.

• Glow-worms are adult beetles that shine in the dark to attract a mate.

• Many sorts of insect live in water when young, such as the nymphs of dragonflies, damselflies, caddisflies, and mayflies.

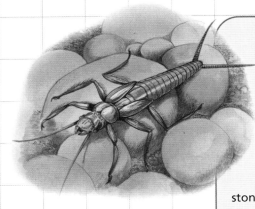

▲ Adult stonefly nymphs rarely fly. Instead they crawl among stream-bed rocks and pebbles.

Incomplete metamorphosis

Stonefly nymphs live in fast-flowing streams. They have wide, low bodies and strong legs with sharp claws to cling to smooth rocks in the rushing water. They grow for two or three years, then emerge and shed their skins to become adult stoneflies. Adult stoneflies look like small, short-bodied dragonflies. They fly, eat and live for only a week or two, so they can breed.

▶▶ ANIMAL REPRODUCTION see pg146 (d2) ▶▶

Hard wings

A beetle has four wings, but the front two, known as elytra, are strong and stiff. They normally lie over the beetle's back and cover and protect the larger, delicate flying wings that are folded beneath. Water beetles hunt tadpoles, worms, and young fish in ponds and streams. They must rise to the surface regularly to refresh their air supplies that are in the form of tiny air bubbles stored under their elytra.

▼ *Water beetles can fly away to another pond if the one they are in dries out.*

▶▶ **Read further › tadpoles**
pg115 (j22)

Pollination

Bees play a vital role in the reproduction of plants. As they visit colorful flowers to collect sweet nectar and tiny pollen grains for food, some pollen from the flower brushes on to the bee's feet and rubs off when it lands on the next flower. This process is called pollination and is how pollen grains are transferred from flower to flower so that flowers can develop seeds. Many other insects, such as flies and beetles, pollinate flowers in the same way.

▼ *A honeybee can make more than 500 visits to flowers in one day. The female honeybee carries pollen in a basket-shaped pouch on the hindlegs.*

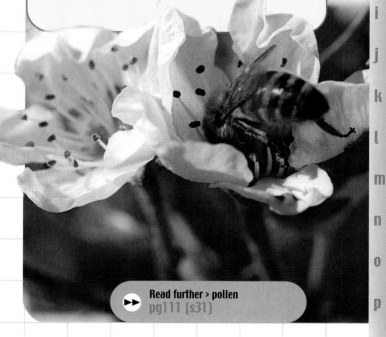

▶▶ **Read further › pollen**
pg111 (s31)

Bugs

More than 80,000 species of insects are known as bugs. Most bugs have four wings and long, thin mouthparts that are like needles to pierce victims and suck liquid food. Pondskaters skim over water to catch and drown their prey. Aphids (greenflies and blackflies), cicadas, and treehoppers suck plant sap; bedbugs feed on human blood; and shieldbugs have a shield-like body covering, which is often brightly colored.

▶▶ **Read further › blood sucking**
pg119 (b35)

▼ *The pondskater glides across water, ready to squeeze its prey, which are usually animals trapped at the surface in its front legs before sucking out the juices.*

🌐 **Check it out!**

- http://www.enchantedlearning.com/subjects/butterflies/toc.shtml
- http://www.uky.edu/Agriculture/Entomology/ythfacts/bugfun/trivia.htm

◀◀ POLLINATION see pg92 (k10) ◀◀

a b c d e f g h i j k l m n o p q r s t u v w

More than eight legs

ARTHROPODS include insects, millipedes (four legs on each body part or segment), centipedes (two legs per segment) and another huge group—the arachnids, which have two main body segments and eight legs. Arachnids include spiders and scorpions, which live on land, and their tiny cousins, mites and ticks, known as false-scorpions, which live in water.

IT'S A FACT

• There are more than 60,000 kinds of arachnids, living in land habitats and a few in freshwater ones, but not in the ocean.

• The centipede group, chilopoda, numbers some 3,000 species.

• There are more than 10,000 kinds of millipedes, diplopoda.

Centipedes and millipedes

"Centipede" means "100 feet" but most centipedes have up to 60 legs. They live mostly in tropical rainforests and are fast-moving night-time predators, using their fang-shaped, first pair of legs to jab and poison prey. The biggest species grow to 12 in long and their bite can cause extreme pain to humans. Some millipedes have only 24 feet, while others have more than 700—but none can run fast. They are protected by their hard body casings and by a horrible-tasting or poisonous fluid that oozes from holes along the body.

▶ Most millipedes feed at night on rotting leafs and old bits of plants.

Read further > biting
pg119 (b35)

▼ Ticks are about 0.4 in long but they grow larger when they have eaten. Mites usually grow even smaller than ticks.

Mites and ticks

Mites are tiny, eight-legged cousins of spiders. Most are smaller than this "o" and live in the soil. A handful of earth from a forest might contain more than 1,000 of them. Other types live as parasites on larger animals, sucking their blood or munching their skin, fur, or feathers. Ticks are also blood-sucking parasites that live on many animals, from sheep to cats, and even occasionally on people.

Read further > blood-sucking
pg119 (b35)

BIGGEST SPIDERS

Spider	Width
South American bird-eating spider	11 in
Central American running spider	10 in
African hercules spider	8 in
Cardinal spider	5.5 in

◄◄ TROPICAL RAINFORESTS see pg98 (o2) ◄◄

Silk-weaving

Spiders have eight legs, a pair of feeler-like palps on their head, and large stabbing mouthparts—chelicerae—that jab poison into prey. All spiders are hunters and spin silk from finger-like parts on their rear body called spinnerets—but not all make webs. Silk is also used to tie up prey, to line the tunnels of the trapdoor and other burrow-living spiders, as a lifeline from which to hang if falling, and by a female spider to protect her eggs.

▸ *If the orb-weaver spider has just eaten, it wraps prey up in silk threads to eat later.*

▶▶ **Read further › eggs**
pg113 (m22)

▶▶ **Read further › insects**
pg118 (d2)

Spiders

The largest spiders, such as tarantulas, goliaths, and bird-eating spiders, mostly from tropical regions. Each are big enough to cover this page. They bite with their huge fangs, overpowering prey the size of small mammals such as mice and baby birds. They are so strong that they do not need powerful poison. Smaller kinds of spiders, such as black widows, are much more poisonous, and their bite can be fatal to humans.

▶▶ **Read further › poison**
pg113 (b22)

▲ *The female tarantula guards her eggs, which are wrapped in a cocoon of silk.*

Scorpions

Like spiders, scorpions have four pairs of legs. They also have powerful biting and chewing mouthparts—chelicerae—and a pair of large, crab-like pinchers known as pedipalps. Many have a sharp poison sting on the tail, which they use mostly to defend themselves. Most scorpions live in hot places and hunt at night for grubs, insects, worms, and other small creatures.

◂ *Scorpions often use their pinchers to grab prey or fight rivals at mating time.*

Check it out!
- http://www.amonline.net.au/
  teachers_resources/background/
  minibeasts.htm#/arachnids
- http://rochedalss.qld.edu.au/
  spider/spider1.htm

▶▶ SPIDER SILK see pg131 (b33) ▶▶

From mollusks to worms

ANIMAL FACTS

• One of the longest but thinnest animals is the ribbon-worm or bootlace-worm (nemertean). This amazing animal lives on the ocean beach, feeds on tiny animals, and may grow to more than 98 in—longer than a blue whale!

• Roundworms (nematodes) are seldom seen, but they live almost everywhere, including water and inside plants and animals. There are more than 20,000 kinds of roundworms, and some grow 3 ft long inside great whales.

CREATURES WITH hard shells, like snails, oysters, mussels, and whelks belong to the huge animal group known as mollusks. However, some mollusks, including slugs and squid, have no outer shell at all. An odd group of animals are the echinoderms, which include starfish and sea urchins. They usually have a radial body shape, like a wheel with spokes, rather than two-sided with a left and right, like other animals. There are also thousands of other types of strange-looking animals like jellyfish and sponges.

▼ Tide pools support a huge variety of life, including crustaceans such as crabs and lobsters, mollusks such as snails and mussels, and sea anemones.

Sea anemones (cnidarian)

● Mollusks

Mollusks range from tiny slugs that are a fraction of an inch long, to giant squid, with a body and tentacles 66 ft long. Most have a hard shell outside or inside the body. Mollusks include many seashore "shellfish" such as clams, limpets, and cowries. Octopus and squid grab victims with their suckered tentacles and bite pieces off with their mouth at their center, which is shaped like a parrot's beak.

▲ Squid are fast swimmers, often reaching speeds of 31 mph.

Starfish (echinoder

● Echinoderms

All echinoderms live in the ocean. Their name means "spiny-skinned"; most sea urchins and a few starfish have sharp spines, sometimes poisonous. Other types of echinoderm include sea cucumbers, which are usually sausage-shaped and look through seabed mud for food particles. Sea lilies are also echinoderms.

▶▶ **Read further › hard shells**
pg113 (m22)

▶▶ **Read further › sharp spines**
pg104 (i15)

All kinds of worms

The most familiar worms, like earthworms, are called annelids. They have a long body made of many sections or segments. Other annelids include ragworms, fanworms, and tubeworms on the seashore and in the sea, and leaf-shaped leeches that suck blood from other animals.

►► **Read further › blood–sucking**
pg119 [b35]

IT'S A FACT

• There are more than 100,000 different species of mollusks.

• The echinoderm phylum numbers over 6,000 species.

• Annelids, such as earthworms, consist of 12,000 species.

Jellyfish

Jellyfish, sea anemones, and coral polyps are all members of the cnidarian group, containing almost 10,000 different species. Most live in the ocean and have a jelly-like body or stalk, and a ring of tentacles that sting their prey. Coral polyps build cup-shaped cases of hard minerals around themselves; most corals gradually build up over time to form the unusual shapes of coral reefs.

►► **Read further › stinging prey**
pg123 [o32]

Cockle (mollusk)

Razorshell (mollusk)

Shell of whelk mollusk used by hermit crab

Periwinkle (mollusk)

Mussel (mollusk)

Sea urchin (echinoderm)

Lobster (crustacean) see pg32 [t7]

Crab (crustacean) see pg33 [d35]

Sponges

Sponges

Sponges have no eyes or ears, nerves or brain, bones or muscles. But, they are still animals. Their bodies are made of many microscopic cells, and they take food into their bodies by "eating." A sponge sucks water into its bag-or flask-shaped body through the many small holes in its wall, absorbs tiny bits of food through the inner lining and squirts the water out through the larger hole at the top.

►► **Read further › squirting water**
pg107 [h32]

Check it out!

►► ANIMAL SENSES see pg136 (d2) ►►

a b c d e f g h i j k l m n o p q r s t u v w

Land movers

MOVEMENT DEFINES what an animal is. In general, animals can move from place to place but plants do not. Creatures travel around to find food and shelter, and to avoid predators. Different types of animals use different parts of their bodies for movement. Most land (terrestrial) animals, from tiny bugs and spiders to large reptiles and mammals, use their legs for moving. But monkeys (see pg145 [e36]) and sloths also swing by their arms, snails slide on their undersides, and snakes use their whole body. All movement takes muscles. Vertebrates (animals with a backbone) have muscles attached to their bones. When the muscles pull on their bones, animals can crawl, walk, fly, or swim.

● IT'S A FACT

• Reptiles were the first creatures to live entirely on land, over 350 million years ago.

• Bears are one of the few animals to walk on the soles of their feet.

• The African fringe-toed lizard has to dance across the hot sand of the desert to keep its feet cool.

● Speed saves

Fast movement is most important in open habitats such as grasslands, where antelopes, gazelles, and zebras need to escape from predators such as cheetahs, lions, and wild dogs. Long, slim legs can be used to attain great speed. The muscles that help these animals to run are mainly in the upper legs and body, leaving the lower legs and feet very light so they can move faster when running at great speed.

▲ The cheetah is the fastest land mammal, able to reach speeds of more than 62 mph, but it can only maintain this speed for less than a minute.

▶▶ **Read further › predators**
pg12 (d2); pg13 (e22)

🌐 Check it out!

• http://www.szgdocent.org/cats/a-chetah.htm
• http://www.saburchill.com/chapters/chap0005.html

◀◀ REPTILES see pg112 (d2) ◀◀

1   2   3   4   5   6   7   8   9   10   11   12   13   14   15   16   17   18   19

◀ *Sloths in South American rainforests are so well camouflaged that they do not have to race away fast to escape from predators.*

Moving through soil

Burrowing animals use various methods of movement. The mole uses its powerful front legs as shovels to clear dirt away as it moves forward. The worm is like a tube of muscle that contracts to make its body hard, like a water-filled balloon, as it pushes its way between soil grains. Mole rats have straight limbs with claws on its five thick toes for digging the soil.

▶▶ **Read further › teeth**
pg130 (n2)

▲ *Naked mole rats of East Africa have massive incisors (front teeth) with which to eat and dig. They are not really naked but have sparse hairs covering their pink bodies.*

Moving in trees

Sloths and gibbons travel through trees in different ways. A gibbon's arms are twice as long as its legs, with hook-shaped hands to hang from branches. Its swinging motion is called brachiation. The sloth hangs with four limbs, moving one at a time, and is the slowest moving animal at just 274 yd/h.

Muscle power

Muscles get shorter, or contract, pulling different body parts, allowing movement. Animals known as vertebrates—fish, amphibians, reptiles, birds, and mammals—the muscles are joined to bones which form an endoskeleton inside the body. In insects and spiders *(see pg131 [j35])* they are joined to the hard outer body casing—the exoskeleton.

▶▶ **Read further › inside the body**
pg134 (f2; s2)

Deltoid (shoulder muscle)

Gluteus (muscle for standing and running)

Temporalis (muscle for chewing)

Triceps (lifts upper front leg)

Rectus (lifts upper rear leg)

Gastrocnemius (tilts back the rear paw)

▶ *Most mammals have a similar body structure, with muscles and limbs that work and move in the same way. This view of the inside of a bear shows some of the main muscles used for movement.*

SPRINT SPEEDS

Fastest land animals	Speed
• Cheetah	62 mph
• Pronghorn antelope	56 mph
• Springbok	50 mph
• Ostrich	47 mph
• Racehorse	43 mph

▶▶ HUMAN MUSCLES see pg158 (d2) ▶▶

a b c d e f g h i j k l m n o p q r s t u v w

Soarers and swimmers

BOTH AIR and water are fluid—unlike solid ground they flow when you push them. So movement in air and water require more muscle power. More than four-fifths of the body weight of a fish is muscle, compared to two-fifths of a land mammal. Fliers and swimmers both use broad pushing surfaces—wings through air, and fins, flippers, and tails through water. These surfaces produce the propulsion (forward movement), while other body parts control steering and slowing down. In a bird, the main wing areas give propulsion, while the wingtips and tail provide control. In a fish, the tail is used for propulsion, and the side fins for control.

To scale
Each square = 20 ft across
Some of the largest whales in the world

Blue whale 98.5 ft

Fin whale 72 ft

Sperm whale 66 ft

Sei whale 52.5 ft

Wing shapes
Hummingbirds and nectar-sipping bats flap their short, broad wings quickly, almost 100 times per second, to push air straight down so they can hover. In contrast, a wandering albatross can soar for hours on its long, slim wings without flapping once. Its 12 ft wingspan glides on the wind from the sea and provides lift (upward force).

▶▶ Read further › nectar eaters
pg133 (f22)

▲ When a hummingbird hovers it tilts its head up and tail down to make its body vertical. Its wings flap in a curved figure eight, and the whole wing twists at the joint with the body at each end of the stroke. This produces a more upward force, or lift, than simply flapping the wings to and fro.

Check it out!

▶▶ PROPULSION see pg186 (k6) ▶▶

◀ *One of the fastest fish, the bluefin tuna, can reach speeds of 44 mph and migrate as far as 6,210 mi across oceans.*

Kicking to swim

Many animals live both on land and in water, so they use their legs and feet to run and swim. The hippopotamus swallows plenty of air so it can remain underwater for a long time. It can run along the riverbed. Otters, crocodiles *(see pg131 [u34])*, and frogs have toes that are joined with flaps of skin, called webbing, to make a broad surface area for kick-swimming.

Powerful rear legs kick off

Webbed rear feet kick to swim and front legs steer through water

Front legs cushion the landing

▲ *Many frogs move by leaping, which enables them to escape quickly from predators.*

Swift swimmers

Water is very dense, so streamlining—a smooth body shape—enables fish, dolphins, seals, and other sea creatures to move through it. Fast fish such as marlin, tuna, and wahoo, have long, slim, tapering bodies that thin into a point. Thrust (the force to move forward) comes from the tail, which is pulled from side to side by huge blocks of muscles along either side of its body.

▶▶ **Read further › dolphins**
pg149 (d22)

◀ *The "flying squirrel" of North America can glide for more than 164 ft, steering with its front legs, and slowing down or stopping by raising its tail.*

Gliders

Flying squirrels, possums, lemurs, fish, lizards, even frogs, do not really fly. The only animals that truly fly with power and control are bats *(see pg136 [h13])*, birds, and insects. The others are gliders, using their broad surfaces like parachutes to swoop down. The best mammal glider, the colugo or flying lemur, can swoop for more than 656 ft.

▶▶ **Read further › bats**
pg136 (j12)

CREATURE COMFORTS

• One of the most adaptable movers has no limbs at all. The golden tree snake can slither fast, swim well, burrow through loose soil, climb trees easily, and even launch itself from a branch and flatten its body so it can glide many feet.

• In habitats like coral reefs, speed is not as important. Fish, like angelfish, move their pectoral (front) fins back and forth like an oar, rather than by switching their tails.

Up and down

A dolphin's tail, called its flukes, looks like a fish's tail. A dolphin swims by arching its body up and down, not bending itself from side to side like a fish. The dolphins flukes are not its "legs"—they have no bones in them. However, its flippers, like a seal's flippers, are its "arms," with hand and finger bones inside the skin.

▶▶ **Read further › swimming**
pg129 (d2)

▶ *Dolphins have long streamlined bodies that are propelled through water by thrusts of their tails.*

▶▶ FLIGHT see pg188 (p2) ▶▶

a b c d e f g h i j k l m n o p q r s t u v w

22 23 24 25 26 27 28 29 30 31 32 33 34 35 36 37 38 39

Meat eaters

ANIMALS THAT eat mainly other animals are carnivores. Some are active predators that hunt down prey, while others use stealth or ambush methods. Meat eaters range from killer whales and sharks in the sea, big cats and wild dogs on land, and eagles and hawks in the air. Much smaller but equally deadly are shrews, bats, frogs, praying mantises, dragonflies, spiders, and even sea anemones. Food, such as flesh, blood, and eggs contain much more nourishment and energy than plant foods. So carnivores only have to spend one-tenth the time eating than herbivores do. Animals, such as monkeys, that eat both plants and meat, are called omnivores.

◄ Bears are the largest meat-eating land animals, feeding on meat, like fish and insects, as well as plants such as fruits, nuts, and leafs. The sharp-ridged shape of their molar teeth has evolved to become more rounded for grinding plants and vegetation.

▼ This lion's skull shows a carnivore's teeth.

Incisors scrape meat from the bone

Canines stab and pierce flesh

Carnassials slide against each other to slice flesh

Hunting tools

Many carnivores have bodily weapons to jab into their prey, wound it, and tear it apart to eat it. These include the strong, sharp, pointed teeth of sharks, alligators, and mammals such as leopards, the fang-like mouthparts in spiders, centipedes, and predatory insects, sharp, hooked beaks of birds of prey, and the toe claws of birds and mammal hunters.

◄ Leopards make large kills about every two days, taking the meat up into trees away from scavengers such as hyenas.

▶▶ **Read further › leopards**
pg143 (k30)

◄ *With a wingspan of up to 7.5 ft, the golden eagle swoops down to snatch its prey such as rabbits, grouse, and other birds, seizing it with its sharp claws.*

Hunting methods

Techniques for catching prey vary greatly. Eagles and owls swoop down on to their prey silently and unseen from above. Wolves and wild dogs chase prey over long distances. Cats creep near to their victims, then rush or pounce on them. Other predators barely move. The shallow-water anglerfish lies camouflaged on the seabed attracting unwary victims with a fleshy blob of "bait" on the end of its fin.

Read further › camouflage
pg142 (g12); pg143 (b22)

Tied in strong silk

Many spiders spin webs and wait for their prey to get caught in them. The spitting spider is more active. It stalks prey and then squirts a glue-like chemical from its fangs, which turns into sticky threads as it flies through the air and lands on the victim. The spider even shakes its head from side to side to make the threads zig-zag, gluing down the prey. Then the spider uses its fangs for their normal purpose, to jab poison into its catch.

▼ *Spitting spiders, can only squirt their "glue" up to one-third of an inch.*

Looks can deceive

Some animals that may not seem to be carnivores really are. A starfish preys on shellfish stuck to the rocks, and they can take a whole day to lever one open and digest it. Sea anemones and jellyfish may look harmless but they actually eat fish, shrimp, and more.

Read further › seabed
pg143 (b22)

Read further › crab spiders
pg142 (s11)

◄ *Sea anemones wait for victims on the seabed and coral reefs, before trapping prey with their sticky, stinging tentacles.*

Feasting

Some hunters kill one large victim which lasts them a long time. A zebra or wildebeest can provide a crocodile with enough energy to last several months before it needs another meal. Other predators catch only tiny prey, but many of them. In one day, a giant anteater consumes 20,000 ants and termites, and a blue whale can gulp in half a million krill, each the size of a child's toe.

Read further › hunting
pg137 (b22)

CREATURE COMFORTS

• Mammals and birds of prey are warm-blooded, so they need to eat more for the energy necessary to heat their bodies, unlike cold-blooded animals.

• For this reason, a big cat must eat about ten times more food a year than a crocodile of similar body size.

▼ *Crocodiles glide underwater unnoticed before surging out of the water to catch their prey.*

◄◄ SPIDERS see pg123 (e33) ◄◄

a b c d e f g h i j k l m n o p q r s t u v w

Plant eaters

MORE THAN three-quarters of all animals are herbivores—plant eaters. In any habitat, there are always more herbivores than carnivores because the carnivore must feed on the plant eater. Plant eaters range from elephants *(see pg146 [p14])* and hippos, to bugs, beetles, moths, and caterpillars. However, few animals can eat all kinds of plants. They have adapted to feed on certain parts. Some eat leafs and flowers, while others chew tough roots or hard-cased nuts.

▲ *Giraffes are "browsers," chewing on vegetation regularly throughout the day. They use their comb-like canine teeth to strip leafs from branches and have a long tongue to gather leafs and shoots from high up in the trees.*

● Living on leafs

Deer, most gazelles, giraffes, and the black rhino are browsers, eating leafs from trees and shrubs. Zebras, wild cattle, and the white rhino are grazers, consuming leafs or grasses from the ground. Most herbivore mammals have straight-edged front teeth for nibbling, and flat-topped cheek teeth, molars, and pre-molars, for thorough chewing.

▶▶ **Read further › teeth**
pg127 (b31)

● Tough to crack

Rodents such as rats, mice, beavers, and squirrels use their long, continuously-growing, front teeth (incisors) to crack the hardest seeds and nuts. Parrots *(see pg149 [b36])* and macaws do this using their beaks, while tortoises use their horn-rimmed, sharp-edged jaws.

▶ *Because of their varied diet, rats spread all around the world, adapting to different conditions. A rat can cover up to 1.8 mi in one night, foraging for food.*

● CREATURE COMFORTS

• The only place on Earth where there are no plant eaters is at the bottom of the sea where there is no light for plants to grow.

• Most deep-sea animals are detritivores, consuming the decaying and rotting remains of dead creatures.

◀◀ PLANT GROWTH see pg88 (d2) ◀◀

◀ *The yellow-bellied sapsucker of North and Central America feeds on sap from broadleafed trees such as poplar, birch, and maple.*

Juice suckers

Sweet, sticky sap from plants and the sugary nectar made by flowers are packed with nutrients. Many plant eaters live only on this sap. The yellow-bellied sapsucker bird drills tiny holes through the trunk of a tree with its long, sharp beak and extracts the sap from inside the tree. Bugs, such as aphids, have needle-like mouths to jab into a stem and suck out the juice.

Read further > nectar
pg128 (n14)

▼ *This horse's skull shows a herbivore's teeth.*

Incisors tear plants from the trees and ground

Row of large, broad-topped, crushing molars to grind plants and vegetation

Gap (diastema) where canines used to be before herbivores adapted to a plant-eating lifestyle

IT'S A FACT

• An elephant can consume up to 330 lb of food daily—the weight of two average-sized adults.

• However, half of this food passes out the other end undigested.

Check it out!

• http://www.saburchill.com/chapters/chap0015.html

• http://www.nhm.org/mammals/page010.html

Changing diet

Some plant eaters change their diet with the seasons. Pikas, which are small-eared relatives of rabbits, nibble buds and shoots in spring and grasses and herbs in summer. In the fall they store grass and leafs in piles near their burrow for the winter. Storing food to eat later in the year is called caching.

▼ *The North American pika chooses its food store for the winter depending on which plants decompose (rot) slowest. This makes sure that their food is not rotten before they can eat it all.*

Read further > winter
pg141 (n27)

"Invisible" plants

Plants are the basic food for all animal life. On land, plants are easily seen. However, in the open ocean, trillions of unseen microscopic plants, called algae, and minute animals, make up plankton, which also supports animal life. They are eaten by whales and by tiny animals, like copepods, which in turn become food for bigger sea creatures.

Read further > underwater food
pg137 (c32)

▶ *Microscopic diatoms and other algae provide food for tiny ocean plant eaters.*

◀◀ ALGAE see pg83 (k30) ◀◀

a b c d e f g h i j k l m n o p q r s t u v w

Digestion and respiration

EVERY ANIMAL needs a vital substance to stay alive—oxygen. It combines with food to make energy for the huge variety of life processes inside the body. Oxygen makes up one-fifth of the air, and is also dissolved in water. Different animals obtain oxygen in different ways, but the parts which do so are always known as the respiratory system. Another main body need is nourishment—nutrients for growth, energy, and day-to-day maintenance. In small and simple animals, nutrients can be taken in or absorbed through the body surface, especially in water where they are in dissolved form all around. Larger animals have a specialized digestive system to obtain food and break it down into tiny parts or molecules, which can then be absorbed into the body.

Brain
Bones and joints
Gullet
Windpipe
Lungs
Kidney
Craw
Gizzard
Liver
Ovary
Heart
Intestine
Cloaca

▲ The lungs of the respiratory system and the heart from the circulatory system take up a lot of the front part of the body in the pigeon's chest. The digestive, excretory, and reproductive systems fill the rear part of the body.

● The digestive system

The digestive tract is a passageway through the body from the mouth to the rear end. Different parts of it are designed for specific tasks. In a pigeon, the craw is like a storage bag for recently eaten food. The muscular gizzard grinds the food into a pulp and the intestine absorbs the various nutrients into the bloodstream. The kidneys are part of the excretory system that filter wastes from the blood to form a liquid—urine—that leaves the body through the cloaca to keep it clear of waste.

▶▶ Read further > urine scent pg139 (b22)

▶▶ DIGESTION IN HUMANS see pg164 (i13) ▶▶

Gills for water

Gills are like "inside out" lungs. They have the same branching, frilly structure, but outside their body, in contact with water. Dissolved oxygen seeps from the water into blood flowing through the gills. Most water-dwellers have some type of gills, including fish, crabs, and molluscs like octopuses and sea-slugs.

▶▶ **Read further › fish senses**
pg137 (c32)

▸ *Most fish have gills. This diagram shows part of a gill. Oxygen, from the water that flows over the gills, passes into the bloodstream of the amphibian.*

Low-oxygen water flows out through gill slit

Gill arch (stiff curve that holds out the gill filaments

Primary gill filament (lamella or "leaf")

Secondary gill filament (smaller lamella or "leaf")

Oxygen in water passes into the blood flowing through gill filaments, turning it red

High-oxygen water flows in through mouth to gill chamber

Not all the same

The axolotl, a type of salamander, keeps its tadpole gills even as an adult. The lungfish has gills but also pocket-like "pouches" with blood-rich linings that branch off the gut. If its pool dries out, a lungfish swallows air into these pouches, which absorb the oxygen.

◂ *The axolotl has visible gills. If the gills become damaged, they quickly grow new ones.*

No special system

Small creatures, like flatworms, have no special parts for respiration. Oxygen can pass through their thin skin. Their flattened shape means no part inside its body is more than half an inch away from the skin, so that oxygen can seep the necessary distance.

▲ *Many types of flatworm are parasitic—they live inside or attached to other creatures.*

Lungs for air

On land, vertebrates such as amphibians, reptiles, birds, and mammals breathe air into lungs. Air tubes inside the lungs branch out and became smaller, ending in millions of microscopic "bubbles," alveoli, which form a huge surface area and have a lot of blood in their linings. Oxygen from air breathed in seeps into the blood and is then spread around the body.

▶▶ **Read further › frogs**
pg129 (c28)

Air spaces inside the lung

◂ *Frogs actually breathe through their skin as well as their lungs.*

Oxygen going into the lungs

Windpipe

Lungs for breathing

Moist skin surface

CREATURE COMFORTS

• The bodies of mammals such as shrews work so fast to stay warm that they need more than 20 times more oxygen, for their body weight, than a large mammal such as a zebra.

• Warm-blooded animals need more oxygen than cold-blooded ones to "burn" food to keep warm. A bird needs 15 to 20 times more oxygen than a lizard of the same size.

▶▶ **RESPIRATION IN HUMANS** see pg160 (m2) ▶▶

Animal senses

OVERALL, OUR own senses of sight, hearing, smell, taste, and touch are good compared to many animals. But the senses of some animals are thousands of times better than ours, while other animals have senses that we do not have, such as being able to detect the natural magnetic force of the Earth. Each animal's senses are suited to its habitat and lifestyle, and especially the way it finds food and communicates. Night-time predators such as owls, cats, and bats have big eyes to gather as much light as possible in the darkness. Creatures of the deepest seabed, where there is no light, have tiny eyes or even none at all.

◄ *The bat moves its head from side to side as it flies. When it hears its high-pitched squeaks come back equally loud in both ears, it is directly facing the source of the echoes—its victim.*

Read further › bats
pg129 (m22)

Sight and sound

Owls are nocturnal—night-time—creatures so they need very acute hearing and large eyes to find their way in the dark. Bats have good sight, yet they cannot see in total darkness. They use their hearing in a system called echolocation to find their way, making high-pitched clicks and squeaks—pulses of ultrasound. When the noise hits an object, it bounces back as an echo and the bat is able to figure out where the object is— even that of a tiny midge no larger than this period.

▸ *The barn owl's ear openings are hidden under head feathers, but its hearing is very sensitive. One ear slightly higher than the other hears sounds coming up from the ground earlier than the other ear. These "offset ears" allow amazingly accurate judgement of the direction of a sound.*

◄◄ MAGNETIC EARTH see pg59 (c28) ◄◄

1   2   3   4   5   6   7   8   9   10   11   12   13   14   15   16   17   18   19

Smelling the air

Most animals have a better sense of smell than humans do. All animals that are hunted, from deer to mice, continually sniff the air for the scent of predators as well as for the smell of food. Smell works in water, too. Many fish have nostrils and can detect scents from many miles away.

▾ *The white-tailed deer is found between the regions of southern Canada and northern South America. It usually faces the wind when it rests and eats so it can detect any signs of danger.*

▶▶ **Read further › scent**
pg139 (j24)

▶▶ **Read further › camouflage**
pg142 (f2)

Taste sensors

In water, taste works on contact and also at a distance, like smell in the air. A catfish is a "living tongue" with taste buds over most of its body. It can also detect tiny electrical pulses passing through water. These come from the living bodies of other creatures nearby in the water, allowing the catfish to find prey that is hidden in the mud.

▲ *The catfish's front end bristles have sensors. It has tiny pits in the skin that detect electricity, smell detectors behind the nostrils, and has touch and taste sensors all over its head, especially on its barbels or whiskers.*

Good vibrations

Like taste, touch works at a distance in water. Moving animals send out ripples that are detected by a fish's lateral line sense. This is a stripe along each side containing tubes or pits with very tiny hairs, which rock back and forth as ripples and water currents pass by them.

Lateral line

▸ *The great barracuda has a strong lateral line sense and is a fast-moving predator, relying mainly on sight in clear tropical waters.*

▶▶ **Read further › movement in water**
pg129 (d22)

CREATURE COMFORTS

• Insects eyes are different from those of other animals. They are made of ommatidia, many tiny parts, like a mosaic, each one detecting just a tiny part of the picture. A dragonfly has the biggest insect eye, with more than 30,000 ommatidia.

• Most insects hear with flexible flaps of skin, "eardrums," which are actually found on the main body rather than on the head. Some grasshoppers have "eardrums" on their knees.

Check it out!

• http://www.earthlife.net/birds/
  vision.html
• http://www.greenscreen.org/
  newsletter/articlesjr/BigEars.html

a b c d e f g h i j k l m n o p q r s t u v w

Communication

COMMUNICATION MEANS passing on messages and information. People communicate by talking, making facial expressions, or using body language such as waving. Animals use sound, sight, and movement to communicate, as well as a range of methods including scent, taste, touch, and the emission of electrical signals. Some messages are understood only between their own kind, for example when a male frog croaks to attract a female of the same species at breeding time. Other messages can be understood by a wide variety of creatures—these are often about matters of life and death.

IT'S A FACT

• Lemurs have different calls that warn members of their troop whether danger is coming from above, along the ground, or hidden in the undergrowth.

• Wolves and wild dogs smell each other's rear ends so that if they find later droppings they will know if a pack member left them—or a stranger.

▼ *The cobra's extended hood reveals the pattern that is on the rear of the hood, but shows through their stretched skin and thin, see-through scales.*

▼ *While some meerkats gather food, others look out for predators, warning the group of danger by barking or shrieking loudly.*

Warning signals

One sight-and-sound communication is widely understood in the animal world. This is rearing or puffing up to look bigger while making a hissing sound. This makes an animal seem larger and more ferocious, to warn off an attacker. A toad puffs up and makes a hissing sound, a cobra rears up, spreads its hood and hisses, and a cat's fur stands on end.

▶▶ Read further > snakes and mimicry
pg143 (c30)

Slap and thump

Sudden danger needs a short, sharp message to warn others in the group, and sound is often used. A meerkat shrieks shrilly, and many birds make a loud "seep" or "tic." The first beaver to notice a predator nearby slaps its flat tail hard on the water's surface. A rabbit thumps the ground.

▶▶ Read further > defending territories
pg144 (f2)

Check it out!

• http://www.teachervision.com/lesson-plans/lesson-142.html
• http://www.enchantedlearning.com/subjects/rainforest/animals/Protection.shtml

▶▶ FACIAL EXPRESSIONS see pg159 (k33) ▶▶

1 2 3 4 5 6 7 8 9 10 11 12 13 14 15 16 17 18 19

Leaving a message

Scent has an advantage over sights or sounds—it lasts after the sender has gone. Rhinos, hyaenas, sheep, foxes, and many other animals spray strong-smelling urine or leave droppings to mark their territory. This shows the sex and age of the animal, and if it is ready for breeding.

◄ *The male white rhinoceros marks his home range by spraying urine, leaving a scent. In order for a female to select a male rhino for breeding, the center of his territory needs to be marked in this way to a distance of about one-third of a sq mi.*

►► **Read further › marking territory**
pg144 (f2; n32)

A series of messages

Animals often give several messages before they take severe action against attackers. A skunk's black and white stripes are easily recognized when it lifts its tail as a warning to other animals to stay away. If an enemy ignores this, the skunk jumps from side to side, turns around, raises its tail, and stands on its front paws before releasing a pungent spray from under its tail that will put off the enemy.

►► **Read further › sense of smell**
pg137 (b22)

▼ *The striped skunk, found across central North America, can eject its foul-smelling spray to a distance of up to 10 ft away.*

Where's the food?

Honeybees indicate the site of a rich food source, to each other such as nectar-laden flowers, by "dancing." The bee flies in figure eight and shakes its body. The angle of the "8" and the number of waggles tell the direction and distance of food from the hive.

►► **Read further › nectar**
pg128 (n14)

▶ *In the bees' honeycomb dance, the angle between the straight crossover part of the "8" and the vertical, tell other bees the angle between the Sun and the direction of the food source.*

CREATURE COMFORTS

• Yellow and black is one of the commonest color combinations used as a warning, telling predators "I taste horrible" or "I am dangerous." This pattern is used by various spiders, wasps, fish, butterflies, caterpillars, frogs, and snakes.

• After an animal has had an unpleasant encounter with a yellow-and-black creature, the animal will avoid similar colors, which helps to protect all species with these colors.

►► HUMAN COMMUNICATION see pg208 (d2) ►►

a b c d e f g h i j k l m n o p q r s t u v w

Hibernation and migration

IN THOSE regions of the world where the seasons are distinct, there are warm, bright summers when food is plentiful, followed by cold, dark winters when living conditions are very difficult. Small creatures, such as insects, can survive the long winter as hard-cased eggs, but mammals and birds cannot. They use two main methods or survival strategies: "stay or go." One is to stay in the region but go into a very deep sleep, known as hibernation, then wake up the next spring. The other is to migrate—travel away on a long journey—returning the following spring.

▲ *Migrating birds have tiny particles of iron-rich chemicals in their brains, which may detect the Earth's natural magnetic field.*

Flying visits

Birds are the main migrants. They can travel long distances quickly. Many types of geese and ducks live in Europe, Asia, and North America, during the winter. Then they fly north to the Arctic in the spring, The brief summer encourages an "explosion" of plants, insects and other foods. The birds nest and raise their young in the Arctic, then fly back again in the fall.

▶▶ Read further > flying
pg128 (f2)

Learning the way

Each spring, caribou, known as reindeer in Europe, trek northward to the treeless Arctic tundra, where mosses, grasses, and other plants grow in the long hours of summer sun. Youngsters learn details of the route each year, and use their experience as they grow older to guide the next generation.

▶▶ Read further > seasonal changes
pg133 (b32)

CREATURE COMFORTS

• Some animals such as lemmings and locusts migrate only occasionally. After several years of good conditions in their home region their numbers grow too high. They run out of food so go off looking for new places to live.

• Some animals actually migrate up and down mountains. Mountain sheep and cattle climb to high pastures in summer and descend to sheltered valleys in winter.

▼ *During migration, some caribou travel up to 40 mi each day. The total journey may be more than 480 mi and take between two and three weeks.*

◀◀ SEASONS see pg61 (m22) ◀◀

| 1 | 2 | 3 | 4 | 5 | 6 | 7 | 8 | 9 | 10 | 11 | 12 | 13 | 14 | 15 | 16 | 17 | 18 | 19 |

▶ *Some salmon are born in freshwater streams, stay for a year or two, then migrate out to sea. Years later, they migrate back to the same stream they were born in, to lay their own eggs and then die.*

● Finding the way

Animals such as whales and birds combine methods of navigating—using the position of the Sun, Moon, and stars, large landmarks such as mountains or cliffs, and even the Earth's magnetic field. In water, migrating salmon and other fish, turtles, and lobsters "smell" and "taste" amounts of natural chemicals that change in different rivers or parts of the ocean.

▶▶ **Read further › birds**
pg136 (j12)

● "Knowing" the way

Monarchs are the champion insect migrants. Each spring these butterflies leave a few over-wintering areas of southwest and North America and fly north, feeding and breeding as they go. Their offspring return in the fall. They do not live long enough to learn the route—instead it is built-in, or instinctive.

▶▶ **Read further › breeding**
pg146 (d2)

▲ *Monarch butterflies can fly up to 48 mi each day.*

▼ *Badgers live and hibernate in "setts" that have many different entrances and tunnels. In mild weather they may wake up from their hibernation and wander outside for a drink and to eat.*

● IT'S A FACT

• The farthest traveling migrant is the Arctic tern that flies from the Arctic to Antarctica and back each year—covering 22,000 mi.

• The birch mouse hibernates up to eight months a year, spending over two-thirds of its life asleep.

● Cold and slow

Only warm-blooded animals truly hibernate. (Winter inactivity of cold-blooded animals is called torpor.) Most are rodents and bats, but badgers and hedgehogs also hibernate. They feed hungrily in the fall to build up stores of fat, then fall into a deep winter sleep. Body temperature drops from about 105°F to as low as 29°F Breathing is very slow and the heart only beats once every few minutes.

▶▶ **Read further › storing food for winter**
pg133 (b32)

● **Check it out!**
• http://www.enchantedlearning.com/coloring/Hibernate.shtml
• http://www.nk.psu.edu/naturetrail/Winter/hibernation.htm

◀◀ MAGNETIC FIELDS see pg21 (b31) ◀◀

Camouflage and mimicry

▲ *Chameleons change color (camouflage) to communicate and control their body temperature (going darker makes them warmer).*

A RAINFOREST OR coral reef may seem empty of creatures—until a closer look reveals "leafs" that are really butterflies (*see pg141 [d37]*), or "seaweed" that is a fish. Blending with the background is called camouflage. It keeps animals hidden from predators—and also helps predators hide from their prey before a catch. Camouflage usually involves colors, patterns, and shapes, but can also include movements, sounds, and smells. Other animals have bright colors and patterns, that act as a warning that they are venomous or have poisonous flesh. When one animal copies another, but is itself harmless, it is called mimicry.

● Master of disguise

The chameleon—a type of lizard—can change its color and pattern in minutes to blend in with its background. It uses tiny colored particles, called pigments, in its skin that can clump together so they are not seen, or spread out to show off their hue. For example, when the chameleon moves from a leafy branch to dry twigs, it changes from green to brown.

▶▶ **Read further › stick insect** pg147 [b30]

IT'S A FACT

• Batesian mimicry is when several harmful, poisonous, or horrible-tasting animals all resemble each other.

• Mullerian mimicry is when a harmless animal avoids being eaten by copying a harmful one.

● Keeping still

▶▶ **Read further › spitting spiders** pg13 [b33]

Movement is an important part of camouflage. A crab spider or flower mantis must keep perfectly still, hidden among the same colored petals. The slightest movement would reveal it not only to its prey—it may become prey for a watching lizard or bird.

◀ *Crab spiders are called this because they can walk sideways (like crabs). Some can even change color to match different flowers.*

Flat as a "carpet"

The carpet shark—or wobbegong—spends most of its time simply lying on the seabed. Its body is flattened and it has lumps and frills in shades of yellow, green, and brown, which resemble the seaweed-covered rocks. As an unsuspecting fish swims up to it, the carpet shark lurches forward and opens its huge mouth to swallow the victim in one gulp.

▼ *Wobbegongs remain close to the shore in shallow water, sometimes partly lying in the open air when the tide falls.*

Read further › anglerfish
pg131 (e22)

Model and mimic

The animal that a mimic copies is called the model. The venomous coral snake is a model for mimics such as the non-venomous king snake or the milksnake. Bigger predators that try to eat a coral snake get bitten, suffer pain, and learn to avoid it and any animal that looks like it. This is how mimics gain protection from predators.

Read further › cobra
pg138 (i12)

▲ *Milksnakes are mostly nocturnal snakes that feed on amphibians and small rodents. The order of the colors in their pattern differs slightly from their model, the coral snake, but is close enough to trick any potential predators.*

Spots and stripes

In the forest, light shines through leafs and creates many patches of brightness and shade thus creating patchy camouflage. Most forest cats, from margays to leopards *(see pg130 [r10])* have spotted coats, as do young deer and baby wild boar, which lie silent and still in the undergrowth while their mothers feed. Animals that live in cold regions are pure or patchy white to blend in with the shade and light of the snow and ice.

Read further › leopard
pg130 (n2)

◄ *The Arctic rabbit of Canada and Greenland has a thick, almost pure white coat to keep warm and blend in with the snow. But its coat may molt to a thinner, gray-brown coat for the summer.*

◄ *Snow leopards have thicker, lighter, coats than other leopards, to blend in with the icy mountain habitat.*

CREATURE COMFORTS

• Many fish are darker on their upper side and lighter on their underside for camouflage in sunlit waters where light comes from above. This is called countershading.

• The mimic octopus can change its colors and move its tentacles to pretend to be a ray, an anglerfish or even a shark, warding off predators.

 Check it out!

• http://www.howstuffworks.com/animal-camouflage.htm
• http://members.aol.com/Art1234567/Camo.html

a b c d e f g h i j k l m n o p q r s t u v w

Courtship and territories

COURTSHIP IS an essential part of male and female animals getting together to mate (breed). Courtship can involve sight, sound, smell, movement, or all of these. Courting partners check that they are both of the same species, fully-grown, able to breed, and are strong and healthy. This gives their offspring the greatest chance of being strong, fit, and healthy. In some animals, breeding also depends on owning a territory. This is an area that the animal occupies and defends against others. Usually it is the male partner that performs the main courtship display and holds the territory.

Breeding requirements

Male antelopes, such as topi, gather in a traditional area and snort, prance, and clash to see who is the biggest and strongest. The winners take charge of small territories, called "leks," at the center of an area, where they are more attractive to females. A lek-less male cannot breed. Birds, such as grouse, also use the lek system.

▲ *A grouse struts around with his head pointed up, whilst fanning his feathers and making bubbling and scraping sounds to attract a female.*

Partners for life

Many animals mate with different partners each year, either one or several. However, some larger birds, such as swans, are monogamous—they mate for life. This means they only have one partner throughout their lifetime. A female swan lays up to eight eggs, which she cares for until they hatch, then both parents look after them.

▶▶ **Read further > breeding**
pg146 (d2)

▼ *Each spring pairs of swans renew their relationship by twining their necks together and calling to each other.*

▼ *Frigatebirds live on the uninhabited islands of the Tropical Pacific, Atlantic, and Indian Oceans. They can form colonies of thousands of pairs at breeding time.*

Putting on a show

Many male birds, such as frigatebirds, put on amazing courtship displays as they puff out their bright red throat pouch to attract a mate. Peacocks fan their feathers, sing loudly and flap or jump. Birds have good color vision, so brightly colored plumage (feathers) is important during courtship rituals. The male robin becomes brighter during breeding time to attract a female.

▶▶ Read further > vision
pg136 (j12)

▶ *The call of the red howler monkey of South America can carry more than 3 mi.*

Morning chorus

Each dawn the forest fills with loud howls, squawks, and songs. Mammals and birds are announcing to others nearby that they are well and healthy and occupying their territories. If a howler monkey does not howl one morning, rivals know the territory is vacant and soon try to take it over.

▶▶ Read further > signs
pg138 (i12)

▲ *A peacock is chosen by a female (peahen) according to how magnificent his brightly-colored tail feathers are and how proudly he displays them.*

CREATURE COMFORTS

• A home range is where an animal roams and feeds. It marks areas with scent, but unlike territory, it is not defended by chasing others out.

• A male Bengal tiger's home range is often more than 39 sq mi; a female's is up to 10 sq mi.

▼ *Rutting between male mammals such as wild goats determines who gets to mate; the loser will have to wait for the chance to compete with another male.*

Fight to the death?

Male mammals such as sheep, goats, cattle, and deer *(see pg137 [i26])* show their strength and fitness by rutting—battling with rivals. The contests look fierce, but there is usually a set of natural "rules" to avoid serious injury.

▶▶ Read further > antelope and deer
pg137 (b22)

🌐 Check it out!

• http://ladywildlife.com/animal/birdcourtship.html

a b c d e f g h i j k l m n o p q r s t u v w

Breeding

BREEDING OR reproduction—making more of the same kind—is essential to all living things. Animals use many different methods. Some small, simple creatures, such as tiny tree-shaped hydras in ponds, simply grow offspring as "stalks" on their own bodies. This is asexual (one-parent) reproduction. But most animals reproduce sexually, when a male and female mate. The male's sperm joins with—fertilizes—the female's eggs. The majority of creatures, from worms to birds, lay eggs. Only mammals and a few reptiles, fish and invertebrates, give birth to babies.

Wrong offspring

Read further › mating pg144 (f2)

The cuckoo is a "reproductive parasite." The female cuckoo replaces an egg in another bird's nest with her own egg, then flies away. The host bird looks after the new egg and chick, which then pushes out the other chicks after it hatches.

▲ *These flycatchers are the host parents of this cuckoo chick, which may eventually grow bigger than them.*

▸ *A baby elephant will stay with its mother for up to two years.*

Parental care

Larger mammals, such as elephants and apes, usually produce just one offspring and care for it over several years. In a herd of elephants, other female elephants (cows) help bring up the young and the "family" members remain close throughout their lives. But smaller mammals, such as rats, may have ten or more babies that grow quickly and become independent within a couple of weeks.

Read further › rhino pg139 (b22)

▶▶ HUMAN REPRODUCTION see pg174 (d2) ▶▶

1 2 3 4 5 6 7 8 9 10 11 12 13 14 15 16 17 18 19

Fatherly duties

Most mammals develop inside their mother, growing as a fetus before being born, and continue growing physically independent of the mother. However, seahorses, though they begin life in their mother, actually develop from eggs inside their father. The female seahorse lays her eggs in a pocket-like pouch on the male's front. The eggs hatch two to six weeks later into young seahorses. Then the father seems to "give birth" as the small babies pop out of his pouch.

▸ The seahorse anchors itself to eel grass using its tail, which is specially adapted for grasping.

Read further › sea creatures pg131 (j22)

No male needed

Some aphids (greenfly), flatworms, leeches, and other smaller animals reproduce by parthenogenesis—the female can produce eggs or babies without having mated with a male. Usually the stick insect lays eggs by parthenogenesis which means the offspring will grow into females. But if the mother has mated with a male, the eggs will hatch into both females and males. Parthenogenesis also occur in some fish, stick insects, and in types of whiptail and wall lizards.

▲ Stick insects often have leaf-like bodies as a camouflage (they adopt the color of their background) to avoid danger.

Read further › camouflage pg142 (f12)

Outside the body

On land, a female and male animal usually mate when the sperm passes into the female's body to fertilize the eggs—internal fertilization. However, in water, many kinds of frogs, fish, shellfish, worms, and other animals simply release their eggs and sperm into the water, and leave fertilization to chance—external fertilization.

▾ The chance of fertilization among frogs is increased by the male releasing his sperm straight onto the jelly-covered eggs that the female lays in the water.

To scale

Each square = 1.5 in across
Different sizes of birds' eggs

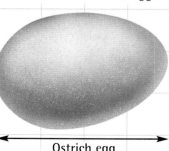

Ostrich egg
6.5 in long

Hummingbird egg
one-third of an inch long

LONGEST GESTATION

Animal	Length of gestation
• Elephant	600–660 days
• Whale	520 days
• Rhinoceros	490 days
• Walrus	480 days
• Giraffe	460 days

Check it out!
- http://www.saburchill.com/ chapters/chap0031.html
- http://www.bornfree.org.uk/ elefriends/elefacts.htm

◂◂ FROG LIFE CYCLE see pg115 (j22) ◂◂

a b c d e f g h i j k l m n o p q r s t u v w

22 23 24 25 26 27 28 29 30 31 32 33 34 35 36 37 38 39

Animals in danger

I N THE next few hours, somewhere in the world, a species of animal will become extinct—completely disappear and be gone for ever. This will probably be because of human activity, such as cutting down more rainforest for farmland or polluting the water the with chemical pesticides. The species may be a rare kind of bird or mammal, but it is more likely to be a small insect such as a bug or beetle. It is likely that the species is not even known to science, because only about 1.8 million animal species have been described and named by scientists. The real number of species living in the world today could be more than 20 million.

CREATURE COMFORTS

• Nearly half of the world's tropical rainforests have been destroyed over the last 50 years for farmland or building.

• In some regions, powdered rhino horn or crushed tiger bones are worth more than gold for the medicinal qualities they are believed to possess.

IT'S A FACT

• It is estimated that one-quarter of all bird species are under some type of threat to their survival, mainly from habitat disturbance.

• Today's "hot spots" of risk include the rainforests of Central and South America, West Africa and Southeast Asia, and the coral reefs across the tropics.

Precious but passing away

The biggest threat to animals is the destruction of their habitat. For example, this occurs when a forest is cut down for timber and new trees are not planted, or when houses, factories, and roads are built through the countryside. When an animal like the golden lion tamarin's natural habitat disappears, it has nowhere to breed or find food, so it may decline in numbers until it eventually dies out completely.

▸ *Golden lion tamarins are victims of habitat destruction in the coastal rainforests of Brazil. However, many have been bred in captivity, then released back into the wild.*

▶▶ **Read further > breeding**
pg146 (d2)

Check it out!

• http://worldkids.net/eac/facts.html

• http://www.5tigers.org/Directory/kids.htm

◀◀ FOREST DESTRUCTION see pg99 (o29) ◀◀

| 1 | 2 | 3 | 4 | 5 | 6 | 7 | 8 | 9 | 10 | 11 | 12 | 13 | 14 | 15 | 16 | 17 | 18 | 19 |

▸ *The pet trade is responsible for capturing many thousands of parrots each year. Some species of parrot have already become extinct due to capture and habitat destruction.*

Varied threats

The rare river dolphins of the Amazon, Ganges and other great waterways, face many problems. Their survival is threatened by water pollution from chemicals that are pumped into the river from factories and dams that block their path. They must compete with fishermen for food supplies and avoid boats with slashing propellers that may harm them and noisy engines that disrupt their sound-sonar communication system. Outbreaks of disease and being hunted for meat are also great threats to their survival.

▸▸ **Read further › dolphins**
pg129 (s22)

▲ *The number of Ganges river dolphin are now fewer than 1,000.*

Rare meat

As people in poor countries struggle to feed themselves, some turn to hunting wild animals for meat or to sell as pets at large markets in towns. This fast-growing trade affects apes monkeys, wild pigs, antelopes, bats, tropical birds such as parrots, lizards, and snakes, especially in poor countries such as those in some parts of Africa.

▸▸ **Read further › snakes**
pg143 (c30)

Hunting and collecting

▸▸ **Read further › pollution**
pg149 (k34)

Tigers are often killed for their luxurious fur, their teeth, which are used in unconventional medicines, and by people who enjoy the "thrill" of hunting dangerous animals. Great white sharks are caught so often, both for "sport" and because they may menace swimmers, that they have become a threatened species.

▾ *The biggest type of tiger, the Siberian tiger, is very rare, with fewer than 200 surviving in the wild.*

Pollution

Power stations and vehicles send fumes up into the air, factory pipes pour poisons into the rivers, lakes, and oceans, and pesticide and herbicide chemicals are washed down from farms. These damaging chemicals, along with disasters such as oil spills, pollute vast areas of the ocean and coastline and can kill fish and clog up birds' wings leaving them unable to fly.

◂ *Oil spills devastate coastal wildlife, killing fish and sea creatures that cannot breathe the contaminated water and so suffocate.*

▸▸ **Read further › damage**
pg149 (d22)

▸▸ OIL REFINERIES see pg205 (r26) ▸▸

a b c d e f g h i j k l m n o p q r s t u v w

22   23   24   25   26   27   28   29   30   31   32   33   34   35   36   37   38   39

Body basics

W E KNOW more about the human body than anything else in the universe. Yet every day we find more detailed information about how the body moves, digests food, gets rid of waste, controls its internal conditions, fights germs and disease, and stays fit and healthy.

We have made amazing discoveries about how the eyes see, how the ears hear, and how the brain thinks and learns. There are exciting new facts about the body's genetic information, made of DNA, which contains all the instructions for how the body grows, develops, carries out its life processes, and survives in today's hazardous world.

Senses (see pg168 [k10]; pg169 [e28]; pg170 [l12])

Skin (see pg154 [t12])

Lungs (see pg160 [n13])

Digestive system (see pg166 [p15])

Heart (see pg163 [k25])

Joints (see pg157 [j35])

Bones (see pg156 [q15])

⬤ ORGANS	
Organ	Weight
• Skin	4,000 g
• Liver	1,600 g
• Brain	1,600 g (males)
• Lungs	1,100 g
• Heart	300 g

⬤ Organs

The body is made of hundreds of different parts, including organs, muscles, and bones. Organs are packed closely together—and they work together, too. They include lungs, liver (see pg165 [d35]), kidneys (see pg166 [e14]), stomach (see pg164 [r11]), eyes, ears, heart, blood (see pg163 [h32]), nerves (see pg173 [g30]), and brain, all wrapped up in the largest organ, the skin. Each of these organs is made from millions of cells.

▶▶ **Read further › cells**
pg152 (g14)

Different outside, same inside

Human bodies have different sizes and shapes—women and men, girls and boys, old and young, wide and slim, dark and light, tall and short—with different clothes and hair styles. But inside, these bodies are almost identical. They all have the same inner parts, or organs, the same muscles and bones, and they work the same way.

Read further › DNA / organs
pg152 (b30); pg150 (j14)

Looking inside the living body

We can see inside living bodies in incredible detail, using various kinds of medical scanners. CT (computed tomography) and MRI (magnetic resonance imaging) scanners show details of the body tissues. PET (positron emission tomography) reveals how much energy is being used, especially in different parts of the brain, and can identify changes in cells that may cause disease.

Read further › ultrasound
pg175 (b34)

‣ MRI scans help diagnose diseases of the brain and nervous system. A computer builds a three-dimensional image using information from the scan.

IT'S A FACT

• Human beings are the most common large, living, creatures on Earth.

• There are more than six billion humans in the world—far more than any other kind of likesized animal, such as lions, dolphins, or even sheep.

• The world's oldest person is a Japanese woman aged about 115.

Social humans

Humans are social beings. Sometimes we want to be alone for a short time. But we usually like to be with other people, especially family and friends, as we can talk, laugh, and have fun together. In the fast-paced modern world, we rush from place to place with less time to spare and the greatest fear some have is being alone.

 Check it out!
• http://www.howstuffworks.com/mri.htm
• http://www.surfnetkids.com/human/.htm
• http://www.kidinfo.com/Health/Human_Body.html

Read further › smiling
pg159 (k33)

▶▶ SCANNERS see pg211 (p22) ▶▶

The micro body

T HE HUMAN body is made up of more than 50 million
million microscopic cells. A typical cell is so small
that about 1000 of them would fit on this period mark.
There are at least 200 kinds of cells in the body, different
sizes and shapes, different functions such as making
products, moving substances around, delivering raw
materials, collecting wastes, or fighting germs. Most cells
do not live long. They wear out and die naturally
at the rate of 50 million every second. However,
specialized types of cells, called stem cells, are always
dividing to produce new cells that replace the old ones.

● Cells and organelles

The cell's outside layer is called the
plasma membrane. Inside, many tiny
organelles (cells with specialized
functions) float in gelatinous
cytoplasm. Sausage-shaped
mitochondria break down glucose
sugar to release its stored chemical
energy, which powers the cell's
processes. Ball-shaped ribosomes are
like tiny factories making new
substances, especially proteins, which
are the cell's main structural parts or
"building bricks."

►► Read further > cells / glucose / nourishment
pg153 (g22); pg167 (j26); pg173 (b34)

◄ *Inside view of a cell showing
parts called organelles—cells
with specialized functions.*

Plasma membrane

Ribosomes

Endoplasmic
reticulum

Lysosomes

Cytoplasm

Nucleus

Mitochondria

Golgi membranes

Muscle layer

Elastic layer

Tough, outer cover

Inner lining

Plasma

Red cell

White cell

Platelets

Types of cells

Each kind of cell is shaped to carry out a particular function. In blood, red cells are round and thin, to absorb as much oxygen as possible through their surface. Some white blood cells *(see pg163 [h34])* can alter their shape to engulf germs. The cells of the blood vessel lining are flattened and joined to make a smooth layer. Many cells of the same kind grouped together are called a body tissue.

▼ *Red blood cells (seen under a microscope) are disc-shaped. Each red blood cell contains almost 250 million hemoglobin molecules, which transport oxygen around the body.*

▶▶ **Read further > muscle / nerve cells** pg159 (b22); pg173 (b34)

Body instructions

The instructions that tell the body how to develop its different parts and make them all work together are called the human genome. They are inside each cell in the body, in the form of the chemical DNA (de-oxyribonucleic acid). The whole genome contains 46 lengths of DNA. Until it unravels to reveal its double spiral shape, each is coiled tightly to form a thicker structure—the chromosome. There are 46 chromosomes inside the nucleus of each cell.

DNA coiled into the chromosome

Single chromosome

DNA unravelling

▶▶ **Read further > egg and sperm** pg175 (k22)

DNA's double helix shape, like a twisted rope ladder

Strands of DNA dividing to make new copies

Strands are linked by chemical subunits called bases

New strands are built upon the original ones

New strands are identical to the original ones

Each of these bases pairs up with only one other base

Check it out!

• http://www.bioanim.com
• http://www.biology.eku.edu/ RITCHISO/301notes1.htm

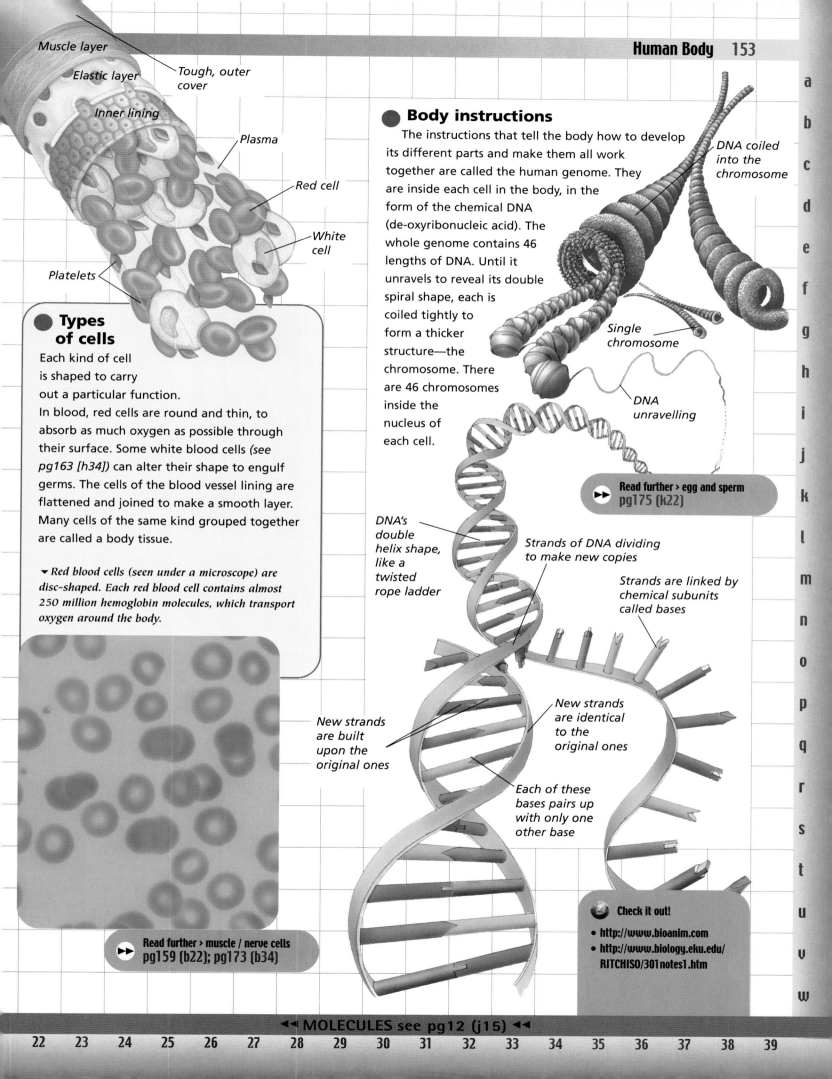

Wrapped in skin

SKIN IS often said to "glow with health." In fact, its surface is dead. The surface of the skin is made of hard, toughened, flattened cells that have filled with the body's protein, keratin, then died. They rub away and flake off in their thousands every minute as we move around, wear clothes, wash, and dry with towels. Just under the skin's surface, more cells are always multiplying, growing, filling with keratin, and dying. They gradually move up to the surface of the skin to replace the old, worn-off, skin. The cycle of skin replacement takes about four weeks.

● BODY TALK

• Human skin is very tough. It can repair many minor cuts and replace itself in grazes. But certain types of damage are more serious. In particular, too much strong sunshine is bad for the skin.

• The sun's invisible rays, called UV-B (ultra-violet B), can harm the fast-dividing epidermal cells just under the skin's surface. This may cause a serious form of cancer called malignant melanoma. Clothing, a hat, and sunscreen cream, or lotion helps to shade and protect skin from powerful sunlight.

● Under the surface

The upper layer of skin is called the epidermis. At its base are fast-multiplying cells that replace the old, keratin-hardened cells that rub off the surface. Under the epidermis is the thicker dermis. It contains strong, stretchy fibers of another body protein—collagen. The dermis also contains microscopic blood vessels (see pg163 pu32]), the growing bases, or roots of hairs, sweat glands, and nerves end in micro-sensors to detect touch.

▶▶ **Read further › nerve signals**
pg173 (b34)

▼ Greatly enlarged view of skin showing its two main layers—epidermis and dermis.

Keratin layer of epidermis

Epidermis

Hair

Basal layer of epidermis where new cells grow

Hair erector muscle

Gland making oily sebum to keep hair and skin waterproof

Dermis

Hair root in follicle (pit)

Sweat gland

Nerve endings

▸ *Microscopic view of a hair growing from its follicle.*

● Hairs

Hairs, like skin, are dead. The only living part of a hair is at its base, where it grows in a tiny pit called a follicle (see pg154 [u10]). The upper part, or shaft, is made of old, dead, stuck-together hair cells. A hair on the head grows at a rate of about 0.2 in every week. Body hairs grow slower; eyelash hairs grow much faster.

▸▸ Read further › microscopic ear hairs
pg169 (b22)

● Cool skin

Skin protects the softer, inner parts of the body from knocks and harm. It keeps in moist body fluids and keeps out dirt, germs, and harmful substances such as strong chemicals. If the body is too hot, for example when exercising (see pg167 [j24]), tiny sweat glands in the skin release watery sweat which oozes onto the surface of the skin. As sweat dries, it draws heat from the body cooling it.

▸ *Sweating helps keeps the body at the right temperature.*

▸▸ Read further › sweat
pg167 (m34)

● Nails

A nail is hard, tough, and dead, made mainly of keratin. The only living part is its root, buried in the skin, which makes new nail tissue as the whole nail grows toward the fingertip or toetip. On average, fingernails lengthen about 0.1 in every month. Toenails grow a bit slower. Both grow faster in the summer. Nails form a stiff backing for the flexible fingertips and toetips, so we can feel, touch, sense pressure, and grip.

▾ *Nails make fingertips strong enough to pluck guitar strings.*

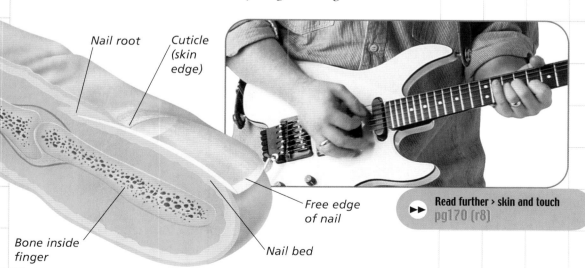

Nail root

Cuticle (skin edge)

Bone inside finger

Free edge of nail

Nail bed

▸▸ Read further › skin and touch
pg170 (r8)

Joint effort

MORE THAN 200 bones form the body's internal supporting framework, called the skeleton. Bones are strong and stiff, giving the body its shape, protecting internal organs and holding together the soft parts such as blood vessels (see pg163 [u30]), nerves, and guts. A single bone is rigid and tough, and can hardly bend. But, the whole skeleton can move because its bones are linked at flexible joints, designed to reduce rubbing and wear. Bones are very strong, yet they are also very lightweight. They are made of active living tissue, so if they break because of too much pressure on them, they can usually repair themselves.

IT'S A FACT

• There are 206 bones in the average skeleton.

• The longest bone in the body is the thighbone, or femur, about one-quarter of the body's height.

• The smallest bone is the stirrup bone in the ear—it is only slightly bigger than this U.

Skull

Collarbone (Clavicle)

Breastbone (Sternum)

Upper arm bone (Humerus)

Rib

Backbone (Vertebrae)

Forearm (Ulna)

Radius

Sacrum

Hip bone (Pelvis)

Thighbone (Femur)

Hand bones (Metacarpals)

Wrist bones (Carpals)

Cranium

Cheekbone (Zygoma)

Orbit

Lower jaw (Mandible)

Kneecap (Patella)

Shinbone (Tibia)

Fibula

Ankle bones (Tarsals)

Foot bones (Metatarsals)

Protection

Some bones protect very delicate body parts. For example, the skull protects the brain and main sensory organs. All but one of the 22 bones in the skull— the mandible—are locked together to make the skull incredibly strong. Two deep bowl-like sockets, called orbits, in the face, protect much of the eyeballs (see pg168 [l9]). The backbone, ribs, and breastbone form a strong cage around the heart (see pg163 [k26]) and lungs (see pg160 [o11]).

▶▶ **Read further › lungs / heart** pg160 (m2); pg163 (b22)

Three layers

Most bones are not solid bone throughout. They have three layers. Outside is a "shell" of hard or compact bone, which is very strong and stiff. Inside this is a layer of spongy, or cancellous bone, with tiny holes so they are lighter. In the middle is the marrow, a soft jam-like substance that makes new red and white blood cells The entire bone is covered by a tough, skin-like layer, the periosteum.

Compact bone
Marrow
Spongy bone
Blood vessel
Osteon (rod-like subunit bone)
Periosteum

▶ Bones grow and harden from birth until about the age of 20.

Read further › bone marrow
pg157 (q34)

▶ The different parts of the knee joint work together to allow freedom of movement.

Joints

Where bones meet in a joint, they are covered with a shiny, slightly softer, substance known as cartilage. Cartilage is moistened by a slippery fluid (synovial fluid) that allows the joints to move smoothly. Ligaments are strips of strong tissue that hold bones together at the joints. Tendons are tough, connective tissue that link bones to muscles (see pg158 [l6]).

Muscle
Kneecap (Patella)
Thighbone (Femur)
Ligament
Cartilage covers bone end
Tendon
Ligament
Cartilage pad
Shinbone (Tibia)

Read further › ball and socket
pg157 (m22)

Joint designs

The body has several different types of joints, which allow different kinds of movements. The hip is a ball-and-socket joint. The rounded end of the femur fits into a cup-shaped socket in the pelvis. This design allows lots of movements—up and down, side to side, and twisting. A hinge joint, such as the knee (see pg157 [j35]), can only move up and down. The elbow is also a hinge joint, which, along with the wrist joint, allows the hand to be turned with the palm facing up or down.

▶ Gymnasts need supple, flexible joints to achieve extreme positions like this.

Read further › muscles
pg158 (d2); pg159 (b22)

Check it out!

• http://www.yahooligans.com/reference/gray/18.html

BODY TALK

• An adult's skeleton has 206 bones—but a baby's skeleton has over 340. This is because as the body grows, some separate bones join together to form one bone.

• Marrow is not found in all bones, and not all marrow is the same. In babies, nearly all bones contain red marrow (which makes new blood cells), but as the body grows some change to yellow marrow (which stores fat).

▶▶ BONES see pg217 (d22) ▶▶

Muscle power

THE BODY'S 650 muscles make up almost half of its total weight. A typical muscle is striped, long, and slim, bulging in the middle, and joined to a bone at either end. However, some muscles are shaped like triangles or sheets and may be joined to several bones, to each other, or not attached to bone at all, such as the layer of muscle in arteries. Muscles are designed to get shorter, or contract. As they contract, they pull on the bones they are attached to, and this moves the body. The contraction of the muscles is controlled by nerve signals sent out from parts of the brain called the motor centers and cerebellum (see pg173 [t27]).

Trapezius turns head

Deltoid lifts arm

Biceps bends elbow

Latissimus dorsi pulls arm back and down (muscle at the back)

Rectus femoris (in front of thigh) straightens the knee

Extensor digitorum straightens fingers

IT'S A FACT

• Muscles make up about 45 percent of male body weight; 40 percent in a female.

• The biggest muscle is the gluteus maximus, in the buttocks.

• The smallest muscle is the stapedius, attached to the stirrup bone in the ear, which is the size of this dash —.

▾ A muscle is a bundle of thousands of myofibers that are grouped into bundles called fascicles.

Epimysium (outer covering)

Tapering end or head of muscle

Body or belly of muscle

Tendon

Actin (thin myofilament)

Myosin (thick myofilament)

Layers of muscles

Just under the skin are dozens of muscles called the outer or superficial layer. Under these is usually another, intermediate layer, there is also a third, or deep, muscle layer. Not all muscle actions cause movement. Several muscles may tense to hold a part steady and still (see pg157 [s30]). For example, when the body is standing, the neck and back muscles tense to keep it upright and balanced.

◀ Front superficial muscles.

▶▶ Read further › joints
pg157 (m22)

Check it out!

• http://www.yahooligans.com/reference/gray/102.html
• http://www.bioanim.com

◀◀ CONTRACTION see pg29 (m22) ◀◀

1   2   3   4   5   6   7   8   9   10   11   12   13   14   15   16   17   18   19

Forward and backwards

A muscle can forcefully pull or contract, but it cannot forcefully push or extend. So, most muscles occur in pairs called antagonistic partners. One pulls the bone one way, and the other, on the opposite side of the bone, pulls the other way. Muscle pairs work together with other pairs as large muscle teams to move bones in many directions. When playing sport, our muscles are working in groups of pairs to respond to the moves we need.

▶▶ **Read further > face muscles**
pg159 (k33)

◀ *More than 50 muscles work in each arm when playing a sport such as volleyball.*

BODY TALK

• Muscles need energy to work. The energy needed comes from glucose, or blood sugar, which is carried by the blood.

• When a muscle is very active it needs much greater supplies of glucose. So the heart beats faster than normal and the blood vessels to the muscles widen, supplying the muscle with three times more blood than it has when it is idle.

Fasciae enclose large groups of muscle fibers

Nerve branches

Muscle fibers (myofibers)

Muscle fibril (myofibrils)

Muscle fibers

A muscle contains bundles of long, thin muscle fibers (myofibers), about the width of human hairs *(see pg155 [b24])*. Each fiber is made of even thinner parts called muscle fibrils (myofibrils). And each fibril contains even narrower parts, myofilaments. There are two kinds of filaments, made of different types of protein: actin, which is thin, and myosin, which is thick. These slide past each other to shorten the fibrils, causing the whole muscle to contract.

▶▶ **Read further > muscle layers**
pg158 (m9)

▶ *The muscles used to smile are called voluntary muscles because we can control how and when we use them, to express how we are feeling.*

Face muscles

Most muscles pull on bones, and the bones work as long levers to move the skeleton *(see pg156 [l14])*. But in the face, several sets of muscles are joined to each other as well as to bones. There are seven muscles on each side of the mouth, which can pull it wider, up, or down. More than 50 muscles are needed to make the facial expressions that show other people our thoughts and feelings.

▶▶ **Read further > bones and joints**
pg156 (d2)

Take a breath

I N AN EMERGENCY, the human body can survive without food for several days, and even without water for a day or two. But it cannot survive without air for more than a few minutes. The air around us contains the gas oxygen. We cannot see, smell, or taste oxygen. But it is necessary for chemical changes inside the body, which break apart the high-energy substance glucose (blood sugar) obtained from food. The energy released from glucose powers almost all of the body's life processes. The parts specialized to take in air and pass oxygen into the blood, for spreading around the body, are known as the respiratory system.

IT'S A FACT

• A pair of adult lungs holds about 5 pints of air.

• Opened out and laid out flat, the alveoli would cover an area about the size of half a football field.

▼ Inside the lungs, the bronchus divides into narrower bronchioles and again into even narrower alveoli.

Trachea

Muscles in wall of bronchus

Right bronchus

Air space inside bronchus

View along inside of bronchus

Right lung

Blood vessel

Alveoli

Bronchiole

Capillaries

Air spaces in alveoli

Respiratory system

The respiratory system consists of the nose, throat, larynx (voice box), trachea (windpipe), bronchi (main airways in the chest), and the lungs. Breathing in, or inspiring, draws fresh air into the lungs, where oxygen is taken in or absorbed into the blood (see pg162 [h17]). Breathing out, or expiring, causes the low-oxygen "used air" to be pushed up along the airways and out of the body. The lungs' airways branch many times, finally becoming too thin to see. At the end of each branch is a group of microscopic air bubbles, called alveoli, surrounded by a network of equally tiny blood vessels, called capillaries. Oxygen seeps or diffuses from the air inside the alveoli, into blood in the capillaries, and is carried around the body.

▶▶ Read further > blood vessels pg163 (p28)

Check it out!

• http://www.yahooligans.com/reference/gray/240.html
• http://www.kidinfo.com/Health/Human_Body.html

◀◀ OXYGEN see pg35 (b22) ◀◀

Absorbing oxygen

The main breathing muscle is the diaphragm, which is dome-shaped and sits under the lungs. When it tenses or contracts, it becomes flatter, expanding the lungs to suck in air. As the diaphragm relaxes again, the stretched lungs shrink back to their original smaller size, pushing out air. Muscles between the ribs also contract when breathing in, to lift the front of the chest and help expand the lungs.

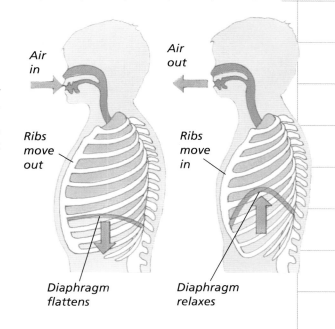

Air in

Air out

Ribs move out

Ribs move in

Diaphragm flattens

Diaphragm relaxes

Read further › muscle contraction
pg159 (b22)

Carrying air

There is no air in space, so astronauts must take their own supply. The air is contained in a special kind of backpack, which holds a main air tank and a reserve air tank. The main tank is connected to the astronaut's helmet. While wearing the helmet, the astronaut is able to breathe in the oxygen pumped into it from the tank. Chemicals inside the tank remove the carbon dioxide that is breathed out, to keep the air in the helmet fresh.

Read further › waste disposal
pg167 (m34)

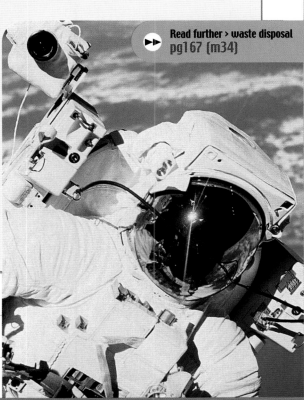

▸ *In order to breathe in space, astronauts have to carry tanks of oxygen.*

Vocal cords

Inside the larynx (voice box), in the front of the neck, two stiff ridges called vocal cords stick out from the sides. During normal breathing there is a triangle-shaped gap for air. To speak, muscles pull the ridges almost together. Air passing through the narrow gap makes them vibrate (shake to and fro rapidly), which produces sound.

When the cords are apart, no sound is made as air can move freely past them

When the cords are pulled together by the laryngeal muscles, air is forced through a small gap and the cords vibrate to create a sound

Read further › baby lungs
pg175 (r26)

BODY TALK

• The bulk of air, almost 79 per cent, is the gas nitrogen, which the body does not use. Fresh air, when breathed into the body contains about 21 percent oxygen and almost no carbon dioxide.

• After air has been in the lungs and breathed out, the proportion of carbon dioxide rises to 4 percent. The proportion of oxygen falls to 15 percent.

a b c d e f g h i j k l m n o p q r s t u v w

Heartbeat

BLOOD FLOWS around and around the body in a system of tubes called blood vessels. Blood is pumped by the heart, which has hollow chambers with strong muscular walls that contract to push the blood through the vessels. Blood carries many substances that are vital for life. These include oxygen and glucose (blood sugar) for energy; nutrients and raw materials for growth and repair; and natural body chemicals, hormones, that control internal processes. At the same time, blood removes wastes and unwanted materials, including carbon dioxide, which is breathed out of the lungs.

The brain receives more blood for its size than any other part of the body

Pulmonary circulation takes blood to and from the lungs

Blood leaves the heart through a giant artery called the aorta

Blood returns to the heart through large veins called venae cavae

Radial artery

Iliac vein

Femoral artery

Saphenous vein

Peroneal artery

● IT'S A FACT

• In most people, blood forms about one-twelfth, (about 8 percent) of total body weight.

• An average adult man has a blood volume of 9 to 10.5 pints.

• An average adult woman has a blood volume of 4 to 9 pints.

• Compared to an adult, a baby has slightly less blood for its body size.

● Circulatory system

The heart sends blood out into thick-walled vessels, called arteries. These branch and divide as they spread around the body, becoming thinner until they are microscopic blood vessels only one-hundredth of a millimeter across, called capillaries. Capillary walls are so thin that oxygen and other substances can easily seep out to the parts around it. Capillaries join to make wider vessels, veins, that return blood to the heart. On average, a drop of blood takes one minute to travel from the heart, through these vessels and back again. This is the circulatory system at work.

🌐 **Check it out!**
• http://sln.fi.edu/biosci/heart.html
• http://www.yahooligans.com/reference/gray/142.html

▶▶ **Read further › blood vessels** pg163 (p28)

◄◄ ANIMAL RESPIRATION see pg134 (f2) ◄◄

1 2 3 4 5 6 7 8 9 10 11 12 13 14 15 16 17 18 19

Two pumps in one

The heart is not a single pump, but two pumps, because the body has two circulations. The right side of the heart sends blood through pulmonary circulation to the lungs (see pg160 [m14]), to pick up supplies of oxygen. This blood returns to the left side of the heart, which then pumps it all around the body in the systemic circulation, to deliver the oxygen. The blood returns to the heart again to continue its endless journey.

Atria (upper chambers)

Walls of ventricles (lower chambers)

Thin walls of atria stretch as blood enters from the veins

One-way valves inside the heart ensure that blood flows the correct way

Thick muscular ventricle walls contract to push blood into the arteries

►► Read further › lungs
pg161 [b22]

A complex liquid

About half of blood is a watery fluid, plasma, with glucose, hormones, and many other substances dissolved in it. The other half is composed of cells. There are three main types: red cells carrying oxygen, white cells to fight disease, and platelets to help blood clot and seal a wound. One cubic millimeter of blood (the size of a pinhead) contains 5 million red cells, 8,000 white cells and 350,000 platelets.

Red blood cell

Platelets

Types of white blood cells

▲ *There are two main types of white blood cell: monocytes that surround and digest germs, and lymphocytes that use antibodies to destroy germs.*

►► Read further › cells / lymph nodes
pg152 [d2]; pg153 [g22]; pg167 [b34]

▼ *Veins are wide and their walls are thin and floppy.*

Inner lining (endothelium)

Valve in vein

Elastic layer

BODY TALK

• The heartbeat rate, or pulse, is measured in the wrist. It varies with age and activity. A new baby's average heartbeat rate is 120 to 130 per minute, even when asleep. By about the age of seven, this average resting rate has fallen to an average of 80 to 90. In the adult body, the rate is around 70.

• During hard exercise, such as running a race, the adult pulse rate can double, up to about 140.

Blood vessels

Arteries have thick, stretchy, walls to cope with pressure as blood surges out of the heart at high speed. Each heartbeat causes the arteries to bulge all through the body. This bulge or pulsation is easily felt in the wrist on the pulse. Capillary walls are only one cell thick. Veins carry slow-moving, low-pressure, blood. Because blood moves so slowly, many veins, particularly in the legs, have valves to stop blood from flowing the wrong way.

Thin muscle layer

Capillaries

Vein

Artery

Thick muscle layer

►► Read further › blood
pg163 [b30]

►► CIRCULATION see pg217 [b32] ►►

Eating for life

THE BODY takes in a huge range of foods, including meat and fish, bread, rice and pasta, and fresh fruits and vegetables. But the journey for all food is the same. It passes into the digestive tract, which is a passageway looped and coiled within the body. As foods pass along the tract they are broken down or digested into smaller, simpler substances, called nutrients, which can be absorbed into the blood stream. The whole journey for food, from one end of the tract to the other, lasts up to 48 hours.

Three pairs of salivary glands make saliva

Swallowed food goes down the esophagus (gullet)

Liver (plays an important part in processing digested food)

Pancreas (secretes pancreatic juices)

Stomach

Large intestine

Small intestine

Appendix

Rectum

Anus

▲ A balanced diet including fresh vegetables, for essential minerals, and carbohydrate, for energy, is vital for a healthy digestive system.

 Check it out!
- http://www.geocities.com/Area 51/Dunes/9641/digestive.htm
- http://www.borg.com/~lube hawk/hdigsys.htm
- http://www.yahooligans.com/ reference/gray/241.html

◄◄ ANIMAL DIGESTION see pg134 (s2) ◄◄

IT'S A FACT

- In an adult the whole digestive tract is about 10 yd long.

- The longest part of the digestive system is the small intestine, measuring 7.5 yd.

- The large intestine is about 2 yd long.

Digestive system

In the mouth, foods are chewed and moistened by saliva (spit). They are swallowed down the esophagus (gullet) into the stomach, and are churned around with gastric juices that contain chemicals called acids and enzymes. These enzymes turn food into a thick, soup-like substance, called chyme, which oozes into the small intestine. Here nutrients are absorbed into the blood. Waste is stored in the rectum and leaves the body through the anus.

 Read further › excretory system pg166 (m2)

BODY TALK

- During a large meal, the stomach stretches to hold about 9 pints of chewed food. Its lining makes a powerful acid—hydrochloric acid—to attack and digest food. This acid also helps to kill germs in the food.

- The stomach does not digest its own lining because it is coated with a layer of slimy mucus, which resists an acid attack.

1 2 3 4 5 6 7 8 9 10 11 12 13 14 15 16 17 18 19

Liver

The liver is not part of the digestive tract, but it is part of the digestive system. It receives nutrient-rich blood from the small intestine. The liver makes a green liquid called bile, which breaks down fatty foods. Bile is stored in the gall bladder. To the left of the liver and behind the stomach is another digestive organ, the pancreas. It produces powerful enzymes to aid breakdown of food in the small intestine.

▶▶ **Read further › digestion / waste**
pg164 (i13); pg166 (m2)

Right lobe

Left lobe

Dividing ligament

Hepatic artery (brings oxygen-rich blood from the heart)

Bile duct

Gall bladder

Hepatic portal vein (carries food-rich blood from the small intestine)

▼ Inside a tooth, many blood vessels and nerves pass through the pulp into the jaw bone.

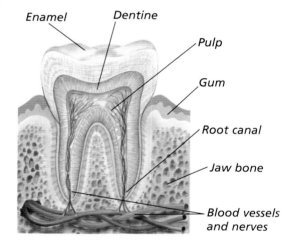

Enamel

Dentine

Pulp

Gum

Root canal

Jaw bone

Blood vessels and nerves

Teeth

A person has 52 teeth, but not at the same time. The first, baby teeth, set begin to appear soon after birth and finally there are 20. These deciduous teeth begin to fall out when children areabout six years old,and are replaced by the second, adult, or permanent set of 32 teeth. Each tooth is covered by enamel *(see pg165 [i23])*, the hardest substance in the body. Under the enamel is slightly softer dentine. The center of the tooth has living pulp of blood vessels and nerves.

▶▶ **Read further › blood vessels**
pg163 (p28)

First incisor

Second incisor

Canine

First and second premolars

First and second molars

Third molar (wisdom tooth)

▲ The adult teeth in one half of the lower jaw.

Small intestine

Most nutrients are absorbed through the small intestine lining into the blood flowing through its walls. The lining is folded into ridges called plicae, and the surfaces of the plicae are also folded, into tiny finger-like structures the size of a period mark, called villi. Similarly, the surface of each villus is covered with thousands of microvilli. The plicae, villi and microvilli make a huge surface area for absorbing nutrients— more than 20 times the body's whole skin area.

Villus

Blood vessels inside villus

Plicae

Wall of intestine

▶ Villi line the intestine.

▶▶ **Read further › digestive system**
pg164 (i13)

To scale
Each square of the grid = 0.4 in

Average baby molar tooth is 0.25 in

Average adult molar tooth is 0.75 in

a
b
c
d
e
f
g
h
i
j
k
l
m
n
o
p
q
r
s
t
u
v
w

Water and waste

THE BODY'S thousands of internal chemical processes are known as its metabolism. This produces wastes of many kinds. Two main systems get rid of such body wastes. The digestive system removes not only bits of leftover and undigested food, but also some wastes of metabolism. The other waste disposal system is the urinary system whose main organs are the kidneys. They filter waste products, unwanted salts and water from the blood, and dispose of them in a watery fluid called urine. The amount of urine that is produced is controlled by hormones.

Adrenal gland

Right kidney

Inside the left kidney

Major artery and vein

Renal artery and vein

Ureter

▸ The urinary system controls the balance of water in the body.

Urethra

Bladder

● Excretion and digestion

About one-fifth of the blood pumped out by the heart *(see pg163 [i25])* goes to the two kidneys. Inside each kidney are about 1 million tiny filters called nephrons. These take waste substances from the blood, along with excess water, to form urine. The urine flows down a tube, the ureter, to the bladder in the lower body. The bladder usually needs to be emptied, through the urethra, when it contains about 0.4 of a pint of urine. Solid wastes are removed from the end of the digestive tract through the anus. They contain mainly rubbed-off bits of intestine lining and undigested bits of food.

▸ Food takes about 48 hours to work its way through the digestive system.

Liver

Stomach

Gall bladder

Pancreas

Small intestine

Large intestine

Read further › digestion
pg164 (i13)
Read further › digestion
pg164 (i13)

Renal artery brings blood to the kidney

Renal vein takes filtered blood away from the kidney

Ureter takes urine to the bladder

Renal capsule (covering)

Anus

Outer layer or cortex containing nephrons (filters)

Inner layer or medulla

▲ Inside the kidneys, the 1 million nephrons filter the blood.

To scale
An adult kidney is about the same size as a small boxing glove—about 2.3 in long

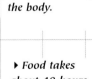

Adult kidney   Boxing glove

a
b
c
d
e
f
g
h
i
j
k
l
m
n
o
p
q
r
s
t
u
v
w

IT'S A FACT

• The kidneys receive more blood for their size than almost any other body organ—about 2 pints per minute.

• All the body's blood flows through the kidneys more than 300 times a day.

White and red blood cells

Lymph duct from node

Outer layer (cortex) of node produces white blood cells

Lymph duct into node

▲ *Lymph nodes are where most of the body's white blood cells are formed.*

Lymphatic system

Lymph is a pale yellow fluid found in the tiny spaces between and around cells and tissues. It oozes into lymph ducts that carry it to lymph nodes. Lymph collects wastes from metabolism and the lymph nodes contain white blood cells *(see pg163 [f36])* that destroy harmful or unwanted substances, especially germs. The lymph ducts and vessels come together to pour lymph into the blood system. During an infection, lymph nodes enlarge with extra fluid and white cells as "swollen glands."

▶▶ **Read further > white blood cells**
pg163 (b30)

Stress and the body

The adrenal glands above the kidneys make hormones that regulate how the body uses water and its reactions to stress. The main stress hormone is adrenaline. In a scary or energetic situation, like playing tennis, it makes the heart beat faster and the liver release glucose for extra energy. More blood flows to the muscles so that the body can quickly take action.

▶▶ **Read further > sweating / pumping blood**
pg155 (b29); pg163 (b22)

BODY TALK

• In an average day of 24 hours, the body produces about 2.5 pints of urine. This amount varies hugely depending on activity and weather conditions.

• When the body is active in hot weather, it sweats to keep cool, and water is lost in the sweat—sometimes 5 pimts or more.

• Sweating and breathing out are part of the excretory system. Both actions remove unwanted substances.

Hormonal system

The hormonal, or endocrine, system consists of glands that make substances called hormones. These pass through the blood and control internal body processes. For example, the thyroid gland in the neck makes thyroxine, which controls how fast cells burn energy. The pea-sized pituitary gland, under the brain, is in overall control of the hormone system. The amount of urine made by the kidneys is controlled by the hormone ADH (antidiuretic hormone). As water is lost in urine or through sweat during strenuous activity, it must be replaced by drinking water.

▶▶ **Read further > substances in blood**
pg163 (b30)

🌐 **Check it out!**

• http://infozone.imcpl.org/kids_kidny.htm
• http://www.yahooligans.com/reference/gray/175.html
• http://www.yahooligans.com/reference/gray/253.html

Sight and sound

IT'S A FACT

• Each eye's retina has more than 130 million light-sensitive cells, rods and cones, in an area slightly larger than a thumbnail.

• Each ear's cochlea has 25,000 auditory cells, with a total of more than 2 million micro–hairs to detect sound vibrations.

MORE INFORMATION about the outside world is taken in by a person through the eyes and ears—from pictures, noises, written words on paper, and everyday sounds—than through all the other senses combined. All the body's sense organs work in the same way. They detect changes or features, and produce patterns of tiny nerve signals that are sent to the brain. The eye detects light as rays of different colors and brightness. The ear detects vibrations of sound that reach it as invisible air waves.

▶ Light enters the eye through the pupil. It then travels through the cornea and lens to form an image on the retina at the back of the eye.

Optic chiasma where signals from each eye partly cross over

Retina – the lining of light-sensitive rods and cones

Choroid layer

Sclera (covering)

Ligaments supporting the lens

Iris

Lens

Optic nerve which carries the signals to the brain

Cornea

Tear fluid gland

Muscles that turn the eye

Pupil

Iris

Tear duct in to nose

Outer sheath of eyeball (sclera)

BODY TALK

• The level of a sound, whether high or low, is called its pitch and is measured in Hz (Hertz or vibrations per second). Most people can hear a range of sounds from about 20 Hz, such as the deep rumble of thunder, to 18,000 Hz, such as the shrill squeaks of a bat.

• However, as the body gets older, its ears and other sense organs stop functioning as well. The ears detect only less high-pitched sounds.

▶▶ Read further › eye color
pg169 (k22)

Check it out!

• http://www.calicutnet.com/
humanbody/eye.htm
• http://www.kidinfo.com.health/
Human_Body.html
• http://www.yahooligans.com/
reference/gray/224.html

Inside the eye

The eyeball, almost 1 in across and has a tough outer cover, the sclera. At the front is a transparent window, the dome-shaped cornea, which lets in light rays. These pass through the lens that bends (refracts) the light to shine a clear image of the world onto the retina lining the eyeball. Here, millions of light-sensitive cells change the patterns of light into nerve signals. The eye's retina has two kinds of light-sensitive cells. Rods are tall and slim, and number about 125 million. They detect shades of light and work well in dim light but cannot see colors. The 7 million cones are shorter and wider and clustered at the rear where the central part of the image falls. They see colors and fine details in bright light.

◀◀ LIGHT see pg31 (b29) ◀◀

1 2 3 4 5 6 7 8 9 10 11 12 13 14 15 16 17 18 19

Inside the ear

Sound waves pass into a slightly S-shaped tube, the outer ear canal, and hit the small, flexible, eardrum at the end. The vibrations pass along three tiny bones—the hammer, anvil, and stirrup—and into the fluid inside the snail-shaped cochlea. The vibrations cause ripples that are sensed by microscopic hairs on auditory cells, and then change into nerve signals.

Outer ear (pinna)

Semicircular canals (balance)

Layers of hair cells in fluid inside the cochlea

Eardrum

Sound wave

Outer ear canal

Cochlea

Hammer

Anvil

Stirrup

Eustachian tube

Read further › nerve signals
pg173 (b22)

Three ossicles

The three ear bones, known as the ossicles, are the hammer, anvil, and stirrup. These are the smallest bones in the body. The surrounding muscles tense to hold them firmly so that they vibrate less when very loud sound waves hit them. These muscles prevent overly loud sounds from damaging the ear. The eustachian tube controls air pressure inside the ear by letting air in and out. The eustachian tube can be opened by yawning or swallowing.

Eye color

The colored part of the eye is the iris—a ring of muscle seen through the clear cornea. The dark hole in the middle of the iris is the pupil, where light passes to the inside of the eye. Nearly all babies are born with blue eyes. After a few months the color may change to a shade of brown, green, or gray, then it stays the same. This color is inherited from parents. If the mother and father are both blue-eyed, their child will almost certainly have blue eyes. However, if one or both parents are brown-eyed, then their child may have brown or blue eyes.

Parents' eye color

Genes for eye color

Possible colors for children

Read further › babies' genes
pg175 (k22)

Laser surgery

A narrow beam of high-power laser light can be aimed accurately into the eye, to carry out treatment for various eye disorders. The heat from the beam can seal a leaky blood vessel, or sculpt and reshape the lens (see pg168 [l18]) and cornea, (see pg168 [m19]) to make vision clearer.

▲ Laser surgery on the retina can mean that glasses or contact lenses are no longer necessary.

Read further › inside the eye
pg168 (o13)

a b c d e f g h i j k l m n o p q r s t u v w

Smell, taste, and touch

BOTH SMELL and taste are chemo-senses. They detect tiny particles of chemical substances—odor molecules floating in the air, and flavor in foods and drinks. The two senses work separately, but they both usually send messages to the brain at the same time, when we eat and drink. So does the sense of touch, as the lips, tongue, gums, and cheeks detect the temperature and consistency of the food. Smell, taste, and touch are all closely linked or associated in the brain—especially when we eat. What we imagine as the "taste" of a meal is really a combination of these three senses.

IT'S A FACT

• The nose can detect more than 10,000 different scents, smells, and odors, using 25 million olfactory or "smell" cells inside the nose.

• The tongue and inside of the mouth have up to 10,000 taste buds, but they sense only four main flavors: bitter, salty, sour, and sweet.

Olfactory bulb

Olfactory tract to brain

Scent-sensitive cells of olfactory epithelium

Mucus lining (inside nose)

Hard palate (roof of mouth)

Nostril

▲ Scent particles dissolve in the mucus lining. The cells at the top of the nose then send signals along the olfactory nerve to the brain.

▶▶ Read further › types of cells pg153 (g22)

Inside the nose

The sensory parts for smell are two patches called olfactory (smell) epithelia. They are in the roof of the nasal chamber, inside the skull behind the nose. Each patch contains millions of olfactory cells (*see pg171 [s25]*), which have bunches of micro-hairs, cilia. These detect certain odor molecules from the air that float up into the nose and land on them.

Epidermis

Keratin layer

Pain sensors

Light touch sensors

Heavy pressure sensors

Skin and touch

The sense of touch uses microscopic sensors at the ends of nerve fibers in the dermis, just under the surface of the skin (*see pg154 [r12]*), to detect a range of physical contacts. These include light touch and heavy pressure, heat and cold, and movements or vibrations. In the fingertips, there are 10,000 micro-sensors in every square millimeter of skin.

▶▶ Read further › dermis layer of skin pg154 (i11)

▲ Some of the microscopic sensors found within the skin.

Tongue and taste

The front, sides, and rear of the tongue have thousands of taste buds set into the surface, scattered between the larger "lumps" called papillae. Each taste bud is one-tenth of a millimeter across. It contains about 25 gustatory (taste) cells, which have tufts of micro-hairs called cilia. These detect chemical flavoring particles in food. The tip of the tongue is most sensitive to sweet tastes, the front sides to salty, the rear sides to sour, and the middle rear to bitter tastes.

Smaller papillae
Large papillae
Taste buds
Inner tongue layers

Large papillae
Bitter
Sour
Small papillae
Salty
Sweet

▲ *The tongue has many taste buds to detect different flavors but its main upper surface has no taste buds.*

Read further › chewing food pg164 (i13)

BODY TALK

• The body has five main senses: sight (visual), hearing (auditory), smell (olfactory), taste (gustatory), and touch (somato-sensory), but there are millions of other tiny sensors inside the body too.

• Sensors in the inner parts of the ear detect the head's position and movements, while those in muscles and joints send information about the position of the body and limbs. This helps balance and posture.

• Other micro-sensors detect internal body conditions such as temperature and blood pressure.

▼ *Smells are scent molecules which are taken into your nose by breathed-in air. A particular smell may be noticeable even when mixed with millions of air molecules.*

Smell cells

Olfactory cells have micro-hairs or cilia facing down into the nasal chamber, which detect smell molecules that land on them. These molecules drift into the nose with breathed-in air and enter the nasal chamber.

Olfactory cell
Bone
Micro-hairs (cilia)

Sensing smells and tastes

It is not clear how the micro-hairs, or cilia, on smell and taste cells respond to chemical particles. It is possible that the surfaces of the cilia have tiny pits in them of different shapes. A certain odor or flavor particle fits into one shape of pit, but not the others—like a key into its own lock. Only when the particle fits properly, is a nerve signal sent to the brain.

Read further › nerve signals pg173 (b22)

Check it out!

• http://www.yahooligans.com/reference/gray/222.html
• http://www.calicutnet.com/humanbody/tongue.htm
• http://www.yahooligans.com/reference/gray/223.html

◄◄ ANIMAL SENSE OF TASTE see pg137 (c32) ◄◄

Nerves all over

THE BODY consists of many different organs and tissues. They must work together in an organized way for the whole body to stay healthy and active. The main system that controls and coordinates all these parts is the nervous system. Like a computer network, it sends tiny electrical signals back and forth, carrying information from one part of the body to another. Electrical signals are called nerve messages, and they travel along wire-like nerves, which spread in a vast network throughout the entire body. Central control of the whole nervous system and the entire body comes from the brain.

Brain
Cranial nerve
Spinal cord
Brachial plexus (nerve junction)
Intercostal nerve
Lumbar nerves
Sacral nerve
Radial nerve
Ulna nerve
Sciatic nerve
Tibial nerve
Peroneal nerve
Lateral plantar nerve

● IT'S A FACT

• The spinal cord is about 18 in long: 31 pairs of main peripheral nerves branche from it.

• The thickest peripheral nerve is the sciatic nerve in the lower hip and upper thigh—almost as wide as a thumb.

▶ *The spinal cord is the bundle of nerves running down the middle of the backbone.*

Spinal cord
Backbone

● The nervous system

The nervous system has three main parts: brain, spinal cord, and peripheral nerves. The brain consists of billions of nerve cells and other tissues in the top half of the head. Its lower part merges into the spinal cord, the body's main nerve. The spinal cord is inside a tunnel formed by the row of holes inside the vertebrae of the backbone or spine. Peripheral nerves branch out from the spinal cord and brain to reach every body part.

▶▶ **Read further > bones and joints** pg157 (b34; m22)

🌐 Check it out!

• http://faculty.washington.edu/chudler/phylo.html
• http://ghs.gresham.k12.or.us/science/ps/sci/ibbio/Anatomy/nervous/neuron.htm

Nerve cells

The nervous system is built up of billions of very specialized cells called nerve cells or neurons. Each has many spider-like branches, called dendrites, that receive signals from other nerve cells. The signals pass out along the nerve fiber, or axon, to other nerve cells. Nerve fibers are too thin to by eye. But some nerve cells are more than 12 in long, making them some of the longest cells in the body.

Read further › waste removal
pg166 (m2)

▼ *The neurons in nerves collect and pass on messages.*

Cell body

Axon

Nucleus

Dendrites

Myelin sheath

Axon terminals connect at synapses (links)

How the brain works

Nine-tenths of the brain consists of the cerebrum, composed of two large, dome-shaped, wrinkled parts called cerebral hemispheres. At the lower rear is a smaller wrinkled part, the cerebellum. It makes muscle-powered movements smooth, skillful, and coordinated. The central parts of the brain, such as the thalamus, are involved in awareness, memories, and emotions. The lowest part is the brain stem, which is responsible for automatic body processes such as digestion and heartbeat.

Thalamus affects sensory levels, awareness and alertness

Cerebrum is the site of mental activity such as thinking and learning

Limbic system affects body functions and emotions

Hippocampus, linked to mood, willpower, learning, and memory

Cerebellum controls coordination

Hypothalamus controls body heat, water, and hunger, and wakes you up

Brain stem controls heartbeat and breathing

Read further › digestion
pg166 (m2)

Inside a nerve

A nerve has a tough, shiny, grayish covering, called the epineurium. Inside are bundles, or fascicles, of nerve fibers that carry tiny electrical pulses of nerve signals. A thick nerve has hundreds of thousands of fibers, while the thinnest nerves, as fine as a human hair, have just a few. Also, inside the nerve are small blood vessels (see pg163 [u30]) to bring nourishment and take away waste. Nerve signals travel so fast that we can sense a situation and react to it in less than 0.2 seconds.

▼ *Nerves allow us to have split-second reactions—essential for sports such as snowboarding.*

Read further › types of cells
pg153 (g22)

BODY TALK

• Different types of nerve fibers carry signals at different speeds. The fastest signals travel at more than 394 ft p/sec.

• The slowest signals travel at 3 to 7 ft p/sec.

▶▶ CONSCIOUS THOUGHTS see pg225 (i22) ▶▶

22 23 24 25 26 27 28 29 30 31 32 33 34 35 36 37 38 39

a b c d e f g h i j k l m n o p q r s t u v w

Making babies

EVERY SECOND, another three human beings enter the world. They are new babies, born after nine months of growing and developing inside their mothers. The parts of the body that produce new human beings are known as the reproductive system. The reproductive parts are the only body system that is not fully formed and working at birth. The reproductive system completes its development around the ages of 11 to 13 in girls, and 14 to 16 in boys, which is the time known as puberty. The process of reproduction begins with the joining of two single cells—the egg from the mother, and the sperm from the father.

● IT'S A FACT

• The average time from the fertilization of the egg by the sperm, to the time of birth, is 266 days.

• More babies are born between 3 a.m. and 4 a.m. than during any other time of the day or night.

▾ *Babies grow inside the womb for around 40 weeks (9 months), before they are born.*

24 weeks

20 weeks

16 weeks

12 weeks

8 weeks

● Female reproductive parts

The egg cell is relatively large, at a fraction of a millimeter. The main female sex organs, the ovaries, contain many thousands of egg cells. Every month one egg becomes ripe and is released into the oviduct or egg tube (fallopian tube) in a process called ovulation. It passes along the tube, where it may meet a sperm cell *(see pg175 [r24])* and be fertilized *(see pg175 [j29])*.

▶▶ **Read further › sperm cell** pg174 (q13)

Check it out!
• http://www.yahooligans.com/ reference/gray/15.html
• http://www.biology-online.org/ 7/3_birth.htm

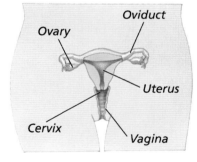

Ovary · Oviduct · Uterus · Cervix · Vagina

▲ *Female reproductive parts.*

● BODY TALK

• During the first nine months of development, a baby's weight increases 5 billion times.

• In the nine months after birth, a baby's body weight increases by about three times.

● Male reproductive parts

Compared to the egg cell, the sperm cell is tiny. The main male sex organs, the testes, make millions of them each day and they live for about 1 month. If the sperm cells do not pass along the ductus deferens or sperm tube, and then out of the body through the penis, they gradually die and break apart as new ones form.

▶▶ **Read further › egg cell** pg174 (m2)

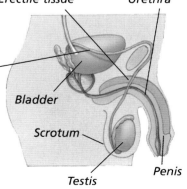

Erectile tissue · Urethra · Vas deferens · Bladder · Scrotum · Testis · Penis

▲ *Male reproductive parts (side view).*

▶ *Between 32 and 36 weeks, the baby usually turns in the womb, ready to be born head first.*

Umbilical cord

36 weeks

32 weeks

Placenta

28 weeks

40 weeks

Cervix (neck of the womb)

In the womb

Inside the uterus the single fertilized egg divides into two cells, then four, eight and so on. After a week it is a ball of a few hundred cells that buries itself in the blood-rich lining of the uterus and takes in nourishment for continued growth. After one month it is hardly larger than a rice grain, but the brain and heart are formed. After two months the tiny baby is still smaller than a thumb, yet all its main parts and organs have formed.

Read further › organs
pg150 (j14)

Sperm

Egg cell's outer coat

Egg cell cytoplasm

Getting together

The egg cell is only able to join with a sperm for the few days when a woman is ovulating (when an egg has been released from the ovary). Thousands of sperm cells swim near to the egg in the oviduct, but only one can join with or fertilize it. Both the egg and sperm contain sets of the parents' genetic material, made of DNA *(see pg153 [n33])*. At fertilization the sets combine to form a unique set of genes for the new baby.

Egg cell nucleus

Read further › DNA
pg153 (b30)

▲ *An ultrasound scan shows the baby growing inside the womb.*

Nucleus with genetic material

Sperm head

▶ *A newborn baby is carefully checked by a doctor to ensure it is healthy.*

New life

In the womb it was warm, wet, and quiet, and oxygen and food came direct from the mother into the baby's blood. At birth a baby is pushed and squeezed into the fresh air, lights, and sounds of the outside world. The baby takes its first gasps of air, often crying as it does so. This is a good sign, since it opens up the baby's airways and lungs *(see pg160 [m11])*. These were not used in the womb, but now the baby must breathe to get oxygen for itself. It also needs food and soon the baby takes a first meal of its mother's milk. The milk provides all the nourishment a baby needs for the first months of its life.

Sperm tail

▲ *Only one sperm can fertilize the released egg.*

Read further › nourishment
pg164 (d2)

◀◀ ANIMAL BIRTH see pg146 (d2) ◀◀

a b c d e f g h i j k l m n o p q r s t u v w

Machine power

MACHINES MAKE it easier to perform jobs that would otherwise be very difficult, even impossible. Machines carry out jobs more efficiently by changing the strength or direction of a force. A machine can be as simple as a door handle or as complicated as a spacecraft, but all include types of six basic machines: the ramp or inclined plane, the wedge, the lever, the screw, the pulley, the wheel and axle. But most machines, even the complex ones, work because of the link between force and distance.

Effort

Load

First-class lever

Effort

▲ *Prizing the lid from a can of paint: the tool acts as a first-class lever with the wrist doing the effort.*

Fulcrum

"Driver" cog is larger with more "teeth"

"Driven" cog has fewer teeth and turns slower but more powerfully

● Gearing up

Gears are used in machines like clocks and cars, which have a rotating mechanism (parts that go round). Gears can alter the power from an engine so that it moves at the right speed and force, and goes in the right direction. Gears are usually sets of wheels called cogs with teeth that "mesh" and turn together (see pg184 [u8]). A big cog turns a smaller cog with less force but faster. A small cog turns a bigger cog slower but with more force.

▶▶ Read further > cars / gears
pg184 (b15; p8); pg185 (l22)

● How levers work

A lever is a bar or rod supported by a fulcrum (central pivot). Effort or force is needed to move one end of the lever to move a load at the other end. The closer the fulcrum is to the load, the less effort is needed to lift it. There are three classes of lever. In first-class levers, such as a seesaw, the fulcrum is in the middle. Second-class levers, such as a wheelbarrow, have the fulcrum at one end, the effort (pushing) at the other end and the load in the middle. In third-class levers, such as a hammer, the effort is between the load and the fulcrum (the hand).

Wheel and axle

Load

Effort

Fulcrum

● Wheel power

A heavy load is very hard to drag uphill, but rolling it in a wheelbarrow is much easier. The wheel reduces the friction (resistance) so that the load can be moved more easily. A ramp makes a job easier by enabling the load to be pulled or pushed up a slope instead of lifted.

Ramp or inclined plane

▶▶ Read further > wheels
pg185 (b22)

▲ *Three simple machines: a wheelbarrow (lever), wheel and axle, and ramp (inclined plane).*

▶▶ WHEEL see pg201 (t22) ▶▶

Weight lifters

A pulley is the best machine for lifting heavy loads. It can be as simple as a rope or chain flung over a bar. Usually, though, the rope runs over a number of grooved wheels. A single pulley wheel helps by changing the direction of the force because pulling down is easier than lifting up. If the rope is looped round and back over several pulley wheels, the load is spread over a long strand of rope, and so is reduced, making the object easier to lift. Pulley "blocks" have many sets of pulleys and can lift very heavy loads with quite a small effort.

▼ *A simple set of pulleys lets a person lift a heavy weight using distance for more force.*

Effort

More pulleys give more force to the person pulling

Load

▶▶ **Read further > weights**
pg179 (b22)

Moving staircase

▶▶ **Read further > elevators**
pg179 (b32)

Escalators—moving staircases—carry people up or down using the power of a pulley. The escalator's pulley is like a bicycle chain wrapped around a cog-like pulley at either end of the staircase. The stairs go around in a loop, moving down on top and coming back up from underneath, in reverse. The weight of the down going stairs pulls the ascending stairs upward. So, the escalator's drive motors only have to lift the weight of the passengers, but not the weight of the stairs.

Ascending or descending stairs

Motor-driven pulley

▼ *This seesaw is a first-class lever, as the fulcrum is between the load and effort.*

Load

Stairs are attached to the pulley with brackets

◀ *Corkscrews are a type of turning wedge.*

▲ *An escalator's steps swivel past each other both ends of the pulley system.*

▶▶ **Read further > weight of loads**
pg180 (d2)

▶▶ **Read further > propellers**
pg186 (i13)

WORK IT OUT

- Many bones in the human body work like levers. For example, the forearm pivots at the elbow, acting as a type of third-class lever to give extra lifting or pushing power.

- Bicycle gears help cyclists pedal between 60 to 90 turns a minute, reducing the necessary effort.

Simple machines

Two ramps (inclined planes) back to back form a wedge for separating or splitting items, like an ax. A wedge wrapped around a pole or rod forms a screw, which changes a turning force into a slow, steady, pulling force.

🌐 **Check it out!**

- http://www.howstuffworks.com/pulley.htm
- http://www.fi.edu/qa97/spotlight3/spotlight3.html
- http://www.galaxy.net:80/~k12/machines/index.shtml

◀◀ FORCE see pg25 (b22) ◀◀

a b c d e f g h i j k l m n o p q r s t u v w

Construction

IN THE past, most big buildings like cathedrals were built of stone, their strength lay in the thick walls. Today, buildings such as skyscrapers get their strength from a framework or "skeleton" of steel girders, beams, and concrete columns, forced into the ground by heavy machinery, like pile-drivers. The skeleton supports the roof, walls, and floors so the walls can be made of glass, when designed to carry no weight. Tunnels and arches are different types of construction, with their strength in curved walls or arches.

● IT'S A FACT

● The world's longest tunnel carries water for 105 mi, from a reservoir into New York City.

● The world's longest underwater tunnel is Japan's Seikan tunnel, which carries a railway 33.5 mi under the Tsugaru Strait between the islands Honshu and Hokkaido.

● Scraping the sky

Skyscrapers are dramatic buildings, often towering many hundreds of feet into the air. To support such a huge structure, every skyscraper must have deep foundations (the part below ground) made of massive concrete or steel piles pushed into the ground. Above these, the walls and floors are attached to a skeleton of steel girders and beams. When a skyscraper is over 40 stories high, the weight of a strong wind blowing against the side of the building is greater than the weight of the actual building. So, architects must make the building horizontally strong as well as vertically strong.

▶▶ Read further › steel girders
pg181 (k22)

5. Facing of glass and concrete walls are added

4. Elevators and other services like electricity and plumbing are installed

3. Concrete and steel frame floors, or decks, are slowly added, starting at the bottom

2. Heavy steel girders are lifted into position by tall cranes as the building rises

1. Foundations are dug and piles are set in the ground

To scale

Two of the world's tallest structures
1 square = 328 ft tall

1,483 ft tall

984 ft tall

Petronas Twin Towers (Kuala Lumpur, Malaysia)

Eiffel Tower (Paris, France)

🌐 Check it out!

● http://www.pbs.org/wgbh/ buildingbig/skyscraper/

● http://www.skyscraperpage. com/

◀◀ CRANES' USE OF ENERGY see pg27 (k23) ◀◀

Pile drivers

Buildings or bridges erected on soft ground are supported by posts called piles. Usually made of steel or concrete, the piles are driven firmly into the ground by pile-drivers. Pile drivers wind up a heavy weight called a pile hammer, inside a frame, then drop it on the head of the pile to smash it into the ground. In 1847, Scottish engineer James Naysmith, invented a steam-driven pile driver that could raise and lower a seven ton weight 80 times a minute. Today, pile drivers use compressed air to raise the hammer, and the drop is precisely controlled by computers.

Read further › compressed air
pg187 (b29); pg189 (b31)

WORK IT OUT

• The first skyscrapers were built in New York and Chicago, U.S.A. The 10-story Home Insurance building in Chicago, was completed in 1885.

• The invention of the safety elevator by Elisha Otis in the 1850s made skyscrapers possible. Today, elevators in skyscrapers can run at speeds of up to 33 ft/sec.

Going underground

Tunnels just below the surface of the ground can be built by the "cut-and-cover" method. This means digging a large, long ditch, then covering it to make the tunnel. But, deeper tunnels must be hollowed out. Tunnels through hard rock are often blasted using explosives. Tunnels through soft rock or soil are dug with a powerful cutting machine called a shield, which is a large drum with disk cutters at the front. As the shield bores forward, debris comes out the back. Ring-shaped steel and concrete supports are put in place to prevent the tunnel caving in.

Building an arch

Arches are usually made of stone or brick and built up from wedge-shaped blocks called voussoirs. While the arch is being built, a wooden frame the same shape as the arch supports the structure. When the frame is removed, the arch is supported by the pressure of either side of the arch against the keystone (center block).

Keystone block in the upper center of arch "locks" structure in place by balancing pressure from either side

Brick or stonework sides prevent the arch collapsing under the weight of structure above

◄ *The world's biggest free-standing arch is the 130 ft-high Gateway to the West arch in St. Louis, Missouri, U.S.A.*

▶ *The shield's rotating cutting head is kept on a straight course by lasers.*

Read further › arch bridges
pg180 (s8)

Read further › bridges
pg180 (d2)

Bridging the gap

Central tower has two cantilever "arms"

Steel beams span length of bridge

Piers on piles support weight of main towers

BRIDGES ARE vital links, carrying traffic—people, animals, and vehicles—over rivers, roads, railroads, or ravines. To be safe, a bridge must be strong enough to bear the weight of the load moving across it, and also its own weight. This strength can be achieved in various ways, but every bridge has massive supports at both ends called abutments. They are embedded in solid ground. In between, there are often extra supports, called piers, linked by short sections of the bridge called spans. There is usually a long, middle span over the deepest water.

LONGEST SUSPENSION BRIDGES

Bridge, Country	Length
Akashi–Kaiko, Japan	6,528.79 ft
Great Belt, Denmark	5,328 ft
Humber Estuary, Britain	4,626 ft
Jiangyin, China	4,544 ft
Tsing Ma, China	4,518 ft

Types of bridge

Traditionally, bridges were simple wooden or stone arches. Modern bridges are built from concrete and steel, and the type of construction depends on the heaviest load it will have to carry and the nature of the place where it is to be built. For example, for a wide span over water, suspension or cable-stayed bridges are usually the best. To carry a very heavy load over a short distance, a beam bridge can be built. To carry a heavy load over a greater distance, a cantilever bridge is often used.

▶▶ Read further > construction pg178 (k2)

▼ Cable-stayed bridges, such as the Queen Elizabeth II Bridge, Dartford, England, hang from steel cables.

▶ Suspension bridges, like the Golden Gate Bridge, San Francisco, have spans that hang on steel wires from a cable spanning two tall towers.

▼ Lifting bridges, such as Tower Bridge, London, use hydraulic power to swing a section of the bridge up to allow tall ships to pass underneath.

▶ Arch bridges, such as London Bridge, England, are very strong because the weight is pushed outwards to the abutments, rather than downward.

▲ Cantilever bridges, such as the Forth Railway Bridge, Scotland, balance the load on two piers.

Check it out!

- http://www.pbs.org/wgbh/ buildingbig/bridge/challenge/ indexp.html
- http://www.howstuffworks. com/ bridge.htm

▲ Beam bridges, such as most city road bridges, rely on the strength of the material—usually steel or concrete—to support a beam between the spans, strengthened by a framework underneath.

◀◀ EFFORT AND LOAD see pg25 (b22) ◀◀

1 2 3 4 5 6 7 8 9 10 11 12 13 14 15 16 17 18 19

Cantilever bridges

Cantilever bridges are built of sections, each with two rigid steel beams on either side of a central tower. Each pair of beams balance one another so that each section of the bridge is an independent cantilever, standing without support from the others. The towers support the weight of the beams with a downward force, so there is no need for central supporting columns.

Supporting tower carries weight of link to bank

Read further › beams
pg178 (d2)

▸ *In a bascule or draw bridge, each half-span is supported only at one end. The middle tilts up out of the way.*

Swinging around

If the banks of a river or canal are very low, one way to ensure that boats can pass beneath without colliding with the bridge is to move the actual bridge. Bascule bridges are built to lift up in the middle. Swing bridges are mounted on a central pier and pivot sideways out of the way, turned by powerful hydraulic (fluid-driven) systems.

Read further › boats
pg186 (d2); pg187 (m32)

Read further › pumping water
pg186 (o16); pg187 (b25)

Building bridges

The first step in bridge-building is to build the piers and abutments. To erect piers in the water, a steel wall or shuttering is built on the riverbed. The water is then pumped out while the pier is built, before the walls can be removed, and the spans laid between the piers.

Steel wall (shuttering)

Water

Collar

Space to accept pier or tower

Footings

River bed

IT'S A FACT

• The largest tilting or draw bridge is in Michigan, U.S.A. It has a 335 ft opening.

• The world's longest arch is the 1,804 ft-long Lupu steel arch in Shanghai, China.

Support tower

Main suspension cable

Vertical stay cable

Suspension

For wide or deep channels, a suspension bridge, with a span of up to 3,937 ft, is often used. The deck (such as a roadway) is held up by steel cables spanning between tall towers. These cables are held in concrete blocks at both ends of the bridge. The deck may be supported by a framework to stop it swaying too much in the wind. The weight of the deck is transferred to the vertical cables, over the towers, and to the concrete blocks at either end.

Read further › frameworks
pg178 (d2; k2)

Support pier

Deck

◂◂ LAKE MICHIGAN see pg75 (c36) ◂◂

22 23 24 25 26 27 28 29 30 31 32 33 34 35 36 37 38 39

On the rails

WORK IT OUT

• The world's fastest scheduled service is the Shinkansen bullet train from Hiroshima to Kokura, Japan. It covers the 119 mi distance in just 44 minutes, averaging 162 mph.

• Across the world, there is about 780,000 mi of railroad track.

A SINGLE TRAIN may carry 200,000 tons of iron ore, while passenger trains often have many carriages that can carry thousands of people. Railroads can carry much heavier loads than road vehicles because they use steel wheels, guided by lips or "flanges" that run along the inside of steel rails, which are tough enough to bear tremendous weight. However, not all rail transport runs on the rails—monorails often run underneath the track and maglevs actually float above it. Because they travel at very fast speeds, trains must be safely controlled by switches and signals.

One-track trains

Monorails are railroads with a single rail. The track is made of steel or concrete sections and the carriages either hang beneath the rail or balance on top of it. When the cars run along the top of the rail, they must be stabilized by guide wheels and gyroscopes—devices that rotate—to keep them from falling over. Monorails are over a century old—the first one was built in Wuppertal, Germany in 1901. Both Tokyo and Seattle have monorail systems in operation.

▶▶ Read further > underground tunnels
pg179 (g33)

▸ Monorail tracks can be held above city streets, avoiding the need to dig deep tunnels.

IT'S A FACT

• The longest train ever was a 660-truck goods train 4 mi long that ran from Saldanha to Sishen, South Africa on August 26, 1989.

• The longest passenger train was a 70-coach train 5,682 ft long that ran from Ghent to Ostend, Belgium on April 27, 1991.

Check it out!

• http://travel.howstuffworks.com/maglev-train.htm
• http://www.csrmf.org/

Gyroscope sensors

Stabilizing side wheels

Monorail section

Weight-bearing drive wheels made of rubber for less noise and vibration

◀◀ STEEL see pg19 (e28) ◀◀

a
b
c
d
e
f
g
h
i
j
k
l
m
n
o
p
q
r
s
t
u
v
w

Signalling

Signals warn train crews of hazards on the track. Track controllers use a "block" system to stop a train entering a block of track that already has a train on it. Some routes in Europe and Japan use Advanced Train Protection (ATP), where the cab picks up signals from the track telling the driver at what speed to travel. If the driver fails to respond, the train slows automatically. In the U.S.A. they are developing Advanced Train Control Systems (ACTS) that will rely on satellites and other high-tech links.

▲ Signal lights are usually red for stop or danger, yellow for warning, and green for all clear.

Read further > satellites
pg193 (k22; p26)

Lifting by magnets

When the same poles of two magnets are placed together, they repel (push each other apart). Magnetic levitation (maglev) trains use this magnetic repulsion to lift the train clear of the track. Very powerful electromagnets lift the entire train so that it floats a fraction of an inch above the track. This cuts down on friction so much that maglev trains can reach speeds of more than 298 mph smoothly and almost silently. Plans are underway to build fast maglev lines from Anaheim, California to Las Vegas, Nevada, and from Tokyo to Osaka, Japan, but they are costly to build and still not totally reliable. So, most maglev systems have been short distance, low-speed train systems, such as the one at the Shanghai Airport, China.

Read further > magnets
pg187 (h22)

Track electromagnets

Concrete T-section track

Support pillar

Train electromagnets

▲ Maglev trains operate in many countries such as China, Japan, Germany, and the United States.

Frog to carry train across old track

Old track direction

Switch rail pivots

Guard rail

New track direction

Slider moves switch rails across

◀ Switches are used to automatically change the direction of a railroad train.

Switch rails

Points and junctions

Occasionally, a railroad train must change tracks in order to change direction. As a train cannot steer, the track branches in two at "turnouts." Here, a switch changes the train from one track to another by moving a pair of rails for the new track direction against the old. The two switch rails pivot at one end and are moved sideways by a slider underneath them at the other end. The slider is usually moved by an electromagnet.

Read further > steering wheels
pg185 (v30)

◀◀ MAGNETS see pg21 (b31) ◀◀

On the road

THERE ARE now more than half a billion cars in the world, and on average two new ones are built every second. There is a huge variety of car transport, from "saloon" (or four-door family) cars with separate trunks, to "all-terrain" or "SUV" vehicles that can be driven cross-country, and motorcycles that can reach high speeds. However, all motor vehicles are built in a similar way. They all need brakes, are all driven by an engine or motor, and most need gears to control the "drive" of the engine.

Brake caliper

Brake fluid under pressure in brake pipe pushes on piston

Brake piston

Piston presses two brake pads together

Brake pads press on brake disc to create friction, thus slowing down wheel

● Putting on the brakes

Stopping a fast-moving car demands great force. When the driver presses the brake pedal, brake fluid is forced through narrow pipes to cylinders on each wheel. The pressure of the fluid presses special pads—brake pads—against the brake discs on the wheels, which slow it down by friction. Many cars have ABS (Anti-lock braking systems) whereby a computer applies the brake automatically within a split second to prevent the car's wheels from locking up and the car from skidding, before it stops.

▶▶ Read further › brake pads
pg185 (v26)

▶▶ Read further › gears
pg176 (n2)

● Geared up

Most cars need gears between the engine and the wheels because engines only work right when running faster within a narrow range of speed. Gears change the drive—the link between engine and wheels—so the wheels turn at different speeds for the same engine speed. Slowing the drive increases the engine's force, so that a small, fast-running engine can power a heavy car. When accelerating or climbing hills, the driver uses the low gears for extra force. In cars with automatic transmission, the right gear is automatically picked.

● WORK IT OUT

• The world's longest car was a limousine built for American, Jay Ohrberg. Over 98 ft long, it had 26 wheels—and a swimming pool with a diving board!

• In 1997, the British jet-powered *Thrust SSC* car broke the sound barrier, traveling across the Nevada desert at over 756 mph.

▲ *Simple cogs reverse the direction of rotation.*

▲ *Rack and pinion change the rotation to a sliding motion.*

▲ *Bevels move the direction of rotation through a right angle.*

▲ *Worm gears bring the rotation down to a slower, stronger rotation at right angles.*

▶▶ WHEEL see pg201 (t22) ▶▶

1 2 3 4 5 6 7 8 9 10 11 12 13 14 15 16 17 18 19

a
b
c
d
e
f
g
h
i
j
k
l
m
n
o
p
q
r
s
t
u
v
w

● Leaning into it

To go round corners, motorbikes' front wheels turn like a car's do. Motorcyclists lean with the cycle on to the slanting edges of its tires. If a motorcyclist tried to turn a corner with the bike in an upright position the force called momentum, which makes the bike carry on in a straight line, would tip it over onto the outside of the curve. So the rider leans the motorbike when turning the corner to counteract the outward force pushing against the bike.

◀ *The faster the bike corners, the greater the outward forces become and the more the biker has to lean over to counter them.*

▶▶ **Read further > wheels**
pg176 (s8)

● Petrol power

Petrol engines burn a mixture of fue, (gas) and air inside the cylinders in the engine. The mixture expands when it is ignited by an electric spark, from the spark plug. This forces a piston down the cylinder to push the crankshaft round to turn the car's wheels through the gearbox. Four cylinders (two- or three-cylinder engines exist) give these power strokes, each at a different time.

▶ *Four-stroke cycle: commonly known as "suck, squeeze, bang, and blow."*

▶▶ **Read further > cylinders / gears**
pg184 (k2; p8)

Valves

Cylinder

Piston

Crankshaft

▲ *Induction stroke—inlet valve opens and the descending piston sucks in the fuel and air mixture.*

▲ *Compression stroke— inlet valve closes and the rising piston squeezes the fuel.*

Spark plug

▲ *Power stroke— spark ignites fuel and expanding gases push down the piston.*

▲ *Exhaust stroke—the exhaust valve opens and the rising piston pushes or blows out the burned gases.*

Gears in the gearbox change the speed engine turns the wheels to suit different conditions

Engine burns fuel to provide power

Car transmission takes power from engine to wheels via the gearbox

Cooling system circulates water to stop engine overheating

Electrical system powers lights and instruments, such as temperature gauge and fuel gauge, on the instrument panel

Ignition system gives an electrical spark to ignite the fuel

Exhaust at back of car carries away waste gases from engine

Suspension softens bumps in road for passengers and keeps wheels in contact with road

Steering gear controls direction by turning front wheels

Wheels are attached to brakes, which slow them down

🌐 Check it out!

- http://www.auto.howstuff works.com/engine.htm
- http://www.innerauto.com/ main.html
- http://auto.howstuffworks.com/ brake.htm

◀◀ MOMENTUM see pg24 (l2) ◀◀

22   23   24   25   26   27   28   29   30   31   32   33   34   35   36   37   38   39

On the water

LIGHT MATERIALS like wood and cork float because they are not as dense (heavy) as water. Ships can be built from heavy materials such as steel, yet still float. This is because the air inside the hull, or body, of the ship makes the ship lighter than the water it displaces. Water travel relies on many methods to move through water. Sailing ships use the power of the wind to travel along. Hydrofoils use "wings" to travel on top of the water. Submersibles and submarines actually let in water to sink, before traveling underwater.

Metal blades or screws slice through water, propelling boat forward

Rudder steers boat left or right

Thrust and drag

Most ships are driven under the water by a screw propeller with slowly turning blades to thrust the ship forward. This system is powerful, but the resistance of the water (drag) slows down the boat. Small speedboats use high-speed jets of water to push themselves along faster.

▶▶ **Read further › propeller blades**
pg188 (j12)

IT'S A FACT

• The heaviest ship ever built is the oil tanker, *SeaWise Giant*, launched in 1976, weighing over 585,015 tons when laden.

• The world water speed record is 318 mph set by Kenneth Warby's *Spirit of Australia* on 8 October 1978, using a "hydroplane" designed to skim across the surface of the water.

How ships float

When launched, a ship pushes water away, but the water pushes back, causing "upthrust." The more water is pushed out of the way, the harder it pushes back. The hull of the ship is hollow, making the density—weight—less than water, so the ship keeps sinking until its weight is matched by the push of the water, then it can float.

Check it out!

• http://www.science.net.org.uk/database/Physics/Original/p00203d.html
• http://oceanexplorer.noaa.gov/technology/subs/subs.html

◀◀ MATERIALS see pg16 (d2) ◀◀

▼ *The first range of submersibles appeared in the 1960s and 1970s. Today's craft are much smaller and more advanced, but still work in the same way.*

Underwater explorer

Submersibles are mostly used for research into the depths of the ocean and undersea wrecks. Remote Operated Vehicles (ROVs) are small robot submersibles, controlled by operators using cameras and virtual reality systems *(see pg190 [o12])*. Submersibles alter their buoyancy—ability to float—to work.

Read further > magnets / virtual reality
pg183 (b30); pg190 (m2)

Propeller for pushing craft through water

Cabin of strong steel to resist intense water pressure

Double hatch containing airlock for divers to exit and re-enter

Powerful electric motor

Searchlights for seeing dark ocean depths

To return to the surface, pilot switches off electromagnets that hold ballast of iron balls in place

Claw for grabbing samples during missions

Float filled with petrol. Since petrol is lighter than water, it helps keep craft afloat

Batteries

Extra-strong Plexiglass dome

Small propellers called thrusters maneuver craft precisely up, down and sideways

◄ *Hovercrafts or "air-cushion" vehicles use a huge fan to blow air downward and lift the craft above the water.*

Read further > wings
pg188 (p2)

Flying on water

The drag of the water slows a boat down. "Hydrofoils" solve this problem with special wings, or foils, attached to the hull by struts. The foils move underwater, working like plane wings to lift the boat. Because only the foils dip in the water, hydrofoils can travel very fast, often at speeds of more than 56 mph.

Surface-piercing hydrofoil   *Fully submerged hydrofoil*

Sail power

Sailing ships rely on wind power to drive them along and can sail in almost any direction except directly into the wind— because the wind does not push the sails but sucks them. As the wind blows over the curve of the sail, it speeds up and its pressure drops, creating suction in the same way that an airplane's wings create lift *(see pg188 [n7])*. However, the sail must be kept at exactly the right angle. Sailors let the sail swing round (comes about) until the angle is right then hold it taut (tight) with ropes.

Read further > air pressure
pg188 (p2); pg189 (b31)

◄◄ UNDERWATER EXPLORATION see pg76 (r14) ◄◄

In the air

AIRPLANES ARE the fastest way to travel, making journeys in just a few hours that would otherwise take days by road or sea. Most modern airplanes are powered by jet engines that can propel some military craft at speeds of more than 1,864 mph—three times the speed of sound. Helicopters rely on their rotor blades to hover in the air. Not all air transport needs an engine—hot-air balloons use hot air and gas to stay aloft.

Swashplate controls angle of blades

Jet turbine engine

Rotor blade

To fly up or down, pilot alters angle or "pitch" of main rotor blades with "collective pitch" control. When blades cut through the air almost flat, they give no lift and helicopter sinks. To climb, pilot steepens pitch to increase lift

To fly forward or backward, pilot uses "cyclic pitch" control to vary rotor pitch as blades go around from one side to the other

▲ *The Sikorsky UH-60 Blackhawk can carry its two crew members and up to 12 soldiers.*

Taking to the skies

Helicopters are able to take off vertically or hover in the air for a long time. They owe this versatile flying ability to big rotor blades, which are like long, thin wings that whirl around at high speed, slicing through the air and providing lift. The blades also act like huge propellors (see pg186 [i13]), hauling the helicopter upward or backward.

►► **Read further › propellors** pg186 (i13)

On the wing

An aircraft's wings are lifted by the air flowing above and beneath them as they slice through it. Because the top of the wing is curved, air pushed over the top is forced to speed up and stretch out, reducing its pressure and pulling from above. The curved shape is called an aerofoil. Under the wing, the air slows down and bunches up, and pressure here rises, pushing the wing up. How much "lift" this creates depends on the angle and shape of the wing, and how fast it moves through the air.

Lift *Drag* *Thrust* *Weight* *Rib* *Spar* *Flap* *Trailing edge* *Aileron* *Tip* *Leading edge*

▲ *Thrust and lift are the main forces that let aircraft to fly.*

IT'S A FACT

• A jumbo jet, sucks in one ton of air per second.

• In December, 1986, the American experimental plane, *Voyager*, flew round the world without landing once.

Check it out!
• http://travel.howstuffworks.com/airplane.htm
• http://travel.howstuffworks.com/airplane3.htm

►► **Read further › lifting** pg183 (b30); pg187 (p23)

◄◄ ANIMAL FLIGHT see pg128 (f2) ◄◄

1 2 3 4 5 6 7 8 9 10 11 12 13 14 15 16 17 18 19

FASTEST JETS

Jet, year flown	Speed
SR-71A Blackbird, 1976	2,193 mph
Mikoyan E-66, 1959	1,483 mph
F-100 Super Sabre, 1955	822 mph
F-86 Sabre, 1948	671 mph
Gloster Meteor, 1946	615 mph

Tail rotor drive shaft

Read further > thrust pg20 (p2)

How jets work

The simplest jets, called turbojets, work by pushing a jet of hot air out the back to thrust the plane forward. Engines like these were used on the supersonic (faster than sound) airliner, Concorde, and some very fast military jets (see pg189 [r28]). Most airliners use quieter, cheaper, turbofans that combine the hot-air jet with the draft from a whirling, multi-bladed fan to give extra thrust at low speeds.

Hot-air balloon

Hot-air balloons get their lift by filling a huge bag made of very light material with hot air from a gas burner. Because hot air is lighter and less dense than cooler air, the bag simply floats up, carrying the basket and passengers with it. As the air cools, the balloon begins to sink. To maintain height, the balloonist relights the burner to warm the air in the bag again.

▲ To descend quickly, the balloonist pulls a cord to let warm air escape through a vent in the top of the balloon.

Read further > air pressure pg187 (m32)

Main shaft — Gases roar past exhaust turbines — "Bypass" air from main fan flows around engine core — Hot gases rush out of engine

Main fan sucks air in

Air is squashed by compressor turbines — Jet fuel is sprayed on to air, and continuous explosion happens — Afterburner burns leftover fuel in exhaust gases

▲ In a typical turbojet, exhaust gases roar out of the back of the engine at more than 994 mph.

Fin (tail)

Rudder turns plane left or right

Jet exhaust

Whole tailplane tilts as elevator to angle plane up or down

Single jet engine within fuselage (main body of plane)

Fuel tanks in wing

Air intake for jet engine

Cockpit

Radar in nose cone to detect other aircraft in the air

▲ The jet-powered American F-16 Fighting Falcon is used by more than 14 countries worldwide.

Soaring forward

Today, nearly all military planes are powered by jet engines. The huge thrust of jet engines means wings can be smaller than on propellor-driven planes. They are swept back to let the planes fly fast with minimum air resistance. The plane's path is directed by control surfaces—movable panels on the wings, tailplane, and fin.

Read further > air-resistance pg187 (m32)

◄◄ DENSITY OF AIR see pg11 (q31) ◄◄

Electronic brains

COMPUTERS HAVE entered our lives both at home and at work and can be used for anything from helping with homework to landing a spacecraft. Over the years, there has been a vast increase in the amount of data computers can store—and the speed with which they work. The advances in the computer world have even led to virtual reality—a way of creating artificial situations—being used for entertainment or business purposes.

► Read further > undersea wrecks / data
pg187 (b29); pg191 (b22)

● WORK IT OUT

• In May 1997, IBM's Deep Blue computer beat the reigning World Chess Champion, Garry Kasparov.

• A "byte" consists of eight on/off instructions or bits in a computer: 1024 bytes make 1 kilobyte (KB); 1024 kilobytes make 1 megabyte (MB); 1024 megabytes make 1 gigabyte (GB); 1 trillion bytes make 1 terabyte (TB).

Special eyepieces show slightly different views of an image to each eye to create illusion of real space

Sound effects are played in stereo through earphones, enhancing experience to make it seem even more realistic

● Is that for real?

Computers can sometimes fool our senses into thinking something is real using virtual reality (VR) systems. VR sends data (information) to our senses that closely mimic reality. A computer or robotic vehicle *(see pg187 [b29])* is sent to explore a situation, like an undersea shipwreck, or is programmed to recreate a fictional situation, such as a tennis match. We can see what the computer sees by wearing a special headset.

● IT'S A FACT

• The world's most powerful computer is the Earth Simulator, built at Kanazawa, Japan to help predict earthquakes.

• IBM are planning to build the world's biggest computer, called Blue Gene, to research proteins.

● Check it out!

• http://www.computer.howstuffworks.com/computer-memory.htm
• http://computer.howstuffworks.com/bytes.htm

▲ A number of pressure and flex (bending) sensors in the glove pick up wrist, hand, and finger movements then send these along the cable to the computer. The computer analyses these movements to determine if the player had moved in the correct way to hit the "virtual" ball, which can only be seen through the eyepieces.

►► LANDING SPACECRAFT see pg213 (c33) ►►

1   2   3   4   5   6   7   8   9   10   11   12   13   14   15   16   17   18   19

Hardware and software

The actual material from which computers are made is called hardware. Equipment such as the keyboard, screen, mouse, printer, scanner, and CD-writer are called peripherals—they sit outside the casing. The instructions or program that make the computer work is called the software. Software packages range from simple text and scanning images to the more challenging creation of graphics and special effects.

Read further › storing data
pg197 (m30)

10100100101010
10001010010101
01010101001010
101
010010010
010101001010010

Zeros and ones

Since electronic circuits can only be switched on or off, computers store and handle data using a "binary" system. This system turns all data into a code of 0s and 1s, or offs and ons. For example, the number five is 0101 in binary code, or off-on-off-on. Each 0 or 1 is called a binary digit or "bit," and they are grouped together in "bytes." Electronic circuits store and process data in this way.

Read further › electrical signals
pg192 (l2); pg193 (b22)

Plastic casing protects components

Chip

◄ *The main part of a computer is the central processing unit, containing a microchip that is no bigger than a fingernail.*

Wire "feet" are connections that attach to other parts in computer

Microchips on circuit board

Main computer casing, to protect all components inside

"Read-only memory" (ROM) is computer's basic working instructions installed in computer at factory

Flat screen monitor

Digital camera or Webcam to record images and send messages or photos over Internet

Inside central processing unit (CPU) is a powerful microchip—a tiny block of complex electronic circuits—that is "brain" of computer and carries out main jobs

Random-access memory (RAM) temporarily stores data as it is being used

Data can be stored as laser guided pits on a CD or DVD that can be inserted into computer in CD or DVD drive (Reader)

Roller sensors

Floppy disk drive where magnetic discs holding data can be inserted

Keyboard to type on or control computer functions

Moving mouse rolls the ball that turns sensors so on-screen cursor moves

►► **INVENTION OF COMPUTERS** see pg207 (h22) ►►

Instant contact

TELECOMMUNICATIONS MAKE it possible to see and talk to people almost anywhere in the world. Some communications, such as phone calls, faxes, or e-mail can be one-to-one. Radio and television (*see pg195 [f33]*) programs are broadcast to millions of people. Cable TV and web-casting (Internet broadcasting) combine both elements. Yet all these forms of communication work in much the same way.

Phones on the move

Mobile or cell phones use low-power radio waves to send messages. Areas across the world are divided into many small sectors called cells, each with an antenna (*see pg193 [s24]*) that picks up signals from phones and sends them out. Because there are so many antennae spread across the world, millions of people can use mobile phones at one time.

Small loudspeaker in earpiece

Mode or function keys

Small microphone in mouthpiece

Number keys

Land lines

Telephones convert sound into an electrical signal. When you speak into a phone, the vibrations of your voice move a tiny microphone that alters the strength of an electrical current. This creates an electrical signal, which is sent to the receiving phone. In the receiver, the changing signal operates a loudspeaker, which vibrates the air and recreates the sound of your voice. Today, many signals are sent as pulses of laser light along special glassy fibers called optical fibers. Signals are also sent as radio waves or microwaves through the air—bouncing off satellites (*see pg192 [p18]*) in space.

Read further > signals
pg183 [b22]

Many communications, such as mobile phone calls and e-mails, are sent on or relayed by satellites in space

Signals from individual transmitters are sent on from a telephone exchange or a service provider

Computer data is translated by a modem into signals that can be carried along phone lines

Read further > electromagnet
pg183 [b30]

TV and radio signals are either broadcast as pulses of radio waves, sent direct via cables or broadcast from satellites

▶▶ COMMUNICATION INVENTIONS see pg208 (n22) ▶▶

1   2   3   4   5   6   7   8   9   10   11   12   13   14   15   16   17   18   19

Instant letter

Fax is short for "facsimile," which means "copy." A fax machine scans a document under a light past a line of sensors. The white parts of the document reflect light so switch on the sensors; the dark parts do not reflect light so switch off the sensors. Thus, a pattern of ons and offs is created and sent to the receiving fax. The receiving fax machine uses heat sensors that pick up the pattern of electrical signals coming through and creates the same pattern on the heat-sensitive paper. More modern machines print on plain paper, using charges of static electricity to attract the toner powder to the paper.

Telephone

Dial pad for typing in fax number

Phone socket that enables fax to connect to a phone line and send and receive messages

Image received is printed on paper from internal roll

Image to be sent is fed through a scanner

Drive rollers, to run document under scanner

Scanner sensors

▶▶ **Read further › on / off patterns**
pg191 (b32)

Bouncing signals

Any telecommunications message needs a transmitter such as a phone; a communications link such as an antenna or satellite; and a receiver or destination, like an e-mail address or receiving telephone number. The message can travel through electrical or optical (fiberoptic) cables, as microwaves or as radio waves, to arrive at its destination.

▶▶ **Read further › telephones**
pg192 (k2)

WORK IT OUT

• A third of the 45 million mobile phones in use in the U.K. are thrown away or lost each year. If you stacked them one on top of the other, the pile of lost mobile phones would be 250 times higher than Mount Everest!

• Most of the 5,000 satellites orbiting the Earth in space are used for telecommunications. Communications satellites use a special orbit, called a geo-stationary orbit, which keeps them in the same place above the Earth constantly.

Electronic letters

A fast and convenient form of communication today is electronic mail or e-mail. The message is typed on a computer or even on some mobile phones and is sent to another e-mail address along a phone line, via a modem, to the central computer of the ISP (Internet Service Provider). The message is stored here until the recipient connects or "logs in" to a computer to receive it.

▶▶ **Read further › computers**
pg191 (b22)

Communications travel via satellites and are beamed up and down from antenna dishes on ground

Telephones link into phone network by a direct cable link. Mobile phones link through the air to local relay towers by radio waves

 Check it out!

• http://computer.howstuffworks.com/e-mail.htm
• http://electronics.howstuffworks.com/cordless-telephone9.htm

▶▶ INTERNET see pg209 (l30) ▶▶

Super vision

MICROSCOPES THAT magnify objects too tiny for our eyes to see and telescopes that magnify things that are far away have been in use since the 1600s. Photography has been recording accurate pictures for more than 160 years. Today, microscopes can show fantastic pictures of minute micro-organisms, or even atoms, and telescopes can reveal the most distant galaxies in the universe. Cameras take higher quality photographs than ever. Digital technology makes it possible for pictures to be scanned into a computer and to be enhanced and even sent across the world instantly via e-mail.

IT'S A FACT

• The world's largest optical telescope is the four-part VLT (Very Large Telescope) on Cerro Paranal, Chile.

• Many ground-based astronomic telescopes use computers to alter how we see the twinkling of stars caused by Earth's atmosphere.

Eyepiece lens

Pentaprism turns image right way round for eyepiece

Zoom ring

Objective lenses gather light rays of scene together and make them converge so that image is smaller

Aperture (hole for incoming light)

Mirror reflects light up to pentaprism

Light from scene

Lenses

Focus ring

▲ Single-lens reflex (SLR) cameras, and simpler compact cameras, use a different technology than more recent digital cameras, which record images electronically on a microchip.

Snap happy

The lens inside a camera is a disk of glass or plastic, especially shaped to focus (bring together) all the light from the scene and create a tiny image (picture) inside the camera. In most cameras, the image is recorded on film coated in chemicals that react to the light that comes in through a hole (aperture). The mirror reflects the light up to a prism and then to the eyepiece so the photographer can see the image. To take the picture, the mirror swings out of the way so that light falls on to the photographic film behind it for a split second.

WORK IT OUT

• A microscope's magnification is limited by the smallest wavelength of light, which is about 4000 angstroms (a millionth of a centimeter). The wavelength of electrons used in electron microscopes is just 0.5 angstroms.

• Individual atoms can be seen with the scanning tunnelling microscope (STM), which scans the surface of materials by tunneling an electric charge into them.

▶▶ Read further › pixels
pg196 (q2)

Farsighted

Telescopes help you see distant things better by focusing (concentrating) the light onto a small area, then magnifying the focused image so it can be seen. In "refracting" telescopes, a large lens focuses the image by bending, or refracting, the rays; then a smaller lens, called the eyepiece, magnifies it. In "reflecting" or mirror telescopes, the image is focused by a large, plate-shaped, mirror onto a smaller mirror then through the eyepiece. Astronomers now use amazingly powerful telescopes to see galaxies billions of light-years away. The image of these galaxies is picked up by light-sensitive pixels and fed into a computer, where it can be electronically enhanced.

Read further › computers
pg190 (b22)

◄ Telescopes allow astronomers to see stars not visible to the naked eye.

▼ Reflecting telescopes have a curved main mirror.

Incoming light

Secondary mirror

Eyepiece lens

Flat mirror

Incoming light

Focused light

Reflected light

Objective (front) lens

Main mirror

Eyepiece lens

◄ Refracting telescopes use only lenses, not mirrors.

Seeing microbes

Powerful "electron" microscopes operate in a different way than optical microscopes. Instead of using lenses to magnify light, they fire streams of particles—electrons—at the specimen (the object being studied) and show the result on a monitor. In a transmission electron microscope (TEM), the specimen is so thinly sliced—usually less than one-thousandth of a inch—that electrons can pass through to cast a shadow, which is picked up by detectors under the image. Chemicals are added to partly block the electron beam and make the shadows stand out more. TEMs can magnify things up to one million times.

▶ A scanning electron microscope (SEM) scans across the surface of the bug to get a very detailed, almost three-dimensional surface view.

Read further › television
pg197 (b22)

Check it out!
- http://www.rmcain.com/mcama/adv/advidxkids.mv
- http://electronics.howstuffworks.com/digital-camera.htm

Round lenses

Glass lenses are shaped to bend light rays in a particular way. Sometimes they are made plate-shaped or "concave"—thin in the middle and thick around the rim. Light rays passing through a concave lens are bent outward, spreading. This means when you see something through a concave lens it looks smaller than it really is. Other lenses bulge outward or are "convex"—fat in the middle and thin at the rim. Light rays passing through a convex lens bend inward, coming together or converging. Objects look bigger when viewed through a convex lens. The point where the converging light rays meet is called the focus.

Image is smaller

Object

Concave lens corrects long-sighted vision

Light rays

Image is larger

Object

Convex lens corrects short-sighted vision

Read further › light
pg194 (o2)

◄◄ LIGHT RAYS see pg31 (b22) ◄◄

Sound and vision

TELEVISION BRINGS pictures and sound from all around the world right into our homes, letting us watch events, such as top sports, as they happen live, across the world. Not only can we watch these events on television, but we can also record events of our own, using personal camcorders. These recordings can be saved on video tape or disk to play back later. Other recordings, such as music or movies can be stored on CD or DVD and played back many times.

▼ A camcorder records images on a small reel of magnetic tape (videotape) or in microchip memory circuits.

Eye piece

Objective lenses

Eyepiece display screen

CCD (charge-coupled device) has an array of pixels that detect light

Electric motors and gears to move lenses for focusing (making the image sharp and clear) and zoom (bigger or smaller)

Camcorders

Digital camcorders have a lens to project a picture that can be recorded using a tiny patch of light-sensitive cells, or pixels. Where the light in the picture is bright, the cell sends out a brief electrical pulse; where it is dark, the cell stays off. As the picture changes, this creates a pattern of electrical pulses. This pattern can then be stored in the camera's memory for playback, or be sent instantly to the camcorder's viewer or a TV screen to be watched as it is being viewed or recorded.

Control buttons

Monitor screen showing what is being viewed or recorded

▶▶ Read further > animated film
pg199 (b25; k27)

▶▶ INVENTION OF DVD see pg212 (t16) ▶▶

On the tube

Older televisions have a slightly curved screen, which is the front end of a device called the tube—like a giant light bulb. Inside the back of the tube are "guns" that create the picture by firing nonstop streams of electrically charged particles, called electrons, at the back of the screen. Where they hit the screen, they make it glow by heating up its coating of phosphor dots. When we look at the screen, we see thousands of these glowing spots of phosphor in the form of a picture. The broadcast, or recorded signal, controls where the beams target the screen, making it glow, and creating the picture.

One electron gun for each color on screen

Antenna to pick up TV signal as radio waves in the air

Red gun

Blue gun

Green gun

Magnetic scan and focus rings to direct beams

Decoder changes signal into right form to control electron guns

Television tube

Screen showing image

Loudspeaker to transmit sound

Screen is coated on inside with millions of tiny phosphor dots

Three electron beams scan to and fro across screen, each hitting only its own color of phosphor dots

Read further > electrical particles
pg195 (k22)

DVDs

Digital Versatile Discs (DVDs), are an efficient way of storing all kinds of data, including music, movies, and video games. Made from plastic, coated with acrylic and sprayed with aluminum, DVDs store data as a spiral track of tiny pits pressed into the otherwise flat (land) surface. When the DVD is played, a laser beam "reads" these pits by scanning the underside of the disc. As light hits land it is read as a binary 1. Light that hits a bump is read as a binary 0.

▼ *DVDs and CDs work in the same way but a CD holds about one-seventh of the information of a DVD.*

Slider carries laser unit across DVD

Laser beam focused by prism

Laser

Beam bounces off DVD

Reflected beam detected by sensor

Laser beam bent by prism

Spinning disc

Spin motor and disc gears

►► INVENTION OF TELEVISION see pg206 (g15) ►►

22 23 24 25 26 27 28 29 30 31 32 33 34 35 36 37 38 39

a b c d e f g h i j k l m n o p q r s t u v w

Mass media

▲ *Animatronic models like dinosaurs are usually filmed against a blue screen, while a background such as a wood is filmed separately. The blue screen is later replaced by the final background.*

DIFFERENT KINDS of media are used for communicating with large numbers of people, whether for entertainment, information, or advertising. Newspapers, books, magazines, movies, cartoons, and the Internet are just some of the many media available to the public. The printing press has made it possible for written media to reach more people, faster than than before. Computers now combine different media to create "multimedia." This combination can be used to create video games, CD-Roms, interactive TV, and computer-animated movies that are more realistic and ambitious than ever before.

● IT'S A FACT

• The light sabres in the *Star Wars* movies are filmed using aluminum dummies, which are then replaced by light on a computer, frame by frame.

• Repeat print-runs of books can be made by simply inserting electronic "smart cards" into the printing machine's computer.

● Straight off the press

Computer technology has revolutionized printing. In the past, pages were printed by spreading ink over metal type (words and letters), which had to be made from scratch using hot metal, and even assembled painstakingly from a stock of letters. Now, an exact picture of all the text and illustrations can be created on a computer screen. This computer picture is then used either to make a film that can set up the printing photographically, or directly control lasers, or jets of ink, as they are printed on the page.

▶▶ **Read further › photography** pg194 [o2]

▼ *The full-color lithoprinter makes colored images out of four colors of ink—cyan (C), magenta (M), yellow (Y), and black (K)—as tiny dots on the page. Four-color or CMYK, printing is used to produce most magazines, books, and newspapers. The fifth press contains a special mix of color or "text black" for printing words.*

Reel of paper can be changed while printing press is still running so no time is lost during printing

Inking rollers make sure ink is spread evenly on paper. Surfaces of roller can be made from rubber or metal

"Paper web" is a very long, continuous, piece of paper that runs through press to be cut into separate sections at end of the press

Transfer roller holds paper tightly in place to ensure everything is printed in the right place and that paper does not move between printing presses

Image to be printed comes from a plate that is placed in press and transferred to rubber blanket roller, which rolls image over paper evenly

Dryer's heated plates dry ink so that it does not smudge when paper is folded

▶▶ PRINTING PRESS see pg208 (k10) ▶▶

1 2 3 4 5 6 7 8 9 10 11 12 13 14 15 16 17 18 19

Bringing dinosaurs to life

Dinosaurs died out 65 million years ago, but amazingly lifelike recreations in movies, on TV and in museums show us what they were really like. These are called "animatronics" and are basically mechanical puppets. From walking to breathing, each movement is created by electric motors and hydraulics, controlled remotely by a team of operators. The initial designs are hand-drawn and then reproduced by computers, which in turn guide the machine to make a mold. This mold is used to make a body shell from stiffened foam rubber.

Read further > hydraulics
pg181 (f32)

Read further > printing
pg198 (k2)

A world in three colors

Almost every color can be printed by combining just three "primary" colors of ink. Three "separations"—versions of the picture in terms of its red, green, and blue content—are created. Layers of yellow, magenta, and cyan inks then soak up the right amounts of blue, green, or red from the light falling on the page.

▸ *Primary colors combine to make white.*

Read further > camcorders
pg196 (q2)

Living pictures

Animation means creating the illusion of movement by showing a sequence of subtly-changing still pictures. In the past, pictures were drawn painstakingly by hand, which could take a long time. The use of computer-generated animations has sped up the process and made a startling amount of realism by scanning real movements into the camera to act as a base for the animation. Since the computer can store a complete three-dimensional image of all the characters and the way they move, the animator has only to drag the character into position on screen to make a new frame (scene).

▲ *The model of a character, such as a monster, is photographed in one pose. A computer scans the photograph and plots the positions of each tiny part of the model's surface into its memory.*

◂ *The model is moved into another position and photographed again. The computer scans this new image, compares it with the first, and "fills in" the missing images so that they differ only slightly from each other.*

Folding unit folds paper so it can be taken off press and packaged right away

Folded pages are cut to right size and stapled or stitched to hold batches together for easy transportation to retailers

WORK IT OUT

• For the *Jurassic Park III* movie, a life-sized animatronic of Spinosaurus—one of the largest meat-eating dinosaurs ever—was made measuring 44 ft long and weighing more than 12 tons.

• The first movie to be made entirely using computer-generated animation was *Disney's Toy Story* in 1995.

Check it out!

• http://actionadventure.about. com/cs/animation
• http://entertainment.howstuff works.com/newspaper.htm
• http://entertainment.howstuff works.com/animatronics.htm

a b c d e f g h i j k l m n o p q r s t u v w

Early inventions

PEOPLE HAVE been inventing things to make their lives easier and more comfortable for about 2.5 million years. Writing was not invented until about 5,000 years ago, so the origins of the earliest inventions were not written down. We only know about them from archeological discoveries. The first inventions were stone tools and weapons made by early hunters and gatherers. Later, people carved needles from bones to sew clothes for warmth. When they began to settle in one place around 10,000 years ago, they invented wheels, plows, and irrigation devices to water their crops. They made jars and pots for storing food, and better weapons to defend their settlements. However, labor saving devices were not developed, possibly because the work was often carried out by slaves.

Digging made easy

The earliest known picture of a plow dates from about 5,500 years ago in the ancient city of Ur (in present-day Iraq). The first plough was wooden, developed from simple digging sticks used to make holes for planting seeds. Its wedge-shaped blade made long furrows in the soil as it moved forward. After the discovery of iron about 2,500 years ago, farmers used iron blades on their plows, which made them stronger than wooden blades and cut deeper into the soil. The first all-iron plough was invented in 1785 by Robert Ransome in Britain.

c.1800

Pile (battery)
Italy

c.1790

Hot air balloon
France

Watch
Italy

c.1450

◄ Farmers used horses to pull the heavy plows while they walked behind, steering the blade through the soil.

►► Read further > seed drills / harvesting
pg202 (o2; r10)

Reading the past

We know about ancient civilizations, such as those of the Sumerians (who lived in part of modern Iraq) and the Egyptians because of the picture writing they left behind. About 5,250 years ago the Sumerians were the first people to write down their language, using pictures to represent words. They developed this into wedge-shaped signs on clay tablets called cuneiform writing (cuneiform means wedge-shaped). The Egyptians developed a form of picture writing known as hieroglyphics (see pg208 [t6]).

▶▶ **Read further › picture writing**
pg208 [m2]

▶ *The cuneiform writing on clay tablets, dating from the 6th century BC, was translated in the 19th century by Henry Rawlinson.*

3000 BC ▲

Abacus Middle East

Glassware Egypt

Spectacles Italy

▼ *2000 BC* ▼

AD 1290 ▲

▲ *The wheel was first invented over 5,000 years ago. Early wheels were made from wooden planks. Around 2000 BC spoked wheels, used on chariots and carts, were invented.*

Lifting water

Archimedes (c.287–212 BC), an ancient Greek mathematician and inventor from Sicily (then ruled by Greece), invented the water-screw. This is a mechanical device used for raising water from a lower to a higher level. Known as the Archimedean screw, it is still used to irrigate fields in the Middle East. The same principle is used in the grain loader of a combine harvester.

▶ *A large screw is set at an angle in a tube that is open at both ends. When the screw is turned water fills the air pockets between the twists and gradually travels upward until it pours out of the top.*

▶▶ **Read further › combine harvesters**
pg202 [r10]

INVENTIVE

• By about 1450 BC, the Egyptians were making glass bottles, shaping the glass by blowing it into molds. Glassblowing (using air to shape very hot glass) was probably invented in Syria about 10 BC.

• To build the city of Jericho in Jordan about 8,000 years ago, bricks were made from clay baked in the sun. About 5,500 years ago, bricks were fired in a kiln to make them harder and waterproof.

🌐 **Check it out!**

• http://www.enchantedlearning.com/inventors

• http://inventors.about.com/cs/famous/inventions

a b c d e f g h i j k l m n o p q r s t u v w

Food and farming

PEOPLE HAVE been inventing ways of growing, cooking, and preserving food for centuries. But, after the invention of plows *(see pg200 [t9])*, there was little advance in farm machinery until the 18th century in Britain—a period known as the Industrial Revolution—when new machinery began to develop rapidly, leading to inventions like the combine harvester. Food and drink, such as sugar and tea, have been available for centuries. More recent inventions, like burgers, chips, and bubble gum, date from the 19th century.

IT'S A FACT

• Coca-Cola was first created by Dr. John S. Pemberton in 1886. He mixed syrup with soda water, to make it fizzy, in a brass kettle.

• The latest combine harvesters have soundproofed cabs and even air-conditioning.

Seed stored in hopper

◀ *Jethro Tull's seed drill made harvesting easier because the seeds were sown in rows.*

Seeds fall down tubes into holes in the soil

Drill digs holes

Sowing seeds

Three thousand years ago, people living in Babylonia (present day Iraq) used a simple device for planting seeds, which dropped them down a tube on top of a plow. In 1660, Taddeo Calvani invented the first seed drill, which was a container with holes in the bottom and mounted on a cart. The vibrations of the cartwheels shook the seeds out through the holes. In 1701, English farmer Jethro Tull invented a much more efficient version whereby seeds dropped down tubes and into furrows in the soil, sown in regular rows. This made it much more likely that seeds would take root, because they had plenty of room in the soil to grow.

▶▶ **Read further > plows**
pg200 (j8)

Harvesting

A combine harvester combines both stages of harvesting: cutting the crop and separating the grain. The first combine harvester (pulled by horses) was designed in 1836 by two Americans, Hiram Moore and John Hascall.

▶▶ **Read further > harvesting**
pg201 (k28)

▼ *The first motorized combine harvesters, produced in 1961, increased the speed at which crops are harvested.*

From pots to burgers

In 1904 Fletcher Davis invented the hamburger. He was a potter who became involved in the burger business by cooking at pottery shows. He also ran a small café in east Texas. His burgers were the classic burger made from ground beef, served on toasted bread with lettuce, tomato, and onion mustard and mayonnaise.

▸ *The word "cheeseburger" was registerd as a trademark in 1944 by Louis Ballast, after he grilled a slice of cheese on top of a burger at his Colorado drive-in.*

Read further > wheels
pg201 (u22)

Shopping on wheels

Sylvan Goldman of Oklahoma, invented the shopping cart in 1936 as a psychological persuasion to buy more in his grocery store. He had noticed that people stopped shopping when their hand-held baskets were full. Goldman's first design, based on a folding chair with wheels on the legs, one basket on the seat and another just above the wheels, was a simple, but very effective idea. Goldman's invention came at the right time because supermarkets were starting to spring up in U.S.A. His invention made him a millionaire.

INVENTIVE

• The popsicle was invented by 11-year-old American boy, Frank Epperson, in 1905 after he left a fruit drink out overnight with a stirrer in it and the drink froze. The popsicle was originally called the Epsicle, after its inventor.

• Inventors are trying to grow square tomatoes, which would be much easier to stack in boxes for shipping.

Double bubble

Bubble gum is extra-strong gum that can be blown into bubbles. First invented in 1906 by an American, Frank Henry Fleer, it was called Blibber-Blubber. It was too sticky—when it popped it was very difficult to peel off the face—and therefore unsuccessful. In 1928, Walter E. Deimer invented a better mixture for bubble gum, which he called "Dubble Bubble."

◂ *Bubble gum is made in all kinds of shapes, colors, and sizes, from simple, round spheres to novelty shapes, like cigars.*

◂ *Farmers across the world look for ways to increase their produce: GM is one way they can do this.*

Genetically modified

One of the most controversial scientific discoveries of the 20th century is the genetic modification (GM) of foods. The genes of every living organism can be altered to change its characteristics. For example, farmers can add anti-pest genes to their crops, which enables them to survive longer or grow unusually big.

🌐 **Check it out!**

• http://www.darex.com/indurevo.htm
• http://www.ideafinder.com/history/inventions/story026.htm

Read further > genes
pg212 (b15)

▸▸ GENETIC MODIFICATION see pg234 (p2) ▸▸

a b c d e f g h i j k l m n o p q r s t u v w

Power it up

INVENTIONS THAT use natural sources of power have been developed over thousands of years to make our lives easier. The ancient Greeks and Romans used water mills to grind grain and olives more than 2,000 years ago. The invention of the steam engine and ways to control gas and create electricity have revolutionized mechanical movement and power. Today, coal and oil is burned in power stations to make electricity and to power engines for transportation, but these sources will eventually run out. So, need therefore to utilise natural energy—solar, wind, and water power are everlasting sources.

IT'S A FACT

• About one-fifth of the world's electricity is generated by hydro electric power.

• It is estimated that we have enough coal to last about 1,500 years and enough oil and natural gas to last for about 60 years.

▸ Before automatic timers were installed in the early 1900s, gas lamps were lit using long torches.

Gas lighting

In 1792, Englishman William Murdock invented a lighting system based on heating coal in a closed vessel and piping the gas it made to the street lights. He later developed a system for producing and storing gas. In the 19th century, coal gas provided many towns with energy for lighting and heating. In 1885, Austrian Carl Auer invented the gas mantle: this was a mesh of carbonized cotton that glowed brightly when heated and was used in street lights.

First engines

The first practical steam engine, invented by Englishman Thomas Savery in 1698, pumped water out of flooded coal mines. Savery's engine cooled and condensed steam (a gas) into water, leaving a vacuum (not a gas), which sucked up the flood water (a liquid). In 1712, Englishman Thomas Newcomen built an improved steam engine. The steam and the vacuum moved a piston up and down, which rocked a crossbeam, which in turn worked a water pump. In 1765, James Watt made improvements to Newcomen's engine. He added a chamber to cool and condense the steam and to change it back into water so that the engine did not have to be heated and cooled all the time.

▸▸ Read further > pumping water
pg201 (k28)

◂ James Watt made the piston on the steam engine move like a wheel, using gears and a connecting rod.

Check it out!

• http://www.bbc.co.uk/history/ society_culture/industrialisation /index.shtml

• http://www.bbc.co.uk/history/ historic_figures/newcomen_ thomas.shtml

Water power

The oldest known dam, made of earth and stones, was built across the Garawi valley in Egypt about 5,000 years ago. Modern arch dams were invented in the 1850s by French scientist François Zola. They resist the force of the water because their shape pushes the water down. In a gravity dam, the great weight of the material they are built from stops the water from pushing its way through.

▲ *Water falling from inside a gravity dam can turn turbine wheels to generate electricity. This is called hydro electric power (hydro means water).*

Read further › use of water
pg213 (r27)

Read further › electricity
pg205 (j32)

▼ *In 1882, Thomas Edison's factories made 100,000 light bulbs. By 1900 over 45 million were needed in the U.S.A. alone to light towns and cities.*

Power of the Sun

The Sun beams a vast amount of energy to the Earth. This energy can be collected and concentrated by photovoltaic (solar) cells to generate electricity. Manufacturing photovoltaic cells was only possible from the mid-1900s when American scientists G.L. Pearson, D.M. Chapin and C.S. Fuller developed a solar battery made up of tiny solar cells. Solar power is safe and environmentally friendly because it does not cause pollution.

▸ *Solar cells can turn about 15 percent of the sunlight that reaches them into electric energy. Scientists hope to improve this percentage.*

Electric city

Before gas and electricity were used, people relied on oil and gas lamps and candles to provide artificial light. The electric light bulb, invented by American scientists Thomas Edison and Joseph Swan in about 1879, was airtight so that it could burn longer. Inside a light bulb, a tiny, thin coiled wire called a filament gets so hot that it glows brightly, giving off light when electricity tries to squeeze through it. The flow of electricity causes the wire filament to glow brightly inside the airless bulb. Made of kind of metal called tungsten, the filament can get very hot without melting.

▼ *Oil refineries produce enough oil to fuel about half the energy we use.*

Read further › gas lamps
pg204 (i14)

Drilling for oil

The Chinese first drilled for oil 2,000 years ago using bamboo and bronze pipes. In 1844, Englishman Robert Beart introduced rotary drilling by using steam engines. A drill bit on the end of a hollow steel pipe forced up the rock (and oil) by pumping water down the pipe. The first offshore oil well was built off the American coast.

INVENTIVE

• In 1867 Alfred Nobel invented dynamite (named after the Greek word for power, *dynamis*). In his will, he requested that it should not be used in warfare.

• Five prizes (Nobel Prizes) are awarded each year for: physics, chemistry, medicine, literature, and the promotion of peace.

◀◀ FILAMENT see pg15 (b29) ◀◀

Electronic media

ELECTRONIC DEVICES such as radios, televisions, and computers change electric signals into sounds and pictures. Inside these devices are electronic components that control the way electricity flows around a circuit, making it perform particular tasks. Early radios and televisions used valves to switch tiny electrical signals, but these valves were large and used a lot of electricity. In the 1940s, American scientists invented transistors that worked like valves but were smaller and more efficient. By the 1960s, transistors and other electronic components, were all placed in one silicon chip 1.25 in square. Today microchips control computers and many other devices.

Televisions

The first televisions relied on the cathode ray tube, invented in 1897 by German physicist Karl Braun. These tubes fired streams of electrons—tiny particles of atoms—at a specially coated screen that made it glow. The first television was presented in 1926 by John Logie Baird. In a color television there are three electron streams: red, blue, and green. These light up phosphor dots on the screen, which blend to form a full color image.

▲ Some flat screen TVs invented in Japan in the 1980s, use liquid crystal displays (LCD) instead of cathode ray tubes.

Early computers

In 1823, English mathematician Charles Babbage invented the first kind of computer—the "difference engine." It proved too complex to complete though, and in 1834 Babbage began constructing his "analytical engine." Data was fed into the engine by hole-punched cards. The results were designed to be printed out. It was never built in full, because it would have been the size of a small train, but Babbage's idea helped others to invent the first working computers.

◀ The engine had a memory that was able to retain up to 100 40-digit numbers and a central processor for calculations.

To scale
1 square across = 6.3 in

Early computer
35.5 in across

Personal Digital Assistant
3.15 in long

Radio revolution

In 1895, Italian inventor Marchese Guglielmo Marconi, was the first person to send signals without wires. Marconi produced invisible radio waves from an electric current that changes direction thousands of times a second. In 1901 he sent radio messages across the Atlantic, from England to the U.S.A. In 1906 people first heard voices over the radio. Today, radio waves are also used in mobile phones.

▲ Early radios were called wirelesses as they used only radio waves, not wires or cables, to transmit sound.

◀◀ COMPUTERS see pg191 (b32) ◀◀

1 2 3 4 5 6 7 8 9 10 11 12 13 14 15 16 17 18 19

● Video games

The first successful video game was invented in 1972 by American computer programmer Nolan Bushnell. The game was a form of electronic table tennis called *Pong*. A video game is controlled by the memory in a silicon chip computer circuit. Most systems are based on the central processing units (CPUs) used in many computers. Video games are controlled by a user control interface, such as a key pad. All game consoles use a video signal compatible with television.

▶▶ Read further › light
pg205 (j32)

▶ *In this game called* Ape Man, *a graphics processor provides texture, color, and other functions while a chip handles the sound.*

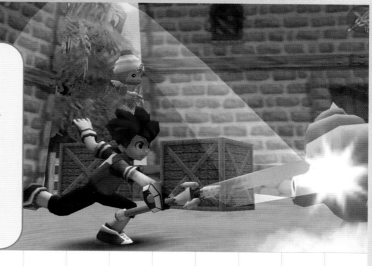

● Clever computers

The first home computer was produced in 1975 by Altair in the U.S.A. and the Apple Macintosh followed in 1984. When computers were first developed in the 1940s they filled entire rooms. The ENIAC (Electronic Numerical Integrator and Calculator), built in 1946, weighed 30 tons. Using 500 mi of wire, and carried out 100,000 tasks per second. Computers are smaller since the invention of the transistor (an electronic switch that detects electric current) in 1948 and in 1957, integrated circuits now. The latest iMacs are flat-screened.

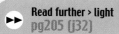

▶▶ Read further › early computers
pg206 (m2)

▲ *A liquid crystal display (LCD) produces images on a flat screen by using electrical current to control the path of light through liquid crystals and colored filters.*

INVENTIVE

• In 1926 the first moving television picture was created by John Logie Baird, using a spinning disc with holes, invented in 1884 by Paul Nipkow.

• Baird's system was later replaced with an electronic system invented by Vladimir Zworykin in the 1920s.

● Moving pictures

Animated films create the impression of movement by showing a quick series of still pictures of cartoons or puppets. The first animated films in the 1900s were cartoons. Cartoons were drawn on transparent sheets of celluloid before being photographed over a still background.

▶▶ Read further › video games
pg207 (b22)

▶ *Today, computers are programmed to draw images made up from thousands of shapes in a structure called a wireframe, where color, texture, shading, and perspective is added to make the image appear three-dimensional.*

● Check it out!

• http://www.computerhistory.org
• http://www.jonesencyclo.com/trends.cfm
• http://www.greatachievements.org

◀◀ ANIMATION see pg199 (k27) ◀◀

22 23 24 25 26 27 28 29 30 31 32 33 34 35 36 37 38 39

Keeping in touch

UNTIL PEOPLE learned to write they could only communicate when speaking face to face. Information passed verbally through the generations, often through story-telling. About 5,000 years ago the Sumerians and ancient Egyptians invented writing. Then, about 4,000 years later, the Chinese invented hand printing. The mechanical printing press was invented about 500 years ago in Europe by Johannes Gutenberg. Other methods of communication, such as Braille and Morse code, were invented in the 1800s. Today, e-mails, telephones, and fax machines connect people around the world, and because of the Internet, information is easier to access than ever before.

▼ The printing press enabled more people newspapers and books, to read.

Printing

Before printing was invented, books were copied by hand. Invented in China before AD 868, "letterpress" printing used letters and pictures carved from blocks of wood, clay, or ivory, which were then covered with ink so that when paper was pressed onto them so that the raised carving was printed. Peking blacksmith Pi-Sheng invented movable type (individual letters on reusable blocks). In 1436 German Johannes Gutenberg invented typecasting, where a large amount of movable type was made quickly and cheaply. In 1886, the linotype machine automatically cast complete lines of type from molten metal.

Read further › writing pg201 (b22)

Clues to the past

Ancient Egyptians used written pictures and symbols, called hieroglyphics, instead of words. They used these for 3,500 years until about AD 400 when Greek became their written language. The Rosetta Stone, discovered in 1799, is written in both hieroglyphics and Greek, providing the key to translating hieroglyphics.

Read further › writing pg201 (b22)

◄ Each hieroglyph (symbol or picture) represents an object or a sound. In total, there are about 700 different hieroglyphs.

COMMUNICATION

Invention	Year first used
Writing	about 3,500 BC
Paper	AD 105
Numbers 0 to 9	about 500
Mechanical clock	1000s
Printing press	1400s

Dot writing

In 1829, Frenchman Louis Braille invented a six-dot coded system of raised dots that could be used so the blind could read. Louis Braille was accidentally blinded when he was three. When he was ten, he was shown a way to write messages with raised dots, originally designed for soldiers to use at night. Braille simplified the system so it was easier to read with the fingertips. Braille is still in use worldwide today.

▼ *Braille is made up of different patterns of six dots, each pattern represents a letter or some short words such as "the."*

▶▶ **Read further › symbols**
pg201 (b22)

Dots and dashes

In 1838 Samuel Morse and Alfred Vail stopped and started an electric current along wires (or telegraphs) to communicate. Named Morse code, the short (on) bursts were dots, and the long (off) bursts were dashes. In 1844, the first telegraph line was opened between Baltimore and Washington, DC, so messages that had taken weeks by post, were sent instantly. Within 30 years, telegraphs covered the globe. Morse code is still used by the Navy today.

Long and short beeps tapped into telegraph machine

Electric current

Message travels along telegraph wires to recipient

▲ *As an electrical current running along a wire is stopped and started, the on and off bursts form the coded messages.*

▶▶ **Read further › radio**
pg206 (q11)

Telephones old and new

Telephones were invented by Scottish-born American Alexander Graham Bell in 1876. Bell discovered how to change the sound vibrations of the human voice into electrical signals, which he then sent along wires to a receiver. Today, pulses of light send telephone calls down fiber optic cables, and electrical signals are sent along copper cables. The word "telephone" comes from the Greek words for "far" and "sound."

◀ *Cell phones, invented in the 1980s, send digital radio signals to base stations, which direct the signal around a network until it reaches the right phone.*

▶▶ **Read further › electricity**
pg205 (j32)

The Internet

The Internet is a worldwide network of computers. Developed in the 1970s by American computer scientist Vinton Cerf and American engineer Robert Kahn, it connects, using phone lines, local networks of computers to special computers called servers. Cerf and Kahn defined the Internet Protocol—the software that controls the Internet. Then, in 1989, English computer scientist Tim Berners-Lee invented the World Wide Web for sharing information over the Internet. At the beginning of the 21st century, more than 25 million computers had access to the Internet, and this number continues to rise.

▶ *The Internet allows people to "surf" (browse) the Internet from all over the world.*

▶▶ **Read further › computers**
pg207 (h22)

To scale
1 square across = 2.3 in

8 in across

Bell's first telephone

Check it out!
- http://www.bbc.co.uk/arts/books/historyofbooks
- http://www.worldalmanacfor kids.com/explore/inventions.html

◀◀ COMMUNICATION see pg192 (l2) ◀◀

a b c d e f g h i j k l m n o p q r s t u v w

Medicine

FROM STETHOSCOPES and vaccinations to contact lenses and forceps, many of the medical inventions of the 19th century are still used today. Before now, there was little understanding of germs or the importance of keeping wounds clean to avoid spreading infection. Without anesthetic to numb the pain of surgery, patients sometimes died from shock. Patients often had to be cut open so doctors could find out what was wrong with them, until instruments such as endoscopes, invented in the 1950s, were able to see inside the body. Body scanners, heart pacemakers, and plastic contact lenses have now been invented.

Magnifying lenses enable surgeons to see small details

Sharp scalpel for cutting through skin, organs and blood vessels

EEG machines monitor patient's heartbeat during operation

Fighting infection

Vaccinations protect the body from diseases, such as smallpox, tetanus, and tuberculosis. Two types of vaccination are used today: "active" immunization is a weak but harmless form of the disease: this tricks the body into producing antibodies to fight it. "Passive" immunization uses antibodies that are already able to fight the disease. When a disease affects someone who has been vaccinated against it, the antibodies are ready to fight.

◄ *The first vaccine was developed by Edward Jenner, about 200 years ago, to fight smallpox.*

▶▶ Read further › treatment
pg211 (j29)

▶▶ Read further › operation
pg211 (b22)

Ancient surgical tools

About 5,000 years ago, the first saws for cutting off limbs were made from wood, bone, or flint, shaped into rows of sharp teeth. Flakes of flint were fixed into straight handles made of wood or bone with sticky tree sap or pitch. Bronze-age patients suffered under a sharp saw to remove limbs without anesthetic. Forceps are metal pinchers that can be used to deliver babies. A hook knife was used to extract organs from a patient's body during an operation.

Iron forceps

Hook knife

Bronze Age saw

▶▶ MEDICAL DEVELOPMENTS see pg224 (d2) ▶▶

1 2 3 4 5 6 7 8 9 10 11 12 13 14 15 16 17 18 19

a
b
c
d
e
f
g
h
i
j
k
l
m
n
o
p
q
r
s
t
u
v
w

Operation

Before an operation, patients are given anesthetics, which cause either loss of feeling in the body, numbing the pain, or put them to sleep temporarily. In 1799, English chemist Humphrey Davey described the benefits of nitrous oxide (laughing gas). It was later used by Horace Wells in 1844.

Read further › ancient tools
pg210 (q10)

◄ *An operating room is kept extremely clean to prevent the spread of infection. Surgeons wear masks, caps, and gowns to avoid spreading infection through by breathing and from any cuts on the skin.*

Very bright lights help surgeons to see clearly during operations

Contact lenses

Contact lenses are tiny lenses that are worn on the eye to help people see clearly. First thought of by Leonardo da Vinci around 1503, glass contact lenses were not actually created until 1887 when Adolf Eugen Fick made heavy, brown glass lenses for animals. Then in 1948, California optician Kevin Tuohy invented plastic lenses. In the 1970s, soft, gas-permeable lenses (that let oxygen pass through the lenses to the eyes) were made from a soft, plastic material. These lenses float on the surface (cornea) of the eye so they can be worn for a longer time.

Read further › spectacles
pg201 (r22)

Medicine

Drugs are used to treat and prevent disease and pain. The oldest list of drugs comes from ancient Babylonia about 3,700 years ago. Today most drugs are chemicals mixed together, or are made from plants or other natural sources.

Read further › Babylonians
pg202 (o2)

▲ *The eye has to be held wide open while putting in contact lenses.*

INVENTIVE

• The two parts of a hypodermic syringe—the needle and the plunger—were invented in 1853 by two people in two different countries: Scotland and France.

• In 1972 Godfrey Hounsfield developed the Computerised Tomography (CT) scan, to take pictures of the insides of the body.

Pacemaker

A person's heart normally beats about 60 to 100 times per minute but sometimes the rate gets too fast or too slow. The rhythm can be corrected or steadied by a pacemaker, which was invented in 1958 by Swedish doctor, Ake Senning.

▸ *The battery operated pacemaker is connected to the heart and sends it timed electrical impulses to help regulate its rhythm.*

Check it out!

• http://www.worldalmanacforkids.com/explore/inventions.html
• http://www.enchantedlearning.com/inventors/medicine.shtml

◄◄ EYES see pg168 (o13) ◄◄

Into the future

TODAY THE pace of new technology moves very quickly, and we take machines for granted that have been invented recently. Future inventions could be more amazing than ever before. Virtual reality, flat-screen televisions, and computer animation have changed the entertainment world. Robotic space explorers may pave the way for human exploration of other planets in the 21st century. Advances in gene therapy and cloning may have had a huge influence on the living world. Inventions, such as personal flying machines and ways to live at sea or on other planets could change our lives forever.

IT'S A FACT

• The first successful gene therapy—replacing faulty genes with new ones—took place on a four-year-old girl who was unable to fight infections.

• The first robot programmed to respond to commands was an artificial duck created in 1738.

• In 2002, a South African millionaire paid $20 million for a 10-day "holiday" in space.

House robots

The invention of the microchip in 1952 enabled the movement of machines, such as robots, to be controlled by computer. In the future, robots, such as this vacuum cleaner, may assist humans in many ways, such as doing housework.

Read further > robots
pg213 [c33]

▾ *This robot vacuum cleaner contains sensors to stop it bumping into things or getting stuck in corners.*

▸ *The Solo Trek XFV is a compact aircraft with vertical take-off and landing. It has a potential 150 mi range and a top speed of 80 mph.*

Flying machine

In 2001, Michael Moshier and Robert Bulaga and their team invented a personal flying machine jet pack that straps on to a person's back: the Solo Trek XFV. On the test flight, Moshier hovered above the ground for only 19 seconds at an altitude of just 2.4 in, but this could indicate the start of a new method of flying.

Read further > flight
pg200 [o16]

▼ 1984 ▼

Personal Digital Assistant (PDA) USA

▲ 1980 ▲

Personal stereo Japan

Microwave USA

▼ 1945 ▼

▴ *DVDs (digital versatile discs) store information such as music and films. DVD players use lasers to "read" the information. DVDs are similar to CDs but have the capacity to store much more information and have excellent sound and picture quality.*

a
b
c
d
e
f
g
h
i
j
k
l
m
n
o
p
q
r
s
t
u
v
w

Living in space

Over the next couple of centuries, explorers may be able to set up colonies on Mars. Future NASA missions are planned to land on Mars with rovers and mobile laboratories with instruments for drilling below the surface, detecting and analysing minerals and water samples. NASA is also developing technology to turn Martian resources into rocket fuel for the return.

Read further › NASA
pg57 (b22)

1816 ▲

*Stethoscope
France*

▼ 1886 ▼

*Escalator
USA*

*Dishwasher
USA*

1907 ▲

▲ *A human colony on Mars could be built in the next 300 years.*

Read further › computers
pg207 (h22)

Intelligent robots

Robots have only been possible since computers were invented, which enabled robots to follow instructions. Robots were first patented in 1961 by American scientists George C. Devol and Joseph F. Engelberger. Today, thousands of robots go to places where people cannot go, such as the deep ocean or other planets. They do tedious and even dangerous jobs, such as handling hazardous, radioactive material. Robots have been used to explore the surface of other planets.

▼ *The robot Sojourner was a space probe sent to the surface of Mars in 1997 to investigate the rock.*

INVENTIVE

• The HelpMate robot works in hospitals delivering meals, letters, and medicine.

• Instead of using PIN numbers, machines may identify people by their eyes or fingerprints.

Floating city

The *Freedom* ship is planned to house up to 50,000 people. It claims to offer a solution to the problem of overcrowding on Earth. The ship is to contain a school, a hospital, yacht marinas, one of the largest shopping centers in the world, sports facilities, theaters, nightclubs, restaurants, and a golf course.

▲ *The Freedom ship will recycle much of its waste, rather than dumping it into the ocean.*

Read further › hospitals
pg211 (b23)

Check it out!

• http://www.newgadgets.
freeserve.co.uk
• http://www.time.com/time/
2001/inventions/
• http://www.wfs.org

◄◄ MARS see pg47 (n22) ◄◄

Great Greeks

THE NATURAL world was studied by many ancient peoples, but it was in ancient Greece that science really began, in about 2500 BC. Ancient Greek thinkers began to look at the world logically—to figure out how natural events occurred by reasoned argument instead of looking for mysterious spiritual forces. Great thinkers such as Plato, Aristotle, Socrates, Euclid, and Archimedes made profound insights into the world around them. Their studies included natural forces, mathematics, the nature of matter, and how the body works. These studies are the foundation of modern science.

IT'S A FACT

• The idea that all matter is made of tiny particles called atoms was developed about 2,500 years ago by Greek thinker, Democritus (c.460–c.370 BC).

• The Greek thinker Empedocles (c.494–c.434 BC) divided all matter into four elements—earth, air, fire, and water—this idea was not contested until the 17th century.

▼ Archimedes discovered the principle of liquid displacement as he saw the water level in his bath rise as more of his body became immersed. He is said to have jumped out of the bath and run naked through the streets shouting "Eureka!" —Greek for "I've got it!"

● Ancient scholars

The ancient Greeks called their thinkers and scholars "philosophers," which means lovers of wisdom. Today we think of philosophy as studies based on thoughts and theories about human existence. Greek philosophers, often while living and studying in Athens, studied all kinds of subjects, including science and mathematics. A temple—the Museion, or Museum—was built in Alexandria, Egypt to celebrate the Greek "muses" thought to inspire ideas and art. The museum had a famous library where scholars from many parts of the world—particularly Greek-speaking countries—came to work.

▼ Greek scholars, such as Plato and Aristotle, developed the idea of intellectual debate.

● Eureka!

Greek scientist Archimedes (c.287–c.212 BC) who lived in Syracuse, in Sicily (then ruled by Greeks), was the first one to apply mathematics to science. He figured out how effective levers and other machines could be. One of his best ideas was the Archimedean screw, still used today, for pumping water. Archimedes demonstrated that objects float because of the weight of the water they displace. This idea is now called Archimedes' Principle.

▶▶ **Read further › House of Wisdom** pg226 (q2)

Check it out!
• http://www.angelfire.com/ca5/ancientgreecescience/
• http://www.utm.edu/research/iep/a/aristotl.htm

▶▶ **Read further › mathematics** pg226 (d2); pg227 (c22)

Early medicine

The ancient Greek doctor Hippocrates (460–379 BC) is often called the father of medicine. He lived at a time when many believed that illness was caused by evil spirits or magic. Hippocrates showed that disease has a physical cause, such as poor diet or dirt. Today, doctors still practice under an updated version of the "Hippocratic oath," undertaking to provide the best care they can for their patients.

▸ *Hippocrates recorded people's reactions to certain treatments, then established medicine on a practical basis.*

Read further › medicine
pg224 (d2; g15); pg225 (i22)

Covering the angles

Though the ancient Egyptians had a good knowledge of angles and triangles so they could build the pyramids, the ancient Greeks created the first systems of geometry—the study of lines and the angles between them. The Greek mathematician Euclid; (c.330–260 BC) who studied and lived in Alexandria, Egypt, wrote *Elements of Geometry*. This gave a clear and thorough analysis of geometric principles. Even today, mathematicians refer to the geometry of flat surfaces— lines, points, shapes and solids—as Euclidean geometry.

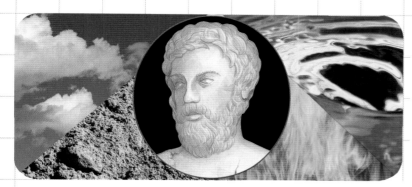

◂ *Aristotle developed Empedocles' idea of the four elements (earth, air, fire, and water) into a coherent and logical argument.*

Aristotle

Ancient Greek thinker Aristotle (384–322 BC) studied many areas of science and philosophy at Plato's academy in Athens and helped to pioneer the study of animals (zoology) and plants (botany). He established a basic approach to science, showing how scientists must observe everything closely, classify these observations, and use logical arguments to understand them. He opened and, for 12 years, directed the Lyceum school in Athens. His ideas remained a key part of university education in Europe for more than 2,000 years.

Read further › classification
pg223 (m22)

Read further › mathematics
pg226 (g15)

▴ *Classic principles of geometry were put into practice in temples such as the Parthenon in Athens, built between c.447–c.432 BC. It has two adjoining square forms topped with a triangular gable.*

GENIUS GENES

• The Greek geographer Eratosthenes (c.285–c.194 BC) measured the Earth's circumference with amazing accuracy 1,800 years before European explorers proved the world is round.

• The Greek scholar Xenophanes realized, thousands of years before Victorian scientists developed the idea, that fossils were rocks containing the remains or imprints of dead plants and animals.

OTHER KEY FIGURES

Date	Name, nationality	Achievements
c.582–c.497 BC	Pythagoras, Greek	Discovered basic mathematical rules
c.390–c.340 BC	Eudoxus, Greek	Worked out the mathematics of spheres
c.265–c.190 BC	Apollonius, Greek	Discovered circles that can be cut from cones, such as parabolas
1st century AD	Hero of Alexandria, Greek	Discovered several uses for steam, such as opening temple doors

◂◂ CONSTRUCTING BUILDINGS see pg178 (l2) ◂◂

Inside the body

FOR 1,500 years medicine was based on the writings of Greek physician Claudius Galen (AD c.130–c.200) who studied animals to support his theories on human medicine. Galen's ideas remained unchallenged until the 15th and 16th centuries when physicians such as Andreas Vesalius and artists such as Leonardo da Vinci began to look at real bodies by dissecting dead human bodies to investigate their structure. This new approach began in Italy at the University of Padua where the great anatomist Vesalius was professor. It spread throughout most of Europe, and later pioneers such as William Harvey and Marcello Malpighi made crucial breakthroughs.

GENIUS GENES

• In the 1820s, Edinburgh medical students needed a lot of bodies to dissect so they could learn anatomy. So, Irishmen William Burke and William Hare began to provide them with extra corpses—first by stealing them from graves, then by murdering people!

• When William Harvey suggested that blood circulated, many people thought he was insane. When he demonstrated blood flowing through a weightlifter's veins, doctor Caspar Hoffman (1572–1648) said, "I see it, but I don't believe it!"

Knife master

Flemish physician Andreas Vesalius (1514–1564) began the first systematic study of human anatomy—the composition of the human body. While lecturing in surgery at Padua University in Italy, Vesalius thought Galen's books inaccurate, as they were based on studies on animals. So Vesalius began to carry out his own dissections, though he was not the first. Vesalius dissected the corpses, often in front of a large audience of students. His findings were published in *De Humani Corporis Fabrica*—"On The Structure of the Human Body"—the first great book of anatomy, which was illustrated by Flemish artist Jan van Calcar.

►► Read further › anatomical drawings
pg217 (d22)

▶ *About 30 years before Vesalius, artists such as Italian Raffaello Sanzio (1483–1520), better known as Raphael, began to observe skeletons to make anatomically accurate drawings of the bones.*

◄◄ BONES see pg156 (d2) ◄◄

1 2 3 4 5 6 7 8 9 10 11 12 13 14 15 16 17 18 19

▶ *Leonardo da Vinci dissected corpses to see how bodies worked. His drawings were revolutionary in their accuracy.*

Drawing the body

The development of accurate anatomical drawings was crucial to our understanding of human anatomy. One of the first great anatomical artists was Italian, Leonardo da Vinci (1452–1519). Leonardo had a great mind and contributed to science in countless ways. Human dissection allowed him to produce detailed anatomical drawings showing how bones and muscles work and how babies grow inside a mother's womb. Accurate drawings enabled physicians to record the results of dissections, and pass on the results on to students and other researchers.

▶▶ **Read further › recording results**
pg215 (b22); pg218 (p11)

Body pump

English physician William Harvey (1578–1657) was the first to show that the heart pumps blood. Physicians already knew that blood moved around the body through veins but thought it moved backward and forward like tides. Harvey showed that valves in the blood vessels allow blood to continually circulate the body in one direction, flowing from the heart through branching arteries and back through converging veins. However, he could not see how blood moved from arteries to veins.

▶▶ **Read further › Malpighi**
pg217 (n22)

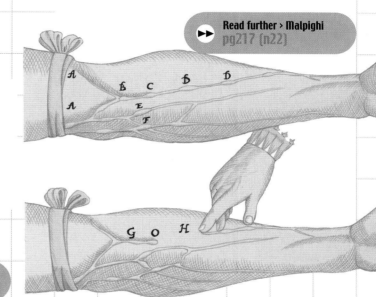

▶ *In describing the circulation of the blood, Harvey labelled veins and arteries to try to understand how blood circulated through the body.*

The final link

▶▶ **Read further › DNA**
pg234 (r8); pg235 (p22)

In 1661, Italian physician Marcello Malpighi (1628–1694) showed how arteries and veins are linked. Using the newly invented microscope, Malpighi saw that arteries and veins are linked by tiny blood vessels, called capillaries, much too small to see with the naked eye. He also used the microscope to study organs like the lungs, kidneys, brain, and skin.

◀ *Microscopes reveal things in the body that are too small for the eye to see, such as tiny blood cells that float through the blood.*

OTHER KEY FIGURES

Date	Name, nationality	Achievements
c.335–c.280 BC	Herophilus, Greek	Began the science of anatomy
c.304–c.250 BC	Erasistratus, Greek	Began the science of physiology
AD c.130–c.200	Claudius Galen, Greek	Collated all the existing knowledge of medicine and the human body
1523–1562	Gabriello Fallopio, Italian	Discovered tiny structures in the ear and female reproductive system
1561–1636	Sanctorius, Italian	Designed a clinical thermometer and studied the body's metabolism
1809–1885	Friedrich Jacob Henle, German	Discovered kidney tubules
1821–1902	Rudolf Virchow, German	Led our understanding of how disease affects body cells
1868–1943	Karl Landsteiner, Austrian-American	Discovered blood groups

Star gazers

ASTRONOMY IS one of the oldest of sciences. It dates back to the earliest days of humankind when hunters gazed into the night sky to figure out which night would give them a full Moon—and more light to hunt by. When people began to form settlements and farm the land, astronomers told farmers when the seasons would come and go. Ancient Egyptians, such as Imhotep, who designed the first pyramid 4,500 years ago, were known for their knowledge of astronomy, so it was already an ancient art by the time the Greek astronomer Hipparchus began to study the sky.

IT'S A FACT

• The Greek astronomer Aristarchus (c.310– c.230 BC) suggested that the Earth revolved around the Sun more than 2,000 years before Copernicus released his theory on this subject.

• In 1918, an unknown American astronomer showed how the Earth is on the edge of our own Galaxy, not at the center.

GENIUS GENES

• In 1593, Galileo invented what could be called the first thermometer—a glass bulb in which colored water moved up and down as the temperature changed.

• When Edwin Hubble (1889–1953) showed that the universe is expanding, Belgian astronomer George Lemaitre (1894–1966) suggested that this was because the universe was originally tiny, before bursting into existence with a mighty explosion called the Big Bang.

◄ As well as plotting the position of about 850 stars, Hipparchus invented trigonometry, which is used to mathematically calculate the angles and lengths of the sides of triangles.

Early star

The ancient Greek astronomer Hipparchus of Rhodes lived during the second century BC. His amazingly accurate observations laid the foundations of astronomy for more than 2,000 years. Using the naked eye and astronomical instruments that he had invented, Hipparchus plotted the positions of all the stars in the sky visible to the naked eye. He used them to work out the length of one year to within less than seven minutes. He also assigned Magnitudes (a measure of brightness) to all the stars. He called the brightest, the Dog Star Sirius, a First Magnitude star and the faintest he could see, a Sixth Magnitude. Astronomers still use the same system today.

▶▶ Read further › Copernicus pg219 (b22)

◄◄ MAGNITUDE see pg51 (f22) ◄◄

1   2   3   4   5   6   7   8   9   10   11   12   13   14   15   16   17   18   19

Moving the Earth

Until the 16th century, most people believed that the Earth was at the center of the universe, and that the Moon, Sun, planets, and stars all revolved around it. But the Polish astronomer, Nicolaus Copernicus, (1473–1543) thought that the occasional backward loops in the movement of some planets through the sky did not support this theory. From his observations, Copernicus developed the revolutionary new theory that the Sun, not the Earth, was at the center of the universe. This idea was so shocking that it was more than 100 years before it was widely accepted.

▼ *Copernicus discovered that the Earth and other planets move around the Sun. He also observed that the Earth takes one year (365 days) to travel around the Sun and that it revolves on its own axis once every 24 hours.*

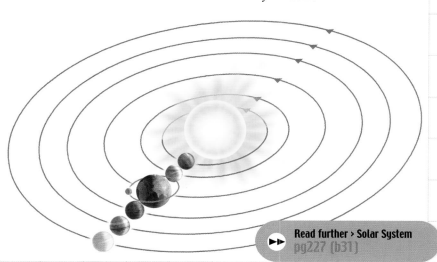

▶▶ **Read further ▸ Solar System** pg227 (b31)

◀ *Copernicus' book, De Revolutionibus orbium coelestium—"On the Revolutions of the Heavenly Spheres"—published in 1543, was placed on the "Index," a list of books banned by the Roman Catholic Church, until 1835.*

Seeing the universe

Less than 100 years ago it was thought that the universe was little bigger than our Milky Way Galaxy. Then, in the 1920s, American astronomer Edwin Hubble (1889–1953) began to study the Andromeda Galaxy. Astronomers had previously thought this was just a cloud of gas called a nebula. But with a very powerful telescope Hubble saw that it was another galaxy full of stars. Soon, many other galaxies were discovered, and it became clear that the universe is gigantic. In 1927 Hubble made another discovery—that all the galaxies are zooming away from us. He realized that the universe is actually expanding all of the time.

▶▶ **Read further ▸ telescope** pg221 (b22)

▲ *Hubble pointed out that the fuzzy patches of light once thought to be nebulae were in fact other galaxies far beyond the milky way.*

OTHER KEY FIGURES

Date	Name, nationality	Achievements
c.2600 BC	Imhotep, Egypt	First known astronomer
270–190 BC	Eratosthenes, Greek, born in Cyrene (now Libya) and lived in Egypt	Made the first accurate measurement of the Earth's circumference
AD 90–170	Ptolemy, Egyptian-Greek	Wrote a guide to astronomy that was the standard textbook for 1,400 years
1546–1601	Tycho Brahe, Danish	First to spot an entirely new star
1571–1630	Johannes Kepler, German	Discovered that planets move not in circles but oval-shapes called ellipses
1738–1822 1750–1848	Sir William Herschel, Caroline Herschel, German-British	Worked together to discover the planet Uranus and over 300 different stars

Check it out!

- http://space.about.com/library/weekly/aa103102a.htm
- http://www.riverdale.k12.or.us/~thasting/astronomy/ancient.htm

◀◀ GALAXIES see pg52 (d2) ◀◀

Three greats

UNTIL THE 17th century, much of our view of the natural world was based on superstition. Then, three of the greatest scientists of all time developed our understanding and perceptions of the world around us. Italian astronomer, Galileo Galilei laid the foundation of our understanding of how things move. Englishman Isaac Newton showed that all things move according to three simple rules, and realized that gravity is a force. Dutchman Christiaan Huygens suggested that light travels as waves.

The great Newton

Born in England, Isaac Newton (1642–1727), was one of the greatest scientists. His highest achievement was his discovery of gravity and the three fundamental laws of motion, which he describes in his famous book published in 1687, *Philosophiae naturalis principia mathematica*—"The Mathematical Principles of Natural Philosophy" —usually called just *The Principia*. But, he made many other important discoveries, including the fact that white light is a mixture of all colors. He found that by shining light through a prism, white light could be split into a spectrum—an array of all seven colors. He also invented the mirror telescope to prevent colored edges on the image. This design is still used in manufacturing many modern telescopes.

▶▶ Read further > telescopes
pg219 (d33); pg221 (b22)

Gravity

Before Newton, no one knew why things fell to the ground or why planets orbit the Sun. Newton said that the idea came to him one day while sitting in an orchard. As an apple fell nearby, Newton wondered if the apple was not simply falling but was actually being pulled down by an invisible force. From this simple idea, Newton developed his theory of gravity—a universal force that tries to pull all matter together.

▶▶ Read further > gravity
pg232 (q12)

◀ As Newton demonstrated, a glass wedge, or prism, bends different colors of light by different amounts, so white light is split into all seven colors of the rainbow (red, orange, yellow, green, blue, indigo, violet).

Check it out!

- http://www.infoplease.com/ce6/people/A0835490.html
- http://www.imahero.com/hero history/galileo_herohistory.htm

Yet it does move!

Galileo (1564–1642) helped us understand how things move, by proving that nothing changes, stops, or starts, goes faster or slower, unless a force is applied. He also found that if something moves faster, the rate at which it accelerates depends on the strength of the force. Galileo also used the newly-invented telescope to discover that Jupiter has four moons and that Venus goes through phases like our Moon. His observations led to the proof that Copernicus *(see pg219 [b28])* was right: the Earth is not at the center of the universe and that it does move around the Sun.

Read further > Copernicus
pg219 (b22)

▲ *In 1609, Galileo made his own telescope. It magnified objects up to 30 times, so that he was able to observe the rings of Saturn and see how many stars there were in the solar system. The scholars he showed it to thought that it was a fraud and that Galileo had painted magnified views on the lens.*

▲ *Galileo is said to have muttered "eppir si muove"—"yet it does move"—after the Catholic Church, who were so horrified by his theory, made him deny it or they would torture him.*

Light waves

Born to a wealthy Dutch family, Christiaan Huygens (1629–1695) was a brilliant scientist who developed Galileo's idea—of using a swinging weight or pendulum to keep a clock on time—to make the first accurate clocks. Like Galileo, Huygens also made his own telescopes to study the night sky and discovered the vague blurs around the edge of the planet Saturn were actually Saturn's rings. His most brilliant insight may have been the theory that light travels in waves and spreads like ripples when a stone is dropped into water.

◄ *Huygens developed the pendulum clock, so time could then be measured accurately.*

Read further > light waves
pg228 (h15); pg229 (d22)

GENIUS GENES

• Galileo is said to have proved that all objects fall at the same rate, by dropping a wooden ball and a cannon ball from the Leaning Tower of Pisa. In fact, it was one of his students who carried out the experiment, because Galileo already knew the result.

• Huygens was the first scientist to write about extraterrestrial life in a book called *Cosmotheoros*.

IT'S A FACT

• In 1699, Newton was asked to supervise the Royal Mint in England, where coins are made, to try to stop counterfeiting.

• Galileo is said to have got the idea for the pendulum clock by watching a bell rope swinging in the cathedral at Pisa, Italy, where he went to university.

◄◄ LIGHT WAVES see pg31 (o22) ◄◄

Evolution

NOWADAYS WE take for granted all kinds of things about the natural world that would have surprised, even shocked, our ancestors. For example, it was only about 350 years ago, that Dutch scientist Anton van Leeuwenhoek discovered the world is teeming with many forms of life too small for the naked eye to see. About 200 years ago, naturalists realized that species of living organisms do not always remain the same but, as Charles Darwin showed, they constantly evolve over time. The classification of species dates back only 250 years to the discoveries of Swedish naturalist Carolus Linnaeus.

▶▶ **Read further > Aristotle and Darwin**
pg215 (m22); pg223 (g29)

GENIUS GENES

• Linnaeus made reproduction and mating the core of his classification system. He liked to talk of the "marriage" of plants, the stamen of the flower, being the groom, and the pistil, the bride.

• After each day's teaching, Linnaeus' students would stand around his house shouting "Long live Linnaeu"—in Latin.

Nature hunters

Our knowledge of the natural world comes from both the work of the great naturalists, and the diligence and interest of countless millions of others. Farmers learned how to turn wild plants to their own uses and early hunters studied the ways of creatures so they could better catch them. But the twin sciences of botany and zoology were further developed in the 18th and 19th centuries, when naturalists, professional and amateur, began to study plants and animals out of pure interest. Some studied the wildlife just a short walk from home. Others, like Charles Darwin, went all the way around the world to bring back exotic species from faraway places to study them.

IT'S A FACT

• In 1683, Dutch scientist Anton van Leeuwenhoek made the first drawings of bacteria—though he had no idea what they were.

• When Linnaeus invented his system, botanists knew of 7,700 plants. Now we know of 275,000.

Check it out!
• http://www.aboutdarwin.com/
• http://www.bbc.co.uk/education /darwin/origin/index.htm

▶ About 2 million years ago, humans learned how to hunt large animals for food. They chipped flakes off of stones to make sharp-edged tools.

▸ *Hooke invented the compound microscope, which had several lenses. This enabled scientists to see tiny microbes and other living things.*

The tiniest creatures

People never suspected that there were organisms too small for the eye to see—let alone living things—until the microscope was invented in about 1590. In the 1670s, Dutch scientist Anton van Leeuwenhoek (1632–1723) became fascinated with what could be seen through the microscope. For 50 years he used his home-made, single-lens microscopes to find microscopic creatures in water. He called them "animalcules," from protozoa to bacteria. In 1665, Englishman Robert Hooke (1635–1703) developed a new version of the microscope to study plant forms.

Read further › microscopes
pg217 (n22)

OTHER KEY FIGURES

Date	Name, nationality	Achievements
c.372–c.287 BC	Theophrastus, Greek	Father of botany
AD 1665–1721	Rudolf Camerarius, German	Showed how plants reproduce sexually
1823–1913	Alfred Wallace, English	Developed theory of evolution
1825–1895	Thomas Huxley, English	Established humankind's link to other mammals

Life-changing

Read further › Church
pg219 (b22); pg221 (b22)

By 1837, naturalists realized that many extinct species, such as dinosaurs, had lived in the past. By studying creatures on his worldwide voyage aboard the HMS *Beagle*, English scientist Charles Darwin (1809–1882) developed the theory of natural selection. This shows that creatures are all born slightly different from each other. Those with a natural advantage, such as being suited to their environment, are more likely to survive and pass on these advantages on to their offspring. Darwin showed that some species evolve while some weaker species do not and so die out. Darwin published these findings in his book *The Origin of Species* in 1859 but it caused a big uproar because it contradicted the Bible about the origin of human life.

▾ *Discoveries of bones have shown how our ancestors evolved over millions of years, learning to walk upright, to use tools, and eventually to use fire.*

Organizing nature

The identification of animals and plants was confusing until Swedish botanist Carolus Linnaeus (1707–1778) devised a system for naming and classifying them, giving two-part names to every species. The first part is for the genus or group of species with similar characteristics; the second part is its own species name. So every plant and animal had its own name— and its own place in the overall scheme of life.

◂ *Capsella (genus) bursa-pastoris (species).*

◂◂ **ANIMAL KINGDOM** see pg103 (m32) ◂◂

Medical matters

DISEASE AND ill-health have not always been understood and so were often untreatable. People died younger, on average, than they do now. In the 11th century, Persian doctor Avicenna wrote the *Canon of Medicine*, a medical textbook used all over the Arab Empire for centuries. In the late 18th century, Englishman Edward Jenner found a way to protect people against some diseases by a vaccine—a small, harmless dose of the disease, often given by injection. Pasteur's realization in the 1860s that germs caused disease was a huge medical breakthrough. This led to the discovery of medicines, such as antibiotics, in the 1920s.

Persian medicine

About a thousand years ago, Muslim physicians began to study the work of the ancient Greeks such as Hippocrates and Aristotle closely to develop many new ideas on medicine. Persian doctor Avicenna or Ibn Sina (980–1037) worked for Persian rulers and wrote more than 200 books on many subjects, including *Canon of Medicine*, which became the standard medical textbook for centuries.

▲ *Avicenna's book* Canon of Medicine, *based in part on the ideas of Aristotle and Galen, about how the body works, included information on anatomy and his observations as a doctor.*

▶▶ Read further › Hippocrates / Aristotle pg215 (b22; m22)

Antiseptic spray

English surgeon Joseph Lister (1827–1912) was appalled at the number of deaths caused by infection after surgery. After reading of Pasteur's discovery that bacteria can be air-born, he developed the carbolic steam spray. This proccess produced a fine mist of mild carbolic acid in the operating room, which killed bacteria, so reducing trisk of infection.

▶▶ Read further › bacteria pg225 (b33)

▶ *By using carbolic steam spray, the death rate among Lister's patients fell from 50 to 5 percent.*

Check it out!

• http://www.pbs.org/wgbh/aso/databank/entries/bmflem.html
• http://ambafranceca.org/HYPERLAB/PEOPLE/_pasteur.html

◀◀ VACCINATION see pg210 (n2) ◀◀

OTHER KEY FIGURES

Date	Name, nationality	Achievements
936–1013	Albucasis (Al-Zahrawi), Spanish Arab	Compiled a 1,500-page surgical encyclopedia and described 200 surgical instruments
1749–1823	Edward Jenner, English	Discovered a vaccine for smallpox
1813–1878	Claude Bernard, French	Discovered how sugars give the body energy
1843–1910	Robert Koch, German	Proved germs cause disease
1854–1915	Paul Ehrlich, German	Developed chemical drugs for diseases
1881–1955	Alexander Fleming, Scottish	Developed a mold—Penicillin *notatum*—that kills bacteria
1898–1968 1906–1979	Howard Florey, Australian Ernst Chain, German	Worked together to develop the first antibiotic, penicillin

The germ of an idea

French scientist Louis Pasteur (1822–1895) discovered that liquids turn sour because of the tiny organisms. He found that these organisms can be killed by heat in a process now known as "pasteurization" in which a substance, such as milk, is heated to a certain temperature, then rapidly cooled. Pasteur's greatest breakthrough was finding that these germs, such as bacteria and viruses, carry disease from one person to another. He showed how a vaccination works by using a tiny amount of the germ to build up the body's defense against it.

◀ *Pasteur discovered a vaccine for cattle and sheep against anthrax, as well as a life-saving cure for rabies.*

Read further › Freudian slips pg224 (s14)

Read further › bacteria pg224 (p2)

Thoughts and feelings

Few scientists have had such an impact on how we think of ourselves as the Austrian psychologist Sigmund Freud (1856–1939). Freud suggested that we have "conscious" thoughts, which we know about, and "unconscious" thoughts, which we are not aware of—but which both influence our behavior. Freud believed that our childhood experiences play an important part in shaping our unconscious thoughts and that our behavior as adults is affected by these thoughts.

▶ *Freud believed in talking to his patients about their problems to find out if any past experiences in their lives affected their behavior as adults.*

Math masters

THE FIRST mathematics were undertaken for entirely practical purposes. Early tax officials—people who collect money for the government—helped develop arithmetic as they worked out tax sums. Ancient Sumerians and Egyptians developed geometry to help them build the pyramids and other buildings. Gradually, people became interested in the theory of mathematics, and many of the great mathematicians through the ages worked on theoretical problems. The achievements of these theorists were less well known than the work of other scientists, as few people then could realise the uses of mathematics.

● IT'S A FACT

• Coordinate geometry is also known as Cartesian geometry, named for Descartes.

• Al-Khwarizmi said, "When I consider what people generally want in calculating, I find that it is always a number."

● Pythagoras

Greek mathematician Pythagoras (c.582–497 BC) developed a mathematical rule regarding the lengths of the sides of triangles. This rule, called Pythagoras' theorem, states that the square of the lengths of the two shorter sides of any right-angled triangle add up to the square of the length of the longest side.

▶▶ Read further › geometry
pg215 (b34)

● Mathematical letters

Algebra is a branch of mathematics that solves problems by substituting letters and other symbols for different quantities. The name comes from the Latin name for the book in which it was first properly described—*Al-jabr*— the full name meaning "The Compendious Book on Calculation by Completion [or Restoring] and Balancing." This is one of the most famous mathematics books of all time, written by an Arabic mathematician, Al-Khwarizmi, in about 830 AD.

▲ *Al-Khwarizmi taught algebra in the House of Wisdom—a mathematical school in Baghdad. He wrote his influential book on algebra between 813 AD and 833 AD.*

▶▶ Read further › mathematics
pg214 (m15); pg215 (b34)

GENIUS GENES

• In 1796, Laplace suggested "the attractive force [gravity] of a heavenly body [an object in space] could be so large that light could not flow out of it" nearly 200 years before astronomers proved it in black holes.

• Descartes said it made sense to think of our bodies and minds as entirely separate. Our bodies and senses are solid, material things, but our minds are something entirely different.

▶ *For more than 2,000 years, Euclid's textbook was used in schools to teach children the basics of geometry.*

Muslim scholars

Greek thinkers, such as Euclid, achieved much in basic mathematics, but more advanced mathematics was mostly developed by Arab scholars. In the 9th century, the caliph (Muslim leader) Al-Ma-mum turned Baghdad into a center of learning. The focus was the Bayt al-Hikma (House of Wisdom). Al-Uqlidisi gave us decimal fractions; Abu'l-Wafa developed the idea of tangents (special angles in right-angled triangles); mathematician and poet, Omar Khayyam made advances in ways to work out complex equations.

Read further > Euclid
pg215 (b34)

Saving the world

French mathematician and astronomer Pierre Laplace (1749–1827) calculated the mathematics of the orbits of the planets and their gravitational pulls in a way that not even Newton had been able to do. In 1773 he showed how one planet would not be thrown off course by the gravity of another as they passed nearby—an effect Newton had feared might lead to the end of the world. Laplace was also the first to suggest that the Solar System was created from a cloud of gas.

▶ *Laplace showed how Saturn does not wobble even when Jupiter passes close by.*

Read further > Solar System
pg219 (b22)

Graphic answers

French philosopher and mathematician René Descartes (1596–1650) is best known for his ideas on the nature of human existence. He is most famous for his argument that everything should be doubted before it was believed, and for stating proof that he existed was his ability to think. From this came his famous quote, *"Cogito ergo sum"*— "I think therefore I am." He also developed a kind of math called coordinate or analytical geometry. This enables scientists and mathematicians to illustrate statistics using lines of geometry on a graph, so that the statistics can be easily understood.

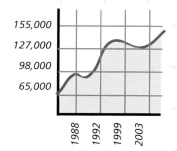

155,000
127,000
98,000
65,000

1988   1992   1999   2003

▲ *Coordinate or analytical geometry allows scientists to analyse how fast things change using Cartesian coordinates, or graphs, to plot statistics.*

Accurate reflections

English friar Roger Bacon (1214–1292) made many discoveries in the geometry of reflections from mirrors and the angles of light rays passing through lenses. Bacon also believed that the world was round. This idea was ridiculed and even got him imprisoned.

Read further > light
pg220 (l2)

▼ *Bacon showed that light rays bounce off of and hit a mirror at the same angle.*

OTHER KEY FIGURES

Date	Name, nationality	Achievements
c.1170–c.1250	Leonardo Fibonacci, Italian	Introduced the Arabic numeral system we use today
1561–1630	Henry Briggs, English	Simplified the idea of logarithms
1601–1665	Pierre de Fermat, French	Introduced probability theory and number theory
1707–1783	Leonhard Euler, Swiss	Developed trigonometry
1777–1855	Karl Gauss, German	Developed theory of numbers
1781–1840	Siméon-Denis Poisson, French	Developed probability theory
1854–1912	Jules Poincaré, French	Invented chaos theory

Check it out!
- http://www.bbc.co.uk/education/maths file/index.shtml
- http://www.allmath.com/biography.asp
- http://www.funbrain.com/numbers.shtml

◀◀ LIGHT RAYS see pg31 (o22) ◀◀

Bright sparks

WE DEPEND on electricity so much today it is hard to imagine a world without it. Yet, about 250 years ago, almost nothing was known about it. Electricity is one of the basic forces of the universe, it exists everywhere. Yet people knew it only as a tiny spark made by rubbing amber or glass against silk. In the 1750s, Benjamin Franklin demonstrated that lightning is electric and, soon after, electricity became a practical reality. Scientists began to make dramatic discoveries about its properties. About 50 years later, Joseph Henry and Michael Faraday, discovered how to generate huge quantities of electricity, and our modern electrical age was born.

IT'S A FACT

• In attempts to repeat Franklin's experiment with a kite in a thunderstorm, many scientists were electrocuted—hurt or killed by the force of electricity.

• Michael Faraday's scientific demonstrations were the top shows of the time, attracting huge audiences.

Flying a kite

There is no more dramatic sign of the presence of natural electricity in the world than lightning. Yet no one realized just what lightning was until the mid-1700s. At that time, scientists were just learning how to make big sparks for the first time by rubbing together materials like glass on sulphur. American statesman and scientist, Benjamin Franklin (1706–1790), wondered if lightning consisted of these same sparks. He conducted an experiment that proved that electricity is produced by lightning. This discovery led to the development of the lightning conductor or rod.

▶▶ Read further > electricity
pg229 (d22)

◀ To test his idea, Franklin flew a kite during a thunderstorm. He tied a metal key to the string with a short silk thread. Electricity from the lightning ran down the wet string to the key and made huge electrical sparks. Franklin had proved his point—but he was lucky to be alive.

▸ *In 1826 Faraday started the tradition of the Christmas lectures at the Royal Institution, London. In these lectures he explained his ideas and discoveries clearly to the public.*

● Magnetic electricity

Chemical batteries such as Volta's *(see pg229 [p38])* made a steady flow of electricity, but only in small amounts. In the 1820s, scientists discovered a link between electricity and magnetism. Then, in 1830, Joseph Henry (1797–1878) in America and Michael Faraday (1791–1867) in England discovered that moving a magnet would create an electric current. Engineers were then able to build machines using moving magnets to generate huge quantities of electricity for the first time. This paved the way for the development of modern electrical appliances, from light bulbs to computers.

Read further › appliances
pg231 (h25)

◂ *Faraday built a dynamo—used to convert mechanical energy into electric energy—by winding coils of wire around a piece of iron and passing electricity through the iron to create a magnet. He then made a hollow coil, and moved the magnet in and out to make the current flow.*

● GENIUS GENES

• In the 1780s, Italian physicist Luigi Galvani (1737–1798) experimented with a dead frog's leg hung on a brass hook and a piece of iron. The frog's leg twitched as the iron touched it, and many people believed it was "animal electricity."

• Following Galvani's idea of animal electricity as a life force, scientists around 1800 tried to bring corpses back to life by electrifying them—a practice made into a vivid story in Mary Shelley's novel *Frankenstein*.

● The first battery

In the 1790s, Italian scientist Alessandro Volta (1745–1827), realized that electricity can be made by mixing the right chemicals. The chemical reaction caused by this mixture makes electricity. By building up alternate layers of copper, and zinc, and then putting them in a jar of salt water, Volta made the first battery. The chemical reaction created the first steady electrical supply.

Read further › electricity
pg228 (d2)

▸ *The first batteries were made by building up layers of copper and zinc, producing an electrical reaction between them.*

● OTHER KEY FIGURES

Date	Name, nationality	Achievements
c.1666–1736	Stephen Gray, English	Showed that some substances conduct electricity and others do not
1698–1739	Charles Dufay, French	Discovered positive and negative electrical charges
1775–1836	André Ampere, French	Found how to measure electric current
1777–1851	Hans Christian Oersted, Danish	Discovered that an electric current is magnetic
1789–1854	Georg Simon Ohm, German	Showed that the flow of electricity in a wire depends on the wire's resistance
1856–1943	Nikola Tesla, Croatian–American	Invented alternating current generators that supply most of our electric power

● **Check it out!**

• http://www.pbs.org/benfranklin/
• http://www.bbc.co.uk/history/historic_figures/faraday_michael.shtml

◂◂ **INVENTION OF BATTERY see pg200 (k17)** ◂◂

a b c d e f g h i j k l m n o p q r s t u v w

Atom experts

I N THE first half of the 19th century, it became clear that gravity is not the only invisible force in the universe. Scientists began to realize that all matter in the universe is held together by the invisible forces of electricity and magnetism. A string of brilliant scientists, such as James Clerk Maxwell in the 1860s and the Curies in the 1900s, illustrated how these forces get their energy from atoms—or from the various particles that make up an atom. Along the way, scientists learned about radiation, nuclear power—and atomic bombs.

Chlorine atom — *Electron*

Nucleus with 17 protons

Sodium atom

Nucleus with 11 protons

Oxygen atom

Nucleus with 8 protons

Carbon atom

Nucleus with 6 protons

Hydrogen atom

Nucleus with a single proton

◄ *Atoms have a nucleus at their centers. Each atom has an equal number of electrons and protons. Electrons have a negative electrical charge and move around the nucleus. Protons have a positive electrical charge and cling to the nucleus.*

IT'S A FACT

• In 1911, Marie Curie was the first woman to win the Nobel prize for chemistry and the first person who won two Nobel prizes in different categories (chemistry and physics).

• Oppenheimer's work on the atomic bomb was code-named the Manhattan Project.

Rutherford and Bohr

By the end of the 1800s, scientists knew that everything is made up of tiny, invisible bits, or "particles" called atoms. In the 1890s, Englishman J.J. Thomson (1856–1940) found there were even smaller particles than atoms called electrons. Then New Zealander, Ernest Rutherford (1871–1937), showed that an atom is mostly empty space—with a tiny, dense blob at the center called the nucleus. By the 1930s, Rutherford was working with Danish physicist Niels Bohr (1885–1962) and together they created a picture of the atom—with tiny electrons circling a dense nucleus made from particles called protons and neutrons. We now know that atoms are very complex, and that there are many particles even smaller than atoms.

►► **Read further > atoms** pg235 (b22)

GENIUS GENES

• As well as discovering radioactivity, the Curies found two entirely new radioactive elements: radium and polonium.

• It was first thought that the atom nucleus was made up of just one kind of particle—a proton. But in 1932, James Chadwick (1891–1974), found another particle, later called a neutron.

OTHER KEY FIGURES

Date	Name, nationality	Achievements
1857–1894	Heinrich Hertz, German	Discovered radio waves
1878–1968	Lise Meitner, Austrian	Worked together on the
1879–1968	Otto Hahn, German	chemistry of radioactivity
1902–1980	Fritz Strassman, German	Discoved nuclear fission

Fields of force

In the 1840s, the great scientist Michael Faraday, brought up the idea of field of force—a region where the effect of an electrical current or a magnet is felt. About 20 years later, young Scottish scientist James Clerk Maxwell (1831–1879), showed how these electromagnetic fields spread out, or "radiate" in invisible waves, like ripples caused when a stone is dropped in a pond. He also demonstrated that these waves travel at the speed of light—and he deduced from this that light is, in fact, an electromagnetic wave.

Read further › light waves / Faraday's dynamo
pg221 (n22); pg229 (d22)

Röntgen's invention of the X-ray allowed [doc]tors to diagnose, illnesses like lung diseases.

Inside view

German scientist Wilhelm Röntgen (1845–1923) discovered X-rays while experimenting with electron beams. He saw that material glowed while the electron beam was on. This was caused by the X-rays that were produced when the electrons made the material fluorescent. Röntgen won the Nobel Prize for physics in 1901.

Atomic radiation

In 1897, French scientist Henri Becquerel (1852–1908), found that the new kinds of radiation being discovered did not always come from electricity. These seemed to appear around uranium atoms. His work influenced Polish–French scientist Marie Curie who, with her husband Pierre, showed that radiation was coming directly from the atoms themselves. The Curies called this atomic radiation "radioactivity." Tragically, Marie Curie died from blood cancer because of her exposure to radioactive substances during her research.

▸ *For their research, the Curies, along with Becquerel, won the Nobel Prize for physics in 1903.*

Read further › radiation
pg233 (i31)

Atomic bomb

Holding the nucleus of atoms together requires an enormous amount of energy. In 1939 scientists split the nuclei of uranium atoms—among the biggest and easiest atoms to break. During World War II, American (Italian-born) Enrico Fermi (1901–1954) made particles fly off, splitting uranium nuclei, which then split other atoms. This set off a "chain-reaction" of splitting that could release huge amounts of nuclear energy.

▲ *In New Mexico in 1942, a team under Robert Oppenheimer (1904–1967) used the "chain reaction" to make the first atomic bomb.*

Check it out!
- http://www.chem4kids.com/index.html
- http://www.pbs.org/wnet/hawking/cosmostar.html/cstars_curies.html

Read further › Einstein
pg233 (b22)

◀◀ ELECTROMAGNETIC RADIATION see pg22 (f2) ◀◀

22 23 24 25 26 27 28 29 30 31 32 33 34 35 36 37 38 39

Time and space

A CENTURY AGO, our idea of the way the world worked was straightforward. It seemed obvious that things happen sequentially. But two extraordinary scientific ideas—quantum science and relativity—have shown that things are not so simple. Quantum science shows that effect does not inevitably follow cause. Relativity turns our common sense view of time, that time runs identically everywhere in the universe, upside down. While these ideas have a very limited impact on our day-to-day lives, they have revolutionized science—from the study of our vast universe to the study of minute atoms.

OTHER KEY FIGURES

Date	Name, nationality	Achievements
1644–1710	Ole Roemer, Danish	Discovered that the speed of light can be measured
1838–1923	Edward Morley, American	Worked together to prove that the speed of light is the same in all directions
1852–1931	Albert Michelson, American	
1902–1984	Paul Dirac, British	Developed quantum physics

▸ *Hawking's research into black holes, relativity, cosmology, and gravitation has earned him numerous scientific awards and honorary degrees. His work provides a strong basis for proof that the universe began with a Big Bang, starting at one point and exploding outward.*

Black holes

Einstein proved that gravity pulls things closer by shrinking the space and time between them. If the gravity is incredibly powerful it will shrink space and time to the point where it disappears. In his book *A Brief History of Time,* English physicist Stephen Hawking (born 1942), suggests that this is what happens in the center of a black hole—a place in space where gravity is so strong that it sucks everything in, including light.

Check it out!
• http://www.eclipse.net/~cmmiller/BH/blkmain.html
• http://www.pbs.org/wgbh/nova/einstein

Read further › Newton and gravity pg220 (l2; n13)

Everything is relative

It would seem to be the case that time is the same everywhere and moves in only one direction, from past to future. German physicist Albert Einstein (1879–1955) showed that this is not so. In his theory of relativity Einstein completely overturned our idea of time and was the first to show that time is relative. Time is not fixed but depends entirely on how it is measured—and you can only measure it relative to something else. Einstein showed that time does not run one-way, but is a dimension, just like length, breadth and depth, and that it can run backward as well as forward.

Read further > atomic bomb
pg231 (n22)

▲ Einstein's equation $E = mc^2$ showed just how much energy there was in an atom, and led to the development of the atom bomb.

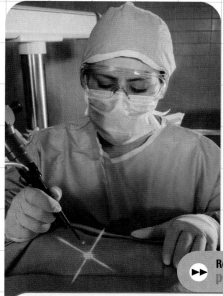

◀ Advanced understanding of quantum mechanics has enabled scientists to develop more effective lasers. Because light does not travel in waves but in quanta, lasers focus the light precisely, allowing surgeons to carry out operations, such as removing birthmarks and treating skin disorders.

Read further > light waves
pg220 (l2); pg221 (n22)

Quantum world

Most scientists once thought light and other kinds of radiation travel in waves. But in the 1890s, German scientist Max Planck, (1858–1947), observed the range of radiation sent out by a hot object—and it did not support the theory that radiation travels in waves. Planck realized that the range of radiation made sense if it was emitted in chunks, or what he called "quanta." Quanta are very, very small. When lots are emitted together they appear like smooth waves; when they are emitted separately, they are like particles. Scientists realized the quantum concept applied to all kinds of particles smaller than an atom, and quantum mechanics became a new science.

GENIUS GENES

• Black holes may be linked by tunnels through space and time called wormholes, to exactly opposite "white" holes. Wormholes may make it possible to travel through time in the future.

• Teleporting may seem to have come straight from *Star Trek*, but scientists have succeeded in teleporting particles. Using a phenomenon called quantum entanglement, particles are destroyed in one place only to reappear instantly some distance away.

▼ Minkowski used geometry to solve problems in number theory, mathematical physics, and the theory of relativity.

Four-dimensional

Hermann Minkowski (1864–1909) developed Einstein's theory of relativity to suggest that space and time were not separate things. Space has three dimensions—up, down, and sideways. Minkowski suggested that time was just another dimension. So it made sense to talk of time as the fourth dimension, and join space and time together to create four-dimensional spacetime.

Read further > geometry
pg215 (b34)

Genetics

THE GREAT biologists of the last few centuries have shown that every living thing is made from thousands, or even millions, of tiny little packages called cells. Each cell carries with it not only its own instructions for life, but the complete instructions for the whole animal or plant of which it is a part. These instructions, called genes, are coded in the structure of a chemical molecule called DNA (deoxyribonucleic acid). DNA works by passing on characteristics from parents to their offspring. Today scientists understand the function of DNA so well that they are beginning to take control of and alter the very materials of life, in a process called genetic engineering.

DNA's double spiral shape

Each base pairs up with another base

● GENIUS GENES

• Crick and Watson's great discovery of the DNA double helix was based on the work of a young expert in microscopy named Rosalind Franklin (1910–1958).

• Some scientists think they may one day be able to duplicate ancient DNA samples from fossils to make dinosaurs live again, like the film *Jurassic Park*.

Rungs made from four different chemical bases

◄ *DNA is structured in bundles called chromosomes. Humans have 46 chromosomes (23 pairs), which control our characteristics.*

Strands of DNA divide to form a template of instruction

● IT'S A FACT

• Genetic engineers put the genes of fluorescent jellyfish in a rabbit, making it glow in the dark.

• In the future, scientists hope to use genetic engineering so that goats will deliver spider's web silk in their milk to use for making ultra-light, bullet-proof vests.

▶▶ Read further › blood cells / vessels
pg217 (b32; n22)

● The amazing spiral

Even under a powerful microscope, the DNA molecule inside every cell looks like little more than a tangled thread. In fact, its chemical structure is a double "helix" or spiral—like a twisted rope ladder. The sequence of the "rungs" is the code that gives the cell instructions by telling it to make particular proteins. When a protein is to be made, the ladder unzips down the middle to expose the code of the rungs. Discovery of this structure was one of the scientific breakthroughs of the 20th century. It was achieved in 1953 by two young scientists working in Cambridge, England: Englishman Francis Crick (b.1916) and American James Watson (b.1928). Their work won Crick and Watson the 1962 Nobel Prize for medicine.

🌐 Check it out!

• http://gslc.genetics.utah.edu/
• http://www.dnaftb.org/dnaftb/1/concept/index.html

◄◄ DNA see pg153 (b30) ◄◄

● Stitching DNA

One of the greatest scientific discoveries of the 20th century was the idea of genetic engineering or modification (GM). In 1972, American biochemist Paul Berg, discovered how to snip a bit of DNA from one bacteria and chemically "stitch" it into the DNA of another. This achievement, known as recombinant DNA, enables the genes for one set of characteristics to be moved from one kind of plant or animal into another. Biotechnology firms use this technique to add qualities, such as pest resistance or more growth, to crops.

4. Bacteria with altered DNA multiplying

Bacteria's ordinary DNA

Read further › DNA
pg234 (r8)

● OTHER KEY FIGURES

Date	Name, nationality	Achievements
1877–1955	Oswald Avery, Canadian-American	Discovered that DNA gave instructions
1905–	Erwin Chargraff, Czech-American	Discovered how DNA bases pair up
1908–1997	Alfred Hershey, American	Developed the idea that DNA gave instructions

DNA plasmid magnified

1. Donor DNA

Gene

2. Opened plasmid

Bacteria

3. Splicing the gene into the plasmid

Altered DNA plasmid less magnified

◄ *This sequence shows the steps in gene splicing. 1. The bit of the donor DNA carrying the right gene is snipped out using restriction enzymes. 2. A special ring of DNA called a plasmid is then broken open. 3. The new gene is spliced into the plasmid, which is sealed up with DNA ligase and introduced into bacteria. 4. The altered bacteria reproduce.*

Read further › offspring
pg223 (g29)

● Mendel's peas

The puzzle of how characteristics are passed on from one generation to the next, or even why some characteristics skip a generation, was solved by an Austrian monk named Gregor Mendel (1822–1884). Mendel grew peas, he studied their sizes and colors.

By recording how these characteristics were passed on from one generation to the next, he worked out a set of basic rules of genetic inheritance—how different characteristics are passed down through the generations.

● Breaking the code

In 1967 two biochemists: American Marshall Nirenberg (b.1927) and Indian-American Har Khorana (b.1922) broke the genetic code. They showed that the genetic code depends on the sequence of four different chemical "bases" down each strand of the DNA molecule. These bases are represented by letters of the alphabet. The sequence is broken up into "sentences" called genes. The code in each gene carries the cell's instructions to make a protein.

◄ *Identical twins share the same characteristics. This is caused by their genetic code.*

◄ *Scientists today use the rules of inheritance to determine whether diseases are likely to be passed on through the generations.*

◄◄ **GENETIC MODIFICATION** see pg203 (q33) ◄◄

22 23 24 25 26 27 28 29 30 31 32 33 34 35 36 37 38 39

a b c d e f g h i j k l m n o p q r s t u v w

Glossary

Abutment A solid structure that supports the end of a bridge or takes the load of an arch.

Abyssal plain Broad plain on the deep seabed, 16,404 ft down and covered in ooze.

Acceleration A change in speed or direction.

Acid A solution made when substances containing hydrogen dissolve in water. Some acids taste sour. Others are highly corrosive.

Acid rain All rain is slightly acidic, but acid rain forms when pollution by sulphur dioxide and nitrogen reacts in sunlight with oxygen and moisture in the air.

Aerofoil A curved surface such as an aircraft wing, which provides control in the air.

Algebra A branch of mathematics that uses letters to represent numbers when making calculations.

Alkali A base that dissolves in water.

Allergy A condition some people experience when they come into contact with a substance such as pollen.

Allotrope One of various forms in which an element occurs. For example, diamond and graphite are allotropes of carbon.

Alloy Metal mixed with another metal or substance. Steel is a tough alloy made from iron, carbon, and traces of other substances.

Alveoli Tiny air spaces or bubbles inside the lungs, where oxygen is taken into the blood from breathed-in air.

Anesthetic A substance, given by medical staff, that stops the body from feeling pain, sometimes making a person unconscious.

Animation Making drawings appear to move, using a series of similar, but slightly different, drawings one after the other.

Annual A flowering plant that completes its life cycle in one year.

Antenna A metal rod or wire for sending and receiving radiowaves or microwaves.

Antennae Long, slim parts on the head of animals, such as insects, often called "feelers" that sense touch, movement, and taste.

Antibiotic A medicine, such as penicillin, which works in the body to kill bacteria.

Antibodies Chemicals produced to attack a particular germ, known as an antigen.

Antiseptic A substance that helps to prevent infection by stopping the growth of germs.

Artery A large blood vessel that carries blood rich in oxygen from the lungs out to the rest of the body from the heart.

Arthropod Any invertebrate animal.

Asexual reproduction When a living thing produces offspring without a mate.

Asteroid One of many thousands of large chunks of rock that orbit the Sun.

Astronaut A person trained to be a crew member in a spacecraft.

Astronomer A person who studies the stars, planets, and other bodies in space.

Atmosphere The thick layer of gases surrounding the Earth.

Atom The smallest particle of an element.

Aurora Colorful glowing lights seen in the sky in the far north and far south.

Bascule A bridge with a highway that can be lifted to allow tall ships to pass through.

Base The chemical opposite of an acid. Weak bases taste bitter and feel soapy. Strong bases are corrosive.

Bases In the genetic material DNA, types of chemical sub units that carry information in the form of a chemical code.

Biennial A flowering plant that takes two years to complete its life cycle.

Big Bang The huge explosion-like expansion of the universe that may have occurred when it began some 15 billion years ago. At first, the universe was a minute, very hot ball of matter and radiation. The universe then expanded and swelled, and stars, galaxies, and planets began to form.

Binary Consisting of two parts or numbers. A computer code of offs or ons, (0s and 1s).

Binary star A true binary is a pair of stars that orbit each other. An optical binary is a pair of stars that look close together in the night sky but are really far apart.

Black hole A point in space where gravity sucks everything in, including light.

Black smoker Small volcanic chimneys on the seabed that throw out black fumes of superheated water.

Brachiation Hanging while swinging with a pendulum-like motion, as when gibbons swing through tree branches.

Broadleaf tree A tree that grows leafs that are wide and flat. It may be an evergreen or deciduous tree.

Browser An animal that eats mainly leafs from taller plants such as trees and bushes.

Buoyancy How well something floats.

Cache A store of something, such as food, by an animal for later use, usually for winter.

Camouflage When an animal is shaped, colored and patterned to merge or blend, in with its surroundings.

Canines Long, sharp teeth near the front of the mouth used to stab and rip at prey.

Cantilever A bracket that supports a shelf or balcony, or a bridge with rigid arms projecting out from piers to meet in the middle.

Capillary Tiny blood vessel in the body that links veins to arteries.

Carbon An element found as coal, diamond, and various other substances. Compounds that it makes are called organic chemicals.

Carnivore An animal that eats mainly meat, usually by catching other animals.

Cell The smallest part of a living thing that contains the chemicals of life, such as DNA, and which make up its tissues, organs, and other parts.

Chain reaction Nuclear reaction that goes on gathering pace by itself.

Chelicerae Fang-shaped or pincer-like biting parts on the head of animals, such as spiders and scorpions.

Chlorophyll A green substance found in plants, which traps sunlight that falls onto the leafs. This helps the plant make food.

Chromosomes Lengths of the genetic material DNA that have been coiled up very tightly to resemble microscopic threads.

Chromosphere The lower layer of the Sun that burns at about 18,000°F, just below the photosphere. The chromosphere's color is a pale red or pink.

Cilia Tiny flexible hairs, usually sticking out or projecting from a cell, that can bend or wave, or detect certain chemicals.

Circulatory system Parts of an animal—usually the heart, blood vessels (tubes) and blood—that spread nutrients around the body, and collect wastes and leftovers for removal.

Class The groups into which a phylum (main group) of animals is divided. For example, the phylum chordata is divided into classes such as amphibians, reptiles, birds, and mammals.

Cloning Making an identical copy of an organism from one of its cells.

Cold-blooded Animals whose body temperature varies with their surroundings. The main group are warm-blooded animals.

Combustion When a chemical reacts with oxygen it creates heat, and often light.

Comet A "dirty snowball" of rock, dust, and ice orbiting the Sun. When its orbit brings it close to the Sun, it partially melts, sending out a giant, shining tail.

Compound Substances made by the atoms of two or more elements chemically bonding.

Compression Squeezing, especially of air or gas, inside a cylinder.

Concave Curved inward like a dish.

Condensation The process by which a gas turns into a liquid, such as air to water.

Conduction The spreading of heat from hot areas to cold areas by direct contact.

Conservation Saving or preserving animals and their natural surroundings or habitats.

Constellation A group of stars that form a pattern in the night sky.

Continental drift The process whereby continents move slowly around the world.

Contraction When something gets smaller, usually as it gets colder.

Convection When warm air or liquid rises through cool air or liquid.

Convex Curved outwards like a ball.

Core The dense, hot center of the Earth.

Cotyledon The food store that is contained in every new seedling.

Crust The solid outer shell of the Earth, varying from 3 to 50 mi thick.

Cuneiform Cuneiform writing was made by making wedge-shaped signs in soft clay.

Decibel A measure of the loudness of sound.

Deciduous tree A tree that loses all its leafs at one time, spends some time with bare branches, then grows new leafs.

Delta A flat piece of land, which has built up from material such as silt that has been deposited by a river as it flows to the sea.

Detritivore An animal that eats rotting bits of once-living things, such as the meat off an old carcass, or tiny edible particles in mud.

Dicotyledon A plant that has two cotyledons, for example a pea.

DNA De-oxyribonucleic acid, a chemical that makes up the instructions or genes for how the body grows and functions.

Drag The way in which air or water slows down an object moving through it. This is sometimes called air or water resistance.

Earthquake A brief, violent shaking of the Earth's surface, typically set off by the movement of tectonic plates.

Echolocation Method used by animals like bats, to find their way and locate objects in darkness, by sending out pulses of high-pitched sounds and listening to the echoes.

Eclipse When one space object blocks the view of another. When the Moon blocks Earth's view of the Sun, it is a solar eclipse. When the Earth blocks the Sun's light from the Moon, it is a lunar eclipse.

Ecosystem A local community of plants, animals, and other living things interacting with their surroundings.

Effort The force to make something move.

Electric motor A device that changes electrical energy into movement.

Electrical charge The force of attraction between certain sub-atomic particles.

Electromagnet Powerful magnet that works when an electric current is passing through it.

Electron The smallest of the particles of an atom. Electrons circle round the atom's nucleus and have a negative electrical charge. Electricity is the movement of electrons.

Electronics The use of electronic components to control the flow of current around a circuit.

Element The simplest possible chemical made of one type of unique atom that cannot be broken down.

E-mail (electronic mail) A way of sending messages over the Internet.

Endoskeleton A skeleton inside the body, consisting of strong supporting parts, usually bones, to hold the body together.

Energy The power to make things happen. Energy cannot be created or destroyed: it can only be converted.

Ephemeral A plant with a life cycle that only takes a few weeks to complete.

Era, geological One of the three major divisions of the last 500 million years of Earth's history: the Palaeozoic, the Mesozoic, and the Cenozoic.

Evaporation When liquid turns to vapor as it gets warm.

Evergreen tree A tree that does not shed its leafs all at once and so remains green throughout the year.

Evolution The gradual changing of species of living things over time, in response to changing conditions.

Excretion Removal of wastes, by-products, and other unwanted substances from the body—by the excretory or urinary system.

Exosphere The layer of the atmosphere above the thermosphere, beginning at about 310 mi up.

Expansion When something gets bigger, usually as it gets warmer.

Extinct When a particular species of living thing has died out and disappeared for ever.

Extrasolar planet A planet outside the Solar System, not circling the Sun but another star.

Fault A fracture in rock where one block of rock slides past another.

Fertilization The process by which the nucleus of the pollen grain fuses with the nucleus of the ovule to make a seed.

Force Something that changes an object's shape or movement by pulling, pushing, stretching, or squashing it.

Fossil the preserved remains of a creature or plant long dead, usually turned to stone.

Fulcrum The point at which a lever turns.

Fungi Living things, most of which have tiny hairs, that feed on dead plants and animals and decompose them.

Fuselage The tube-shaped body of an airplane, excluding the wings.

Galaxy A giant collection of stars in space containing millions of stars. Some are spiral shaped, some are elliptical (oval), and some are irregular in shape. The Sun is part of a local galaxy called the Milky Way Galaxy or just the Galaxy.

Gas Substance without shape or form.

Gastric To do with the stomach, for example gastric juices made in the stomach contain powerful chemicals for digestion.

Gears Wheels with teeth around the edge that fit together to change the speed or direction of movement.

Genes Instructions or information, in the form of the chemical DNA, for how the body develops, grows, and functions.

Genetics The study of genes and DNA.

Genome The full set of all the genes for a human body, which number about 35,000.

Geometry The mathematics of lines, angles, curves, surfaces, and solid shapes.

Germ A microbe that can cause disease and grow into a new organism.

Germination The process that occurs when the seedling breaks out of its case, sending out its root and shoot.

Gills Body parts for breathing underwater. They are usually feathery or frilly and take in oxygen that has dissolved in the water.

Glaciation The molding of the landscape by glaciers and ice sheets.

Gland A body part specialized to make a certain product, usually in liquid form, which can be released directly into the blood flowing through the gland (endocrine gland).

Global warming The process whereby the Earth is becoming gradually warmer. It is believed that this is caused by pollution in the atmosphere, which traps the Earth's heat.

Glucose A type of high-energy sugar, often called "blood sugar," that is broken down inside the cells of the body to release its energy, which powers the cell's life processes.

Gravity The force of attraction between every single piece of matter in the universe. Gravity makes things fall, holds things to the ground, as well as keeping the Earth and other planets circling the Sun.

Greenhouse effect The way certain gases in the atmosphere trap the Sun's heat like the panes of glass in a greenhouse.

Habitat Particular place with its own kinds of animals and plants, such as a pine wood, grassland, desert, seashore, or deep seabed.

Heat The total energy a warm substance has because of the movement of its molecules.

Herbivore An animal that eats mainly plant foods, such as leafs, fruits, and seeds.

Heredity The passing of characteristics, such as eye color, through the generations.

Hibernation When an animal's body temperature falls very low, usually to less than 50°F, and the animal falls into a deep sleep to survive the long, cold season.

Home range An area where an animal usually roams and feeds, but which it does not defend, unlike a territory.

Hormones Natural body substances that control processes such as growth, how fast cells use energy, and the balance of water.

Hydro-electric power Electrical power generated by the force of falling water.

Hydrogen The lightest, most common gas in the universe, and the first to form. Stars are made mostly of hydrogen and another light gas called helium.

Ice age A long cold period when huge areas of the Earth are covered by ice sheets.

Igneous rock Rocks created as hot magma from the Earth's interior cool and solidify.

Incisors Teeth at the front of the mouth, usually shaped like chisels with sharp straight edges for gnawing and nibbling.

Inclined plane A slope that makes lifting easier by sliding or rolling things.

Induction The induction stroke in a car engine is the movement of the piston that draws new fuel into the cylinder.

Industrial Revolution The rapid development of the use of machines in late 18th and early 19th century British industry.

Internal combustion engine An engine that uses a fuel, such as burning gasoline mixed with air, to power a machine or vehicle.

Internet A vast computer network linking computers all over the world via satellites, optical fibers, and telephone wires.

Invertebrate An animal that does not have a backbone (vertebral column).

Involuntary In the muscle system, when a muscle works automatically without need for thought, rather than being controlled.

Irrigation Watering dry land to make it suitable for growing crops.

Keratin A tough substance that forms the horns, claws, hooves, and nails of mammals, the feathers, beaks, claws and scales of birds, and the claws, and scales of reptiles.

Knot A unit for measuring speed at sea or in the air. A knot is about 1.1 mi/h.

Krill Shrimp-like animals that thrive in vast shoals (groups) in the ocean and are food for larger animals, such as penguins, seals, and whales.

Larva The growing stage of a creature, such as an insect, that looks different to its parent, for example, the caterpillar of a butterfly.

Lateral line Line of tiny sensors along a fish's body, to detect movement in the water.

Lava Hot molten rock emerging through volcanoes, known as magma when underground.

Lift Force to lift an aircraft or hot-air balloon.

Light-year The distance light travels in one year—about 5.9 million million mi. Distances to the stars are measured in light-years.

Liquid crystal display (LCD) A display made with liquid crystals. A passing electric current lines them up, blocking the light and so forming patterns.

Lithosphere The rigid outer shell of the Earth, including the crust and the rigid upper part of the mantle.

Lymph A pale fluid that collects between cells and oozes to collect in tubes and lymph ducts, and flow through lymph nodes.

Magma Hot molten rock in the Earth's interior. It is known as lava when it emerges to the surface of the Earth.

Magnetism The force of attraction or repulsion in substances like iron, and around a moving electrical charge or current.

Mammary glands Parts on a female mammal's front that make milk for her young.

Mantle The warm layer of the Earth's interior below the crust. Every now and then parts of the upper mantle melt to form magma.

Marrow Soft, jelly-like substance in the middle of many bones, which makes new cells for the blood (red marrow) or stores energy and nutrients as fat (yellow marrow).

Mass The amount of matter in an object.

Matter Anything of physical substance in the universe.

Medula The inner or lower region of a body part such as the kidney or brain.

Melting The way a solid substance turns to liquid when it reaches a certain temperature.

Mesosphere The layer of the atmosphere above the stratosphere, beginning 30 mi up.

Metabolism All of the body's internal chemical processes that involve changing and breaking down, such as digestion, respiration, and excretion.

Metamorphic rock Rocks created by the alteration of other rocks by heat or pressure.

Metamorphosis When an animal changes its body shape greatly as it grows, instead of the same body shape just growing larger.

Meteor A meteoroid that crashes into Earth's atmosphere and burns up—often seen as a glowing streak in the sky called a shooting star.

Meteorite A rock from space that crashes into the Earth's surface.

Meteoroid A small piece of space rock that crashes into the Earth.

Microwave Radio waves with a short wavelength, which are used in cooking and telecommunications.

Mid-ocean ridge A ridge down the middle of the sea floor where tectonic plates meet.

Migration Long-distance journeys, usually carried out at certain seasons, there and back again each year.

Milky Way The faint band of light stretching across the night sky, made of billions of stars. This is the edge-on view of our own Galaxy, the Milky Way.

Mimicry When one animal looks like another (the model) to gain an advantage, for example pretending to be a poisonous animal when it is not itself poisonous.

Minerals Substances in the soil that a plant needs for healthy growth.

Model In animal mimicry, the creature that the mimic looks like or pretends to be.

Molecule The smallest bit of a substance that can exist by itself.

Momentum Makes an object move at the same speed and in the same direction.

Monocotyledon A plant with only one cotyledon, for example a grass plant.

Motor In the body, to do with muscles and movements, for example motor nerves carry signals from the brain to muscles to tell them when to contract and by how much.

Muscle Part inside an animal's body that gets shorter, or contracts, to move the body.

Myofibers Muscle fibers, which are bundled together inside a muscle—"myo" is to do with muscles.

Natural selection Strong features of living things are naturally selected because those possessing them survive to pass them on.

Nebula A cloud of dust and gas in space. Some glow because they contain young stars. Some glow because they reflect light from other stars.

Neurons Nerve cells, specialized to receive and pass on information in the form of tiny electrical signals called nerve impulses.

Neutrino One of the tiniest of all particles from which matter is made.

Neutron With protons, one of the two basic particles that make up an atom's nucleus.

Neutron star A very small and dense star formed when a large star explodes.

Nuclear energy Energy released by splitting or fusing the nuclei of atoms.

Nucleus (plural nuclei) The core of an atom, made from protons and neutrons.

Nutrients Substances in digested food that are useful to the body, such as providing energy for growth and repair of body parts.

Nymph The growing stage of an animal, such as an insect, which resembles its parent in general shape.

Ommatidia Tiny rod-shaped parts that together form the eye of an insect.

Omnivore An animal that eats a wide range of foods, both meat and plant matter.

Optical fiber Special glass cable that transmits signals using laser light.

Organelles Cell parts, such as the nucleus or control center, and the folded sheets of membranes called endoplasmic reticulum.

Organs Major parts of the body such as the heart, lungs, or stomach, which are usually made of several different kinds of tissues.

Oxygen A gas making up one-fifth of air, which has no color, taste, or smell but is needed in continuing supplies by the body to break apart substances such as glucose.

Ozone layer A layer of gas called ozone (a form of oxygen) high up in the Earth's atmosphere that absorbs most of the Sun's harmful ultraviolet radiation.

Parasite A parasitic animal gains nourishment or shelter from another living thing, called its host, and in doing so, can damage or harm the host.

Parthenogenesis When a female animal is able to produce offspring without a mate.

Particle A tiny piece of matter.

Pasteurization Liquids, such as milk, are heated to a certain temperature and then rapidly cooled in order to destroy germs.

Patent The exclusive right to make, use, or sell an invention for a set number of years. Inventors must apply for a patent.

Perennial A plant that lives for many years.

Period, geological One of the major periods of time into which the Earth's history is divided, each lasting many millions of years.

Periodic Table The table of chemical elements arranged in order of the number of protons in the nucleus of their atoms.

Pheromone A chemical substance produced by an animal, which affects t he actions and behavior of others animals of its kind.

Photon One of the tiny particles or "packages" that light travels in.

Photosphere The surface of the Sun, which is made from churning, hot gases.

Photosynthesis The process by which plants make food using water, sunlight, and carbon dioxide from the air.

Phylum The main groups into which the animal kingdom is divided, such as sponges mollusks, echinoderms, and annelid worms. Each phylum is divided into various classes.

Planet A large world that revolves around the Sun or another star.

Planetary nebula A gigantic ring of clouds of gas emitted at speed that form around the outside of a supernova.

Planetesimal One of the small lumps of rock circling the early Sun which later clumped together to form the planets.

Plankton Tiny plants and animals that drift in the water of seas, oceans, and large lakes.

Plasma Special form of gas at very high temperatures, full of charged particles.

Plasma The liquid part of blood without the microscopic cells (red cells, white cells, and platelets).

Pole, Magnetic The region of a magnet where the magnetism is strongest. Every magnet has north and south poles.

Pollen Tiny capsules made by the stamens. To reproduce, plants must pass pollen between flowers. Pollen is carried by the wind or other insects to other plants.

Pollination The process by which the pollen moves from the stamens to the stigma of the same flower or a different flower on the same kind of plant.

Pollution The introduction into an environment of substances harmful to living things.

Polymer Substance such as plastic made from long chain or branchlike molecules.

Positron A particle identical to an electron but with a positive electrical charge.

Predator An animal that hunts and catches other creatures, called prey, for its food.

Prey A creature that is hunted or caught as food by another animal, called the predator.

Prism Wedge of glass that splits white light passing through it into different colors.

Program Coded instructions, which are carefully writted, telling machines, such as computers, how to work. Computer programs are written in binary language.

Proton With neutrons, one of the two basic particles that make up an atom's nucleus.

Pulley Wheel with a grooved rim that guides a rope to make it easier to lift things.

Pulsar A neutron star that spins rapidly sending out regular pulses of radio waves.

Pulse rate The number of times per minute that the heart beats and sends blood, causing pulsations (pressure waves) in the arteries.

Pupa A hard-cased, inactive stage in the life of an insect before it becomes an adult.

Quantum (plural quanta) A tiny package of light, energy, or matter.

Quasar A small, very distant object that looks like a star but is hundreds of times brighter than galaxies. Most quasars are billions of light-years away, the furthest things visible in the universe.

Radiation Energy emitted from particles as electromagnetic waves such as light and radio waves, or as radioactive particles.

Radio waves Electromagnetic waves with the longest wavelength and lowest frequency, including microwaves and those used for radio and TV broadcasting.

Radioactivity The break-up of atomic nucleus, sending out energetic particles that are very dangerous to animal life.

Reaction, chemical The joining of two or more chemicals when at least one of the chemicals changes.

Recombinant DNA The way scientists take DNA from one thing and add it to the DNA of another to alter its life instructions.

Recycling Using the same materials, such as newspaper, over and over again.

Red giant A huge red star at least ten times as big as the Sun, formed when a medium-sized star, such as the Sun, begins to burn out and swell up.

Red shift The change in color as light from galaxies turns redder because the waves are stretching away from us.

Reflection The bouncing back of light or other waves when they hit a surface.

Refraction Light rays bend as they pass from one transparent substance to another.

Relativity The theory that you can only measure time relative to something else.

Renewable resources Materials, such as the sun, wind, and water, that can be used and replaced naturally, without being used up.

Respiratory system Parts of an animal that take in oxygen from the air.

Root The part of a plant that holds the plant in the soil and takes up water and minerals for the plant to use.

Satellite Any object orbiting a star, planet, or asteroid. Man-made satellites orbiting the Earth are used to gather scientific data or receive and transmit radio signals.

Scales Small, hard parts, usually in overlapping rows, covering the bodies of animals such as reptiles and fish.

Seed A capsule, which forms from the ovule after fertilization and contains a tiny plant with a foodstore.

Sepal A small leaf that forms part of the covering of the flower bud.

Sexual reproduction When a living thing produces offspring with a mate.

Solar cell A cell that converts the Sun's energy into electricity.

Solar System The collection of planets, moons, and smaller objects that orbit (circle) the Sun.

Solid State of matter with a shape and form.

Solution Liquid in which a solid, a liquid, or a gas is broken up and intermingled so it behaves as part of the liquid.

Space probe An unmanned spacecraft sent from Earth to investigate the Solar System and beyond.

Space station A spacecraft, big enough for people to live and work on, which orbits the Earth.

Species The groups into which animals are divided. All members of a species can breed together, but they cannot breed with members of other species.

Spectrum The range of colors created when light is split by a prism.

Spiral galaxy A rotating galaxy with a spiral shape like a giant spinning wheel. The Milky Way is a spiral galaxy, and the Sun is on one of its arms.

Spore A tiny capsule made by non-flowering plants such as mosses and fungi. It contains a piece of the parent plant or fungus, which can break out and grow into a new plant.

Stamen The part in the flower that produces pollen.

Static electricity Electricity that builds up when things rub together but do not move.

Steam Gas formed by evaporating water.

Stigma The part of the flower on top of the ovary, which receives pollen.

Stomata Holes on the underside of a leaf that let air and water in and out.

Strata Layers of sedimentary rock.

Stratosphere The layer of atmosphere above the troposphere, beginning 6 mi up, where temperatures rise with height.

Sub-atomic particles Particles that are even smaller than an atom.

Subduction The bending of a tectonic plate beneath another as they collide.

Sunspot A dark spot that develops on the surface of the Sun, which interrupts the flow of gases.

Supernova A gigantic explosion caused when a giant star runs out of energy. It throws off its outer layers and burns as bright as billions of ordinary stars.

System Several parts such as tissues and organs that work together to carry out one major, vital function.

Tectonic plate The 20 or so giant slabs of rock that make up the Earth's surface.

Tendon A strong, rope-like part where the end of a muscle narrows to join to a bone.

Terrestrial An animal that lives on land.

Territory An area or place where an animal lives and feeds, and which it defends by chasing away others of its kind.

Testa The protective outer casing of a seed.

Theory A carefully thought out idea to explain a particular scientific phenomenon.

Thermosphere The layer of the atmosphere above the mesosphere, beginning 50 mi up.

Thorax The name for the middle or chest region of the body in many kinds of animals. In an insect, the legs and wings join to the thorax.

Thrust The force driving something along.

Tissues Parts of the body formed of many cells of the same kind, such as muscle cells (fibers) that make up muscle tissue.

Tropical rainforest A forest that grows where the weather is always hot and wet.

Troposphere The lowest layer of the atmosphere existing up to 6 mi.

Vaccination Injecting a substance into the blood so that it produces antibodies, which provide protection against a disease.

Veins Main blood vessels or tubes that carry blood towards the heart.

Vertebrate An animal that has a backbone (vertebral column), usually as part of its inner skeleton of bones.

Virtual reality A computer recreates a three-dimensional space, so that it seems as if you are actually in the space.

Voluntary In the muscle system, when a muscle can be controlled at will or by thinking, rather than working automatically without the need for thought (involuntary).

Warm-blooded When an animal's body temperature stays the same, despite changing temperatures in its surroundings. The two main groups of warm-blooded animals are mammals and birds.

Warning colors Usually bright colors and patterns to warn other creatures that an animal is harmful, such as being poisonous.

Wavelength The length from the crest of one wave to the crest of the next.

White dwarf A small, dense star formed when a medium-sized star such as the Sun runs out of fuel.

X-ray High energy electromagnetic radiation used to take pictures through the body of bones and other structures.

Index

Acknowledgments

The publishers would like to thank the following
artists who have contributed to this book:
Lisa Alderson, June Allan, Julie Banyard, Mark Bergin, Syd Brak,
John Butler, Steve Caldwell, Martin Camm, Jim Channell, Kuo Kang Chen,
Peter Dennis, Richard Draper, James Evans, Nick Farmer, Wayne Ford,
Nicholas Forder, Chris Forsey, Mike Foster, Mark Franklin, Luigi Galante,
Roger Goode, Jeremy Gower, Peter Gregory, Alan Hancocks, Alan Harris,
Ron Hayward, Robert Holder, Ian Jackson, Rob Jakeway, Emma Louise
Jones, Roger Kent, Mick Loates, Kevin Maddison, Alan Male, Maltings,
Janos Marffy, Doreen McGuiness, Alessandro Menchi, Andrea Morandi,
Helen Parsley, Sebastian Quigley, Terry Riley, Steve Roberts, Eric Robson,
Martin Sanders, Peter Sarson, Mike Saunders, Rob Sheffield, Guy Smith,
Sarah Smith, Roger Stewart, Rudi Vizi, Christian Webb, Steve Weston,
Mike White, Tony Wilkins, Paul Williams

The publishers wish to thank the following
sources for the photographs used in this book:
p37 (b/r) DreamWorks Pictures; p72 (b/l) AFP; p181 (t/r) Vince
Streano/Corbis; p185 (t/l) Patrick Ward/Corbis; p192 (c/r) Nokia;
p198/199 (c/t) Universal; p206 (c/r) Sony; p207 (c/l) Courtesy of Apple;
p207 (t/r) Sony Computer Entertainment; p209 (b/r) Nokia; p212 (c/r)
Casio; p212 (b/l) Electrolux; p212 (c) Trek Aerospace

All other photographs are from:
Castrol, Corbis, Corel, DigitalSTOCK, digitalvision, Dover,
Flat Earth, John Foxx, Hemera, ILN, MKP Archives,
NASA PhotoAlto, PhotoDisc, STOCKbyte